Inhabitants
of
Cecil County
Maryland

1649-1774

Henry C. Peden, Jr.

HERITAGE BOOKS
2006

HERITAGE BOOKS
AN IMPRINT OF HERITAGE BOOKS, INC.

Books, CDs, and more—Worldwide

For our listing of thousands of titles see our website
at
www.HeritageBooks.com

Published 2006 by
HERITAGE BOOKS, INC.
Publishing Division
65 East Main Street
Westminster, Maryland 21157-5026

International Standard Book Number: 978-1-888265-82-5

CONTENTS

PREFACE

Cecil County was created in 1674 from Baltimore County and Kent County; however, land patents and certificates date from 1649 in the area that now comprises Cecil County.

The lists in this volume were gathered from a variety of sources: Land Patents Index, 1649-1774 (as published in *Land Patents of Cecil County*, compiled by Cecil County Genealogical Society); Colonial Naturalizations, 1660-1729; New Munster Petitioners in 1722; St. Mary Ann's Parish Religious Oaths, 1742-1774, Cohabitants, 1749-1774, Bachelors, 1759-1765, and Sundry Persons, 1754-1774; St. Stephen's Parish Pewholders, 1747, and Bachelors, 1763; Tax list of 1761; Militia List of 1740; Fines, 1746-1773; Tavern Licenses Granted, 1759-1773; Amerciaments, 1756, 1771-1774; Court Justice Papers, Juror Lists and Overseer Lists, 1767-1768; Bohemia Manor Day Book, 1735-1761; Tax List of 1759; Elk Forge Tax List, 1762; Insolvents, 1764-1765, 1768; Tax List of 1766; Overseers of Roads, 1760-1773; Constables 1760-1771; North East Forge Accounts, 1764-1774; Bohemia Manor Tenements, 1768; Debt Books, 1734-1766; Tax list of 1752; Civil and Military Officers, 1696; Sundry Persons List, 1749; Bondholders, 1755; Petitioners, 1737 and 1761; Assemblymen, 1674-1774; and, Alienated Lands List, 1763. Not included in this volume are the Rent Rolls, 1658-1724.

The records used in compiling this book can be found in the following locations: Maryland Historical Society, Manuscripts Division (MS.174, MS.231, MS.1117, MS.1556, MS.1929); Maryland State Papers; *Maryland Historical Magazine*, Volumes 5 and 6; Parish Registers of St. Mary Ann's and St. Stephen's P. E. Churches; Archives of Maryland, Volumes 20, 46, 52; and, The Maryland State Archives.

Researchers should also consult other published sources for information on early Cecil Countians in addition to the records mentioned above, primarily: *Cecil County Bible Records*, by Gary L. Burns (Cecil County Genealogical Society, 1990); *Land Patents of Cecil County* (Cecil County Genealogical Society, 1986); *Early Anglican Church Records of Cecil County*, by Henry C. Peden, Jr. (1990); *Quaker Records of Southern Maryland, 1658-1800*, by Henry C. Peden, Jr. (1992); *Nottingham Quakers, 1680-1889*, by Alice L. Beard (1989); *Revolutionary Patriots of Cecil County, 1775-1783*, by Henry C. Peden, Jr. (1991); *The 1693 Census of the Swedes on the Delaware*, by Peter S. Craig (1993); and, *History of Cecil County, Maryland*, by George Johnston (1881).

For additional information on Swedish and Finnish families moving to Cecil County from the Delaware Valley in the 17th and 18th centuries, the reader should consult Peter S. Craig, *The 1693 Census of the Swedes on the Delaware* (1993) and George Ely Russell, "The Swedish Settlement in Maryland," *The American Genealogist*, 54:203-210 (1978).

It is hoped that persons using this book of lists will learn more about their colonial ancestors and their Cecil County connection.

Henry C. Peden, Jr.

LAND PATENTS AND CERTIFICATES
IN CECIL COUNTY, 1649-1774

Abraham Bondwell - 1743 - "Abraham's Promise" - 300 acres.

Elizabeth Harris - 1702 - "Abram's Promise" - 300 acres.

Philip Holleadger - 1686 - "Addition" - 300 acres.

Charles Carroll - 1713 - "Addition" - 300 acres.

James Heath - 1722 - "Addition" - 80 acres.

John Bannington - 1716 - "Part of Addition" - 100 acres.

Domonick Carroll - 1730 - "Addition" - 360 acres.

James Magregar - 1667 - "Addition" - 500 acres.

Richard Leake - 1670 - "Addition"- 100 acres.

William Harris - 1708 - "Addition" - 298 acres.

Archibald Armstrong - 1770 - "Addition to Addition" - 3/4 acre.

Matthias Johnson - 1753 - "Addition to Batchelors' Content" - 33 acres.

John Campbell - 1734 - "Addition to Campbell's Dividend" - 100 acres.

Henry Ward - 1753 - "Addition to Chance" - 3 acres.

John Passmore - 1765 - "Addition to Consent" - 51 acres.

John Ruston - 1735 - "Addition to Forge Mills" - 100 acres.

John Brice - 1750 - "Addition to the Forrest" - 13 acres.

Ann Fulton - 1773 - "Addition to Fulton's Desire" - 8 3/4 acres. Certificate in the name of Francis Fulton.

James Heath - 1718 - "Addition to Heath's Third Parcel" - 330 acres.

James Healty - 1722 - "Addition to McHealty" - 1530 acres.

Robert Mercer - 1764 - "Addition to Mount Harmon" - 8 1/4 acres.

Charles Rumsey - 1763 - "Addition to New Hall" - 27 acres.

John Passmore - 1762 - "Addition to the Partner's Parcels" - 144 acres.

Benjamin Pearce - 1725 - "Addition to the Rounds" - 126 acres.

Andrew Pearce - 1756 - "Addition to the Rounds" - 16 acres.

Augustine Herman - 1665 - "The Adjunction" - 100 acres.

Charles Ramsey - 1701 - "Adventure" - 100 acres.

Edward Jones - 1680/1 - "The Adventure" - 187 acres.

William Willson - 1695 - "Albany" - 367 acres.

William Fisher - 1665 - "Albens" - 80 acres.

Thomas Aldridge - 1674 - "Aldridge's Lott" - 100 acres.

Andrew Alexander - 1753 - "Alexander's Chance" - 67 acres.

Mark Alexander - 1769 - "Alexander's Lot" - 109 acres.

David Alexander - 1769 - "Alexander's Lott" - 11 1/2 acres.

Martin Alexander and Francis Alexander - 1732 - "Alexandria" - 130 acres. Certificate in the name of Samuel Alexander and John Holtham.

Thomas Johnson - 1713 - "Amster" - 200 acres.

Daniel Carnell - 1679 - "Anchor and Hope" - 500 acres.

Benjamin Pearce - 1730 - "Andrew's Square" - 58 acres.

Richard Angell - 1684 - "Angell's Lott" - 1200 acres. Certificate in the name of Bryan Omealy.

Bryan Omealy - 1684 - "Angell's Rest" - 1200 acres.

George Hack - 1659 - "Anna Catharina Neck" - 400 acres.

Simon Carpenter - 1683 - "Anna Catharina Neck" - 400 acres.

William Rumsey - 1732 - "Ant Castle" - 500 acres. Certificate in the name of Stephen Hollingsworth.

William Rumsey - 1733 - "Antego" - 250 acres. Certificate in the name of Stephen Hollingsworth.

James Frisby - 1723 - "Ariana" - 240 acres. Certificate in the name of Peregrine Frisby.

Edward Armstrong - 1753 - "Armstrong's Fortune" - 72 acres.

Johannas Arrant - 1760 - "Arrant's Chance" - 814 acres.

Johannas Arrant - 1763 - "Arrant's Chance" - 598 acres.

E. Alexander - 1724 - "Arthur Ehaston" - 260 acres.

John Browning and Henry Denton - 1688 - "Askmore" - 550 acres.

John Brown - 1753 - "Augustine's Defiance" - 138 acres. Certificate in the name of John Lusby.

Bartholomew Etherington - 1767 - "Augustin's Oversight" - 21 1/2 acres.

Henry Baker - 1741 - "Baker's Addition" - 42 acres.

John Bing - 1742 - "Baker's Addition" - 40 acres. Certificate in the name of Henry Baker.

Henry Baker - 1756 - "Baker's Meadow" - 12 1/2 acres.

Thomas Baldwin - 1768 - "Baldwin's Choice" - 340 acres.

John Baldwin - 1726 - "Baldwin's Dispatch" - 340 acres.

John Baldwin - 1728 - "Baldwin's Inlargement" - 45 acres.

John Baldwin and William Rumsey - 1732 - "Baldwin's Lott" - 10 acres. Certificate in the name of John Baldwin.

Rowland Chambers - 1729 - "Balteagh" - 150 acres. Certificate in the name of Edward Griffith.

James Frisby - 1696 - "Baltimore Field" - 33 acres.

Peregrine Frisby - 1746 - "Baltimore Field's Resurveyed" - 118 acres.

Darby Nolan - 1688 - "Bandon Bridge" - 60 acres.

Thomas Bastick - 1664 - "Banks" - 200 acres.

Thomas Tarrey - 1724 - "Part of the Banks" - 147 acres.

William Rumsey - 1739 - "Barbadoes" - 180 acres.

Christopher Hendrickson - 1713 - "Barbados" - 79 acres.

Thomas Love - 1770 - "Barroner's Limited" - 40 acres.

Andrew Barry - 1745 - "Barry's Venture" - 14 acres. Certificate in the name of James Porter.

Andrew Barry - 1747 - "Barry's Meadow" - 10 acres.

Richard Clayton - 1728 - "Batchellor's Funn" - 400 acres.

William Currier - 1762 - "Batchelor's Content" - 96 acres.

Nathaniel Hynson - 1720 - "Batchelor's Folly" - 100 acres.

Gunning Bedford - 1721 - "Batchelor's Hope" - 400 acres.

William Bateman - 1743 - "Bateman's Tryall" - 66 acres.

Godfrey Bailey - 1659 - "Bayley" - 300 acres.

Alexander White - 1723 - "Bear Point" - 106 acres.

Joseph Phips and Eleanor Phips - 1757 - "Beaver Dam" - 136 acres.

Christopher Wilkinson - 1760 - "Beaver Dam" - 146 acres.

Joseph Gilpin - 1763 - "Beaver Dam" - 294 acres.

John Howell - 1683 - "Beaver Dam Neck" - 50 acres.

Andrew Barrett - 1767 - "Beaver Island" - 4 3/4 acres.

Philip Stoops - 1765 - "Beck's Meadow" - 232 acres.

Jonathan Beck - 1717 - "Beck's Meadows" - 210 acres.

Edward Beck - 1680 - "Beckworth" - 150 acres.

Osgood Gee - 1745 - "Beddington Park" - 360 acres.

Gunning Bedford - 1714 - "Bedford's Chance" - 20 acres.

John Beedle - 1757 - "Beedle's Promise" - 169 acres.

Alexander Boulding - 1738 - "Beetle's Intent" - 33 acres.

George Talbott - 1638 - "Bellaconell" - 2000 acres.

Jonathan Beck - 1716 - "Benjamin's Levill" - 115 acres.

Richard Bennett - 1749 - "Bennett's Grove" - ? acres.

Richard Bennett - 1707 - "Bennett's Ridge" - 484 acres.

John Whitkinson - 1759 - "Beverdam Resurveyed" - 146 acres.

John Hammond Dorsey - 1746 - "The Biter's Bitt" - 27 acres.

John Wills - 1714 - "Black Marsh" - 200 acres.

Andrew Alexander - 1749 - "Blackenstine Park" - 170 acres.

Andrew Wallace - 1749 - "Blanesteen's Park Resurveyed" - 234 acres. Certificate in the name of Andrew Alexander.

William Blankenstein - 1687 - "Blankenstein's Parke" - 400 acres.

Matthias Vanbibber - 1724 - "Blankenstein Forrest" - 209 acres.

Beall Bordley - 1748 - "Blenheim" - 523 acres.

Augustine Herman - 1662 - "Bohemia Manor" - 4000 acres.

Augustine Herman - 1676 - "Bohemia Manor" - 6000 acres.

Augustine Herman - 1682 - "Bohemia Manor" - 6000 acres.

Augustine Herman - 1682 - "Bohemia River Middle Neck" (or "Little Bohemia") - 1000 acres.

Thomas Bolding - 1768 - "Bolding's Choice" - 9 acres.

Nicholas Painter - 1680 - "Bollen's Range" - 150 acres.

George Gouldsmith - 1666 - "Bonnington" - 200 acres.

Richard Bennett - 1731 - "Bonnington" - 210 acres.

Stephen Bordley - 1763 - "Bordley's Meadow" - 41 acres.

William Borne - 1696 - "Borne's Forrest" - 400 acres.

John Thomas - 1723 - "The Bottle" - 100 acres.

William Boulden - 1734 - "Boulden's Rest" - 330 acres.

John Steel - 1745 - "Bourn's Forrest and Addition" - 521 acres.

Richard Bowdy and John Greenwood - 1694 - "Bowdy's Folly and Greenwood's Advancement" - 200 acres.

John Stockton - 1768 - "Brereton Resurveyed" - 111 1/2 acres.

John Brice - 1763 - "Brice's Triangle" - 23 acres.

John Brice - 1764 - "Brice's Discovery" - 140 acres.

John Brice - 1765 - "Brice's Purchase" - 25 acres.

John Bristoe - 1716 - "Bristoe's Conveniency" - 10 acres.

Thomas Boldin, Thomas Beetle and Thomas Boldin, Jr. - 1746 - "Bristole" - 500 acres.

Nicholas Painter - 1683 - "Brostoll" - 150 acres.

Joseph Wallace - 1754 - "Broad Axe" - 150 acres.

John Collett - 1664 - "Broad Neck" - 300 acres.

James Brooks - 1744 - "Brooks' Meadow" - 100 acres.

John Brooks - 1744 - "Brooks' Range No. 91" - 127 acres.

Samuel Wheeler - 1687 - "Browning's Neglect" - 482 acres. Certificate in the name of James Sparnon and William Blankenstein.

John Browning - 1685 - "Brownley" - 100 acres.

Bryan Omealy - 1684 - "Bryan's Lott" - 400 acres.

John Buchanan - 1714/5 - "Buchanan's Endeavor" - 100 acres.

John Buchanan - 1732 - "Buchanan's Endeavor" - 100 acres.

Thomas Wroth - 1755 - "Buckler's Hill" - 85 acres.

Daniel Kennedy - 1723 - "Buck Range" - 200 acres.

John Jones - 1734 - "Buckshead Hill" - 100 acres.

William Budd - 1740 - "Budd's Misfortune" - 1500 acres.

Andrew Alexander - 1740 - "Bulling's Range" - 129 1/2 acres. Certificate in the name of Samuel Alexander.

Abraham Strand - 1667 - "Buntington" - 200 acres.

Henry Pennington - 1730 - "Buntington" - 350 acres.

Henry Pennington - 1734 - "Buntington Resurveyed" - 350 acres. Certificate in the name of Henry Benntington [sic], Jr.

Henry Pennington, Jr. - 1734 - "Buntington's Addition" - 20 acres.

Richard Edmonds - 1674 - "Burcklere Hill" - 200 acres.

Robert Burle - 1658 - "Burles' Journey" - 500 acres.

James Mofit - 1721 - "Cadey" - 50 acres.

John Wild - 1716 - "Cafinryo" ["Cofin Ryers"?] - 64 acres.

John Campbell - 1725 - "Campbell's Dividend" - 300 acres.

Thomas Canker - 1664 - "Canker's Neck" - 100 acres.

Henry Morgan - 1679 - "Cardigan" - 50 acres.

Benjamin Hazelhurst - 1739 - "Carigeen" - 31 acres.

William Russell - 1716 - "Carlo" - 100 acres.

Martin Cartnill - 1724 - "Cartnell's Addition" - 24 acres.

Andrew Wallace - 1713 - "Castle Fine" - 500 acres.

Susanna Lowe - 1688 - "Castle Greene" - 150 acres.

George Catto and wife Araminta Catto - 1756 - "Catto's Range" - 1049 acres.

Oliver Caulk - 1762 - "Caulke's Addition" - 3 acres.

Matthew Smith - 1701 - "Cedar Branch Neck" - 841 acres.

William Rumsey - 1742 - "The Center" - 15 acres. Certificate in the name of William Pearce.

Jonas Chambers - 1764 - "Chamber's Fourth Vacancy" - 63 acres.

Jonas Chambers - 1767 - "Chamber's Fifth Discovery" - 19 1/2 acres.

Jonas Chambers - 1774 - "Chamber's Sixth Discovery" - 34 acres.

James Chambers - 1763 - "Chamber's Venture" - 42 acres.

Henry Eldasly - 1675 - "Chance" - 200 acres.

John Briscoe - 1683 - "Chance" - 65 acres.

John Cocks - 1683 - "Chance" - 65 acres.

James Corss - 1686 - "Chance" - 50 acres.

William Bateman - 1702 - "Chance" - 66 acres.

Margaret Lusby - 1740 - "Chance" - 50 acres. Certificate in the name of Roger Laramore.

Augustine Laramore - 1742 - "Chance" - 50 acres. Certificate in the name of Roger Laramore.

Alexander Mackdowell - 1752 - "Chance" - 10 acres.

John Land - 1755 - "Chance" - 20 acres. Certificate in the name of John Thomas.

David Price - 1773 - "Chance" - 15 1/2 acres. Certificate in the name of William Husbands.

Henry Ward - 1750 - "Chance Resurveyed" - 250 acres.

Andrew Wallace - 1723 - "Charlemount" - 70 acres.

Charles Jones - 1685 - "Charles' Camp" - 100 acres.

Jacob Johnson - 1762 - "Chestnut Ridge" - 52 acres.

John Highland - 1728 - "Chestnutt Levell" - 280 acres. Certificate in the name of Nicholas Highland.

Francis Child - 1676 - "Child's Harbour" - 500 acres.

Thomas Hollingsworth - 1714 - "Choice" - 400 acres.

Samuel Thompson - 1755 - "Choice Addition" - 31 acres.

William Hill - 1679 - "Civility" - 400 acres.

George Clark - 1773 - "Clark's Adventure" - 4 acres.

Ralph Rutter - 1708 - "Clay Banke" - 100 acres.

Francis Clay - 1651 - "Clayfall" - 500 acres.

Peter Numbers - 1732 - "Clemenson's Addition" - 10 acres.

Andrew Clemenston - 1664 - "Clemenston" - 400 acres.

Clement Michaelson - 1658 - "Clement's Hill" - 50 acres.

James Armstrong and Zebulon Hollingsworth - 1743 - "Clements' Venture" - 200 acres. Certificate in the name of Michael Clements.

John Larkin - 1686 - "Clifton" - 883 acres.

Beale Bordly - 1750 - "Coaster's Harbour" - 297 acres.

William Digges and Charles Digges - 1736 - "Coaster's Refreshment" - 1600 acres.

Henry Ward - 1682 - "Cobham" - 1000 acres.

John Cox - 1665 - "Cockatrice" - 200 acres.

Henry Hendricks - 1763 - "Cockatrice" - 364 acres.

Henry Hendrickson - 1716 - "Cockatrice Addition" - 27 acres.

William Pearce - 1734 - "Colchester" - ? acres.

Michael Manycozens and John Bedle - 1725 - "Colleston" - 194 acres. Certificate in the name of Roger Laramore.

Peregrine Ward - 1750 - "Colleton" - 320 acres. Certificate in the name of Michael Earle.

John Collett - 1672 - "Colletton" - 250 acres.

Richard Collett - 1664 - "Collettson" - 700 acres.

John Collett - 1664 - "Collettson" - 300 acres.

William Beedle - 1759 - "Colliston" - 214 acres.

William Rumsey - 1731 - "Concord" - 300 acres. Certificate in the name of John Thomas.

William Rumsey - 1739 - "Concord" - 305 acres.

Robert Holly - 1730 - "Confusion" - 220 acres.

Henry Toules [Joules?] - 1678 - "Conneticott" - 200 acres.

Henry Joules [Toules?] - 1675 - "Connecticut" - 200 acres.

William Ward - 1766 - "Connecticut" - 205 acres.

George Robinson - 1713 - "Consent" - 800 acres.

John Passmore - 1765 - "Consent Resurveyed" - 1406 1/2 acres.

Moses Musgrove - 1713 - "Contencon" - 600 acres.

Griffith Nicholls - 1722 - "Contention" - 66 acres.

Robert Mackay - 1769 - "Contention" - 25 acres.

Robert Kemble - 1686 - "Contrivance" - 100 acres.

John Collett and George Gouldsmith - 1665 - "Convenient" - 400 acres.

John Coppen - 1728 - "Copping's [or Coppin's] Chance" - 32 acres. Certificate in the name of Ephraim August Herman.

John Copson - 1727 - "Copson's Forrest" - 70 acres.

John Copson - 1728 - "Copson's Intent" - 13 1/2 acres.

William Currier - 1764 - "Copson's Intent" - 18 acres.

John Hazlehurst - 1739 - "Corengimm" [or "Corengem"] - 31 acres. Certificate in the name of Benjamin Hazlehurst.

Henry Hendrickson - 1716 - "Corkatine Addition to Crouches Oversight" - 78 acres.

Mathias Cornelius - 1658 - "Corneliaston" - 150 acres.

Mathias Mathiason, freeman - [Note: Name in the record looks like Mathiason Mathias Freemans] - 1727 - "Cornelinston" - 140 acres. Certificate in the name of Walter Mathiason.

Emanuell Grubb - 1713 - "Cornwall" - 200 acres.

Emanuel Grubbs - 1716 - "Cornwall's Addition" - 100 acres.

Daniell Mekery and Hugh Cornelius - 1665 - "Corobough" - 300 acres.

John Baldwin - 1726 - "Part of Corrobough" - 100 acres.

Abraham Morgan - 1664 - "Coster's Harbour" - 300 acres.

William Coursey and Thomas Coursey - 1695 - "Coursey's Triangle" - 200 acres. Certificate in the name of William Coursey.

William Cox - 1716 - "Cox Prevention" - 250 acres.

William Cox - 1717 - "Coxes Fancy" - 250 acres.

James Knox - 1763 - "Coxes Prevention" - 250 acres.

Richard Bennett - 1730 - "Coxes Purchase" - 424 acres.

John Cox - 1683 - "Cox's Forrest" - 500 acres.

John Copson - 1728 - "Cox's Park" - 469 acres.

John Howell - 1683 - "Cranberry Neck" - 150 acres.

Edmund O'Dwyer - 1686 - "Crossayle" - 575 acres.

Isaac Crouch - 1773 - "Crouch's Addition" - 27 1/4 acres.

Henry Hendrickson - 1716 - "Croutches Oversight" - 78 acres.

William Currier - 1762 - "Currier's Addition" - 32 acres.

William Currier - 1763 - "Currier's Lott" - 42 acres. Certificate in the name of Henry Baker.

Bryan Daley - 1673 - "Daley's Desire" - 500 acres.

George Spencer - 1683 - "Danby" - 500 acres.

John Hause - 1740 - "Daniel's Den" - 280 acres.

Daniel Silvane - 1670 - "Daniel's Den" - 400 acres.

Daniel Silvane - 1672 - "Daniel's Hope" - 200 acres.

William Dare - 1680 - "Dare's Desire" - 200 acres.

Thomas Jacob - 1719 - "Dare's Desire" - 190 acres.

Thomas Jacobs - 1735 - "Dare's Desire" - 190 acres.

Thomas Jacobs - 1738 - "Dare's Desire" - 225 acres.

Samuel Davidson - 1752 - "Davidson's Fancy" - 17 acres.

John Baldwin - 1725 - "Davidson's Part of Consbough" - 100 acres.

David Alexander - 1724 - "David's Purchase" - 296 acres.

William Rumsey - 1733 - "David's Sheepfold" - 100 acres.

William Claw - 1674 - "Dayley's Desire" - 500 acres.

William Currier - 1758 - "Deer Harbour" - 36 acres.

John Lusbey- 1746 - "Defiance" - 138 acres. Certificate in the name of John Brown.

Robert Williams - 1671 - "Denby" - 700 acres.

George Holland - 1679 - "Denton" - 382 acres.

William Fitzredmond - 1717 - "Derry Heel" - 1900 acres.

James Mofitt - 1721 - "Derry Hinah" - 146 acres.

Nicholas Sewall - 1728 - "Divident" - 377 acres.

Campbell Veasey - 1733 - "Deviding" - 900 acres.

Mathias Vanbebber - 1714 - "Deviding" - 600 acres. Certificate in the name of Casparus Harman.

John Veazey - 1725 - "Part of Deviding" - 300 acres.

John Veazey - 1758 - "Dividing" - 326 acres.

Cornelius Archvanhoofe and Henry Sewall - "The Divident" - 400 acres. Certificate in the name of John Bateman and Henry Sewall.

Gasper Guerin and Thomas Edmonds - 1664 - "The Dividing" - 600 acres. Certificate in the name of Gasper Guerin.

Samuel Maffit - 1769 - "Division" - 13 acres.

Augustine Pasmore - 1768 - "Doe Hill and Bear Point"- 421 1/2 acres.

George Robinson - 1713 - "Doe Hill" - Resurvey - ? acres.

Alexander White - 1720 - "Bear Point" - Resurvey - ? acres.

John Thomas - 1730 - "Dole Dyfr"[?] - 180 acres.

Thomas Wiles - 1713 - "Dollvane" - 200 acres.

Stephen Hyland - 1774 - "Donohoe's Purchase" - 103 acres.

William Dorson - 1755 - "Dorson's Point" - 28 acres. Certificate in the name of Moses Jones.

Nathaniel Dougherty - 1732 - "Dougherty's Endeavour" - 50 acres.

William Palmer - 1678 - "Dover" - 200 acres.

George Robinson - 1716 - "Doe Hill" - 275 acres.

James Curthey [Carthey?] - 1720 - "Drum Greena" - 100 acres.

John McKinley - 1748 - "Drum Greena" - 100 acres. Certificate in the name of James Cathey and Benjamin McKinley.

William Smith - 1702 - "Duck Neck" - 100 acres.

Robert Evans - 1759 - "Duck Neck" - 109 acres.

Hugh Macgregar - 1687 - "Dunbar" - 228 acres.

John Dunn - 1696 - "Dunn's Folly" - 120 acres.

William Fitzredmond - 1717 - "Durrow" - 350 acres.

Robert Dutton - 1713 - "Dutton's Mill Dam" - 50 acres.

Robert Story - 1736 - "Dutton Port" - 117 1/2 acres.

Henry Stedham - 1773 - "Eagle's Nest" - 212 acres.

Lulef Stedham - 1741 - "Eagle's Nest" - 104 acres.

John Lithcoe - 1680 - "Eagle's Nest" - 169 acres.

John Edwards - 1752 - "Edward's Fancy" - 4 acres.

David Thomas and Company - 1764 - "The Elk Company" - 440 acres.

William Alexander - 1736 - "Elk Plains" - 149 acres.

George Emery - 1716 - "Emery's Endeavour" - 100 acres.

George Emery - 1695 - "Emery's Satisfaction" - 60 acres.

Abraham Hollingsworth - 1732 - "Enlargement" - 40 acres.

Joseph Ensor - 1762 - "Ensor's Lot" - 31 acres.

William Brookers - 1673 - "Essex Lodge" - 700 acres.

Thomas Etherington - 1753 - "Etherington's Hope" - 18 acres.

Thomas Etherington - 1762 - "Etherington's Chance" - 15 1/2 acres.

Thomas Etherington - 1762 - "Etherington's Tryal" - 57 1/2 acres.

John Simpers - 1760 - "Evans' Purchase" - 78 acres.

Robert Evans - 1767 - "Evans' Success" - 46 acres.

Henry Ward - 1683 - "Eyla" - 90 acres.

John Campbell - 1683/4 - "Eyla" - 190 acres.

John Hollingsworth - 1716 - "Fair Hill" - 200 acres.

William Boulding - 1720 - "Fateague" - 100 acres.

Richard Fedderay - 1757 - "Fedderay's Meadow" - 5 acres.

James Heath - 1714 - "Fifth of Heath's Parcel" - 75 acres.

Abram and Stephen Hollingsworth - 1719 - "First Part of Partners" - 400 acres.

Nathaniel Stiles - 1667 - "The Fishing Pond" - 250 acres.

Thomas Ricketts - 1760 - "Flint Hill" - 55 acres.

Richard Bennett - 1665 - "The Folly" - 400 acres.

Michael Byrnes - 1728 - "The Folly" - 82 acres.

George Ford - 1772 - "Ford's Desire" - 200 1/4 acres.

James Alexander - 1724 - "Foretress" - 444 acres.

Richard Leake - 1683 - "The Forke" - 300 acres.

William Pierce - 1683 - "The Forke" - 200 acres.

Henry Eldersley - 1697 - "The Forlorn Hope" - 150 acres.

Thomas Phillips - 1731 - "Forrest" - 30 acres.

William Blankenstein - 1687 - "The Forrest" - 400 acres.

Walter Mickes - 1682 - "The Forrest of Dean" - 300 acres.

William Harris - 1705 - "The Forrest of Dean" - 600 acres.

Edward Truson and Henry Truelock - 1683 - "Forrester's Delight" - 400 acres.

Joseph Wallace - 1774 - "Fox Den" - 17 1/2 acres.

Jacob Vanpoot - 1749 - "Fox Harbour" - 169 acres. Certificate in the name of Amey Lewis.

Joseph Wood - 1749 - "Francina" - 858 acres.

Francis Alexander - 1734 - "Francis' Marsh" - 50 acres.

William Freeman - 1735 - "Freeman's Park" - 300 acres.

William Abbitt - 1739 - "Freeman's Park" - 190 acres.

George Holland and Joseph Spernon - 1680 - "Friendship" - 200 acres.

William Painter - 1681 - "Friendship" - 1400 acres.

Osgood Gee and Company (Lease) - 1745/6 - "Friendship" - 350 acres.

William Beedle - 1759 - "Frier's Hills" - 204 acres.

John Money - 1760 - "Frier's Neglect" - 38 acres.

James Frisby - 1670 - "Frisby's Addition" - 300 acres.

James Frisby - 1682 - "Frisby's Farme" - 300 acres.

James Frisby - 1683 - "Frisby's Forrest" - 370 acres.

James Frisby - 1684 - "Frisby's Meadows" - 1000 acres.

James Frisby - 1702 - "Frisby's Point" - 80 acres.

James Frisby - 1675 - "Frisby's Prime Choice" - 400 acres.

James Frisby - 1684 - "Frisby's Purchase" - 50 acres.

James Frisby - 1719 - "Frisby's Ramble" - 423 acres.

James Frisby - 1678 - "Frisby's Wild Chase" - 200 acres.

Ariana Frisby - 1722 - "Frisby's Venture" - 300 acres.

John Brice, William Harris and Daniel Cheston - 1743 - "Frisby's Neglect" - 71 acres.

Arianna Jennings - 1738 - "Frisby's Forrest" - 657 acres. Certificate in the name of Arianna Frisby.

Stephen Knight - 1747 - "Frisby's Ramble" - 473 acres.

John Hyland - 1680 - "Fryer's Hills" - 250 acres.

Michael Earle - 1772 - "Frog Moor" - 70 1/2 acres.

Benjamin Bravard - 1768 - "Frog's Quarter" - 35 acres.

John Hyland - 1666 - "Fryer's Hills" - 250 acres.

Francis Fulton - 1773 - "Fulton's Desire" - 31 1/2 acres.

William Galloway - 1695 - "Galloway's Farm" - 286 acres.

Rebecca Campbell - 1685 - "Garden" - 190 acres.

James Steel - 1716 - "Gardiner's Forrest" - 40 acres.

Samuel Johnson - 1716 - "Gardner's Advice" - 200 acres.

William Wallace - 1714 - "Gardner's Gift" - 60 acres.

William Wallis - 1725 - "Garner's Gift" - 60 acres. Certificate in the name of Andrew Wallace [Wallis].

James Gault - 1774 - "Gault's Purchase" - 274 acres.

John England and others - 1720 - "Geefarrison" - 5743 acres. Certificate in the name of John Copson.

George Oldfield - 1680 - "George's Friendship" - 100 acres.

Thomas Pearce - 1751 - "Gibson's Dream" - 181 acres.

Daniel Smith - 1680 - "Gibson's Green" - 150 acres.

Thomas Jacobs - 1716 - "The Gift and Jacob's Chance" - 70 acres. [Note: Index mistakenly shows name as Thomas Smith].

Thomas Jacobs - 1719 - "The Gift and Jacobs' Choice" - 170 acres.

Henry Gilder - 1724 - "Gilder's Forrest" - 100 acres.

Joseph Gilpin - 1773 - "Gilpin's Addition" - 103 1/2 acres.

Nicholas Hyland - 1766 - "The Girdle Oak" - 80 acres.

William Dare - 1680 - "Glance" - 200 acres.

John Macknett - 1716 - "Glasgow" - 90 acres.

Richard Gray - 1678 - "Glass House" - 500 acres.

Nicholas Painter - 1683 - "Gloster" - 750 acres.

Miles Godman - 1725 - "Godman's Lott" - 1 acre.

John Cock - 1675 - "Goe Look" - 200 acres.

James Paul Heath - 1744 - "Goe Look" - 97 acres.

Jonas Chambers - 1764 - "Golden Ball" - 60 acres.

Richard Patten - 1744 - "Golden Point" - 40 acres.

John Cox - 1676 - "Good Luck" - 75 acres.

William Freeman - 1737 - "Good Luck" - 103 acres.

John Veazey - 1745 - "Good Luck" - 340 acres. Certificate in the name of John Thompson.

James Porter - 1757 - "Good Luck" - 50 acres.

John Veazey - 1759 - "Good Luck" - 307 acres.

John Veazey - 1761 - "Good Luck Addition" - 76 acres.

James Porter - 1768 - "Good Neighbor" - 50 acres.

Thomas Maffit - 1768 - "Good Neighbour" - 254 acres.

Adam Dobson - 1760 - "Good or Bad" - 23 1/2 acres.

Adam Cartmill - 1716 - "Good Will" - 100 acres.

Alexander White - 1738 - "Gorey" - 183 acres.

Henry Baker - 1763 - "Gorry" - 251 acres.

Robert Weller - 1677 - "Gotam Bush" - 100 acres.

Chris. Geist and Thomas Humphreys - 1724 - "Gratitude" - 420 acres.

Abraham Pennington - 1714 - "Greenberry" - 241 acres. Certificate in the name of Casparus Harman.

John Larkin - 1671 - "Greenfield" - 750 acres.

Alexander Freeny - 1720 - "Green Meadows" - 160 acres.

Nathaniel Utye - 1661 - "Green Oake" - 450 acres.

Samuel Hill - 1680 - "Green Spring" - 200 acres.

William Savin - 1758 - "Green Spring" - 177 acres.

Daniel Nowland - 1760 - "Green Spring" - 141 acres.

Griffen Jones - 1734 - "Griffin" - 1000 acres.

Phillip Calvert - 1658 - "The Grove" - 1000 acres.

Peter Hack - 1684 - "Hack's Addition" - 150 acres.

George Hack - 1662 - "Hackston" - 800 acres.

Sepherin Hack - 1666 - "Hackston" - 800 acres.

John Nicholas Hack - 1676 - "Hackston" - 800 acres.

Edward Ellis - 1723 - "Haile Hill" - 50 acres.

Richard Hall - 1679 - "Hall's Choice" - 400 acres.

Elihu Hall - 1752 - "Hall's Fishery" - 6 acres.

Elihu Hall - 1767 - "Hall's Hope" - 328 acres.

Richard Hall - 1679 - "Hall's Lott" - 600 acres.

James Stanley - 1677 - "Hampshire" (or "Child's Harbour") - 500 acres.

Richard Leake - 1671 - "Happy Harbour" - 400 acres.

William Hargraves - 1670 - "Hargraves' Choice" - 350 acres.

Ariana Margaritta Harris - 1751 - "Hargraves' Choice" - 390 acres.

Casparus Harman - 1689 - "Harman's Arcadia" - 243 acres.

Harman Kinkey - 1764 - "Harman's Addition" - 28 1/2 acres.

Godfrey Harmer - 1658 - "Harmer's Mount" - 150 acres. J. Brice, W. Harris, and D. Cheston - 1743 - "Harris' Venture" - 20 acres.

William Harvey - 1774 - "Harvey's Purchase" - 169 1/4 acres.

Richard Loes - 1667 - "Hasell Moore" - 600 acres.

Richard Foster and Thomas Wamsley - 1667 - "Hassel Branch" - 300 acres.

William Salsbury - 1683 - "Have At [It?] All" - 100 acres.

John and Mary Lusby - 1740 - "Hazel Branch" - 286 acres.

Garrett Othosun - 1719 - "Head of the Pond" - 58 acres.

Garat Othoson - 1739 - "Head of the Pond" - 58 acres.

John Money - 1763 - "Head of the Pond" - 53 acres.

Dennis English - 1678 - "Heart's Delight" - 200 acres.

Thomas Heath - 1677 - "Heath's Adventure" - 200 acres.

James Heath - 1700 - "Heath's Chance" - 200 acres.

James Heath - 1727 - "Heath's Levell Parcell" - 980 acres.

James Heath - 1703 - "Heath's Outlett" - 1000 acres. Certificate in the name of Thomas Hughes.

James Heath - 1714 - "Heath's Parcells" - 1100 acres.

James Heath - 1705 - "Heath's Range" - 1850 acres.

Hendrick Hendrickson - 1663 - "Hendricks" - 50 acres.

Hendrick Hendrickson - 1664 - "Hendrickson" - 50 acres.

Hendrick Hendrickson - 1667 - "Hendrick's Choice" - 100 acres.

Hendrick Hendrickson - 1679 - "Hendrick's Addition" - 100 acres.

Henry Hendrickson - 1716 - "Hendrickson's Addition" - 50 acres.

Christopher Hendrickson - 1722 - "Hendrickson's Choice" - 8 acres.

Christian Hendrickson - 1717 - "Hendrickson's Choice Resurveyed" - 260 acres.

Thomas Etherington - 1746 - "Hendrickson's Oversight" - 12 acres.

Henry Hendrickson and John Ward - 1716 - "Henry and Ward" - 134 1/2 acres.

Herman Husband - 1756 - "Herman's Ramble" - 30 acres.

Richard Dobson - 1771 - "Herring Pond" - 18 1/4 acres.

John Highland - 1714 - "Highland" - 2305 acres.

Nicholas Highland - 1714 - "Highland" - 100 acres.

Michael Offley - 1679 - "High Offley" - 100 acres.

George Emmery - 1695 - "High Park" - 222 acres.

Richard Nash - 1683 - "High Parke" - 200 acres.

Nikolas Hiland - 1716 - "Hiland's Forrest" - 100 acres.

Nathaniel Hillen - 1680 - "Hillen's Adventure" - 600 acres.

John Hance - 1750 - "Hill's Adventure" - 68 acres.

James Hughes - 1769 - "Hill's Adventure" - 75 1/4 acres.

David John - 1754 - "Hill Foot" - 150 acres. Certificate in the name of William John.

Henry Baker - 1767 - "Hinton's Conveniency" - 86 acres.

Reese Hinton - 1719 - "Hinton's Convenience" - 86 acres.

Robert Hodgson - 1716 - "Hodgson's Choice" - 250 acres.

James Husband - 1737 - "Hog Pen Neck" - 140 acres.

William Holeman - 1658 - "Holemandton" - 200 acres.

George Holland - 1649 - "Holland's Delight" - 343 acres.

George Holland - 1677 - "Holland" - 650 acres.

Hugh Walker, Rowland Chambers and William Edmondson - 1737 - "Hollingsworth's First Parcel" - 85 acres. Certificate in the name of Abraham Hollingsworth.

Zebulon Hollingsworth - 1734 - "Hollingsworth's Second Parcel" - 100 acres. Certificate in the name of Abraham Hollingsworth.

Abraham Hollingsworth - 1716 - "Hollingsworth Parcells" - 400 acres. Patent to Zebulon Hollingsworth and others.

Zebulon Hollingsworth - 1716 - "Hollingsworth's Inspection" - 25 acres.

Stephen Hollingsworth - 1715 - "Hollin Point" - 40 acres.

Stephen Hollingsworth - 1713 - "Hollowing Point" - 300 acres.

Martha Mounts - 1723 - "Hollowing Point" - 22 acres.

Robert Holly - 1727 - "Holly's Expedition" - 100 acres.

Richard Bennett, Jr. - 1664 - "Holmondston" - 650 acres.

Thomas Paine - 1672 - "Holt" - 700 acres.

Robert Holy - 1746 - "Holy's Contrivance" - 68 acres.

Gabriel Brown - 1666 - "Homeley" - 150 acres.

John and Thomas Severson - 1729 - "Homely" - 150 acres.

Edmund Perke [Parks?] - 1724 - "Honney Island" - 39 acres.

Richard Hall - 1678 - "Hope" - 400 acres.

Mathias Vanbibber - 1716 - "Hopewell" - 544 acres.

Sampson Currier - 1751 - "Hopewell" - 200 acres.

James Porter - 1747 - "Hopewell" - 366 acres.

Humphrey Kytely - 1680 - "Hopewell" - 200 acres.

Joseph Hopkins - 1677 - "Hopkins' Addition" - 70 acres.

John Collett and George Gouldsmith - 1665 - "Hornes" - 150 acres.

Francis Smith - 1714 - "Horn Point" - 42 acres.

Matthias Vanbibber - 1722 - "Horseshoe" - 344 acres.

Nathaniel Howell - 1688 - "Howell's Addition" - 40 acres.

John Howell - 1683 - "Howell's Adventure" - 100 acres.

Thomas Howell - 1671 - "Howell's Farme" - 300 acres.

John Howell - 1687 - "Howell's Range" - 150 acres.

William Ewing - 1771 - "Huckleberry Meadow" - 108 acres.

William Hudle - 1677 - "Hudle's Right" - 200 acres.

Joseph Husband - 1770 - "Husband's Discovery" - 6 1/4 acres.

Edward Husbands - 1679 - "Husbands' Rest" - 1630 acres.

David Hutton - 1762 - "Hutton's Grudge" - 85 acres.

Nicholas Hyland - 1696 - "Hyland's Addition to Harris Point" - 26 acres.

Nicholas Hyland - 1754 - "Hyland's Chance" - 49 acres.

John Hyland - 1724 - "Hyland" - 100 acres.

Nicholas Hyland - 1766 - "Hyland's Discovery" - 245 acres.

Richard Leake - 1672 - "Indian Range" - 300 acres.

John Hagley - 1685 - "Indian Range" - 300 acres.

David Witherspoon - 1749 - "Indian Range" - 440 acres.

Abraham Hollingsworth - 1732 - "Inlargement" - 40 acres.

John Smith - 1738 - "Inspection" - 100 acres.

William Alexander - 1738 - "Inspection" - 100 acres.

Mathias Vanbebber - 1732 - "Intention" - 60 acres.

Thomas Hollingsworth - 1723 - "Jacob's Adventure" - 50 acres.

George Robinson - 1714 - "Jacob's Bottom" - 25 acres.

Thomas Jacob - 1716 - "Jacob's Chance" - 25 acres.

Thomas Jacobs - 1719 - "Jacobs' Choice and the Gift" - 170 acres.

Thomas Kelton - 1703 - "Part of Jamaicoe" - 185 acres.

Richard James - 1669 - "James' Adventure" - 200 acres.

Samuel Beedle - 1752 - "James' Adventure" - 83 acres.

James Alexander - 1724 - "James' Inheritance" - 170 acres.

John James - 1694 - "James' Inspection" - 47 acres.

James Coppen - 1753 - "James' Lott" - 370 acres.

James Wallace - 1753 - "James' Venture" - 23 acres.

John Baldwin - 1727 - "Jawert's Delight" - 130 acres.

John Hyland - 1679 - "John and Mary's Hyland" - 1000 acres.

Edward Johnson - 1752 - "Johnson's Addition" - 278 acres.

Nicholas Hyland - 1766 - "Johnson's Adventure" - 222 acres.

Jacob Johnson - 1762 - "Johnson's Purchase" - 55 acres. Certificate in the name of William Hull [Hall?].

Thomas Jones - 1738 - "Jones' Addition" - 31 acres.

Moses Jones - 1764 - "Jones' Discovery" - 142 acres.

William Harris - 1704 - "Jones' Green Spring" - 400 acres.

William Jones - 1747 - "Jones' Venture" - 75 acres.

Joseph Alexander - 1724 - "Joseph and James' Settlement" - 710 acres.

Edmund O'Dwyer - 1683 - "Kappagh" - 1593 acres.

Thomas Casey - 1686 - "Kappagh" - 1593 acres.

Katharine Masse Demondedesse - 1680/1 - "Katharine's Delight" - 100 acres.

Katharine Masse Demondedesse - 1680 - "Katharine's Lott" - 100 acres.

Robert Kemble - 1685 - "Kemble's Addition" - 300 acres.

Hugh Kenneday - 1720 - "Kenneday's Adventure" - 500 acres.

George Talbott - 1683 - "Kildare" - 700 acres.

William Kilgore - 1770 - "Kilgore's Liberty" - 15 3/4 acres.

William Fitzredmond - 1717 - "Killavilly" - 200 acres.

Thomas Rumsey - 1681 - "King's Aime" - 500 acres.

Thomas Davis - 1741 - "King's Delight" - 69 acres.

Thomas King - 1673 - "King's Delight" - 50 acres.

Elias King - 1705 - "King's Land" - 400 acres.

Garrit McKinney - 1750 - "Kinney's Meadow" - 14 acres.

Joseph Carter - 1735 - "Kinsley" - 700 acres.

Adam Wallace - 1713 - "Kirkington" - 530 acres.

Adam Wallace - 1731 - "Kirkminster" - 200 acres.

Robert Crocker - 1737 - "Knavery Outdone by Justice" - 68 acres.

Richard Edmonds - 1679 - "Knowlwood" - 1000 acres.

Pearce Lamb - 1694 - "Lamb's Meadows" - 215 acres.

Pearce Lamb - 1683 - "Lamb's Range" - 100 acres.

Griffiths Nicholls - 1722 - "Land Dour" - 244 acres.

Thomas Lytfoot - 1683 - "Land of Delight" - 600 acres.

Roger Larramore - 1666 - "Larramore's Neck Enlarged" - 800 acres.

John Thomas - 1737 - "Larenim" - 100 acres.

Benjamin Pearce - 1728 - "Larenim's Conveniency" - 200 acres.

John Largant - 1721 - "Largant's Neck" - 100 acres.

John Larkin - 1677 - "Larkin's Desire" - 300 acres.

Roger Larramore - "Larramore's Addition" - 109 acres.

George Lawremore - 1663 - "Lawremore's Neck" - 250 acres.

John Lawson - 1732 - "Lawson's Chance" - 200 acres.

Matthew Chapman - 1683 - "Lee" - 500 acres.

Reece Jones - 1727 - "Lee" - 466 acres.

Charles Carroll - 1732 - "Lee" - 500 acres.

James Harris - 1732 - "Lee" - 486 acres.

Moses Andrews - 1744 - "Lessroon" - 75 acres. Certificate in the name of James Scott.

Thomas Lindsey - 1695 - "Level" - 100 acres.

William Husband - 1731 - "Level's Addition" - 260 acres.

William Husbands - 1746 - "Levell" - 959 acres.

John Cox and Andrew Peterson - 1671 - "Levell" - 300 acres.

Peregrine Browne - 1685 - "Levell" - 500 acres.

Casparus Herman - 1695 - "Levell" - 900 acres.

Henry Ward - 1683 - "Levell" - 500 acres.

James Murphy - 1684 - "Levell Ridge" - 1000 acres.

Michael Lum and Johannes Arrance - 1750 - "Lum's Adventure" - 137 acres.

William Rumsey - 1735 - "Little Addition" - 37 1/2 acres. Certificate in the name of Edward Rumsey.

Henry Baker - 1762 - "Little Anglesey" - 50 acres.

Henry Baker - 1762 - "Little Angle" - 50 acres. Patent in the name of Price Winton.

William Rumsey - 1738 - "Little Chance" - 20 acres. Certificate in the name of Edward Rumsey.

Robert Mackey - 1769 - "Little Venture" - 10 acres.

Benjamin Griffith - 1771 - "Littleworth" - 187 acres.

Thomas Lloyd - 1763 - "Lloyd's Discovery" - 15 acres.

Mathias Vanderhyden - 1688 - "Locust Neck" - 120 acres.

Sarah Pearce - 1726 - "Locust Point" - 132 acres. Certificate in the name of Francis Smith.

John Ward - 1725 - "Locust Thicket" - 510 acres.

William Ward - 1687 - "Locust Thicket" - 500 acres.

Thomas Nichols - 1695 - "Londonderry" - 200 acres.

Henry Ward - 1682 - "Long Acre" - 900 acres.

John Thompson - 1749 - "Long Lane" - 78 acres.

William Ewing - 1757 - "Long Lane" - 27 1/2 acres. Patent in the name of James Porter.

Hugh Macgregar - 1687 - "Long Lane" - 78 acres.

John Brice - 1765 - "Long Neglected" - 11 acres.

Andrew Poulson - 1680/1 - "Long Point" - 100 acres.

Thomas Love - 1755 - "Love's Arrowood" - 33 acres.

William Dare - 1681 - "Lower Triumph" - 500 acres.

Vincent Lowe - 1683 - "Lowe's Lott" - 500 acres.

Samuel Lowman - 1714 - "Lowman's Addition" - 100 acres.

John Holtham - 1753 - "Luck" - ? acres.

John Bailey - 1773 - "Luck" - 440 1/2 acres.

Lydia Hollingsworth - 1714 - "Lydia's Chance" - 27 acres.

Lydia Hollingsworth - 1724 - "Lydia's Joynture" - 400 acres.

Stephen Hyland - 1761 - "Mackenny's Desire" - 54 acres. Certificate in the name of Alexander Mackenny.

David Mackie - 1769 - "Mackie's Part 6" - 19 acres.

Hugh Mackgregory - 1695 - "Mackgregory's Delight" - 240 acres.

Samuel Maffitt - 1769 - "Maffitt's Restitution" - 26 acres.

Edward Gunnell - 1679 - "Maidenhead" - 200 acres.

George Collings - 1724 - "Maidenhead" - 76 acres.

Joseph Spernon - 1684 - "Manchester" - 245 acres. Certificate in the name of Joseph Spernon and Thomas Hinton.

Richard Hill - 1678 - "Manwaring Hall" - 400 acres.

Dr. Hugh Matthews - 1731 - "Manwaring Hall" - 1000 acres.

John Collett - 1672 - "Mapleton" - 200 acres.

Philip Stoops - 1751 - "Mapleton" - 64 1/2 acres.

Thomas Larkin - 1705 - "Margarett's Delight" - 1000 acres.

Richard Bennett - 1730 - "Markesfield" - 56 acres. Certificate in the name of Benjamin Cox.

Marcus Syfrayson - 1658 - "Markfield" (Kent County, now Cecil County) - 100 acres.

Thomas Frisby - 1706 - "Marksfield" - 50 acres.

Richard Leake - 1674 - "The Marshes" - 200 acres.

George Martin - 1734 - "Martin's Delight" - 200 acres.

George Martin - 1735 - "Martin's Enlargement" - 100 acres.

Otho Pennington - 1764 - "Martin's Nest" - 108 acres. Patent originally in the name Lodowick Martin.

Thomas Beard - 1763 - "Martin's Nest Resurveyed" - 127 1/2 acres.

Lodowick Martin - 1680 - "Martin's Rest" - 100 acres. [See the entry for "Otho Pennington, 1764, "Martin's Nest," q.v.].

Jane Martinson - 1661 - "Martinson" - 50 acres.

Jonathan Beck - 1716 - "Mary's Jointure" - 57 acres.

Henry Hendrickson - 1725 - "Mary's Park" - 130 acres.

John Gray - 1740 - "Mathias Hills" - 256 acres. Certificate in the name of Rees Jones.

Henrick Mathyason - 1658 - "Mathayson" - 100 acres.

Hugh Matthiason - 1741 - "Matson's Town" - 130 acres.

Henrich Freeman - 1683 - "Mattson's Range" - 30 acres.

Francis Maulding - 1725 - "Mauldin's Forest" - 200 acres.

Charles James - 1688 - "Mayford" - 100 acres.

Hugh Mecgregory - 1683 - "Mecgregory" - 80 acres. [Note: This tract is the same one by the name of "Long Lane"].

Peter Meekins - 1738 - "Meekins' Adventure" - 70 acres.

William Harris - 1743 - "Mesopotamia" - 340 acres. Certificate in the name of Edward Jones.

Nicholas Dorrell - 1687 - "Mickum" - 100 acres.

Jonathan Beck - 1718 - "Middle Ground" - 320 acres.

James Halloway and Thomas Pearce - 1695 - "Middle Grounds" - 200 acres.

Jarvis Morgan - 1670 - "Middle Neck" - 600 acres.

James Heath - 1726 - "The Middle Parcel" - 290 acres.

Andrew Woodberry - 1672 - "The Middle Plantation" - 300 acres.

Susanna Maria Bennett - 1658 - "Midland" - 250 acres.

Matthias Vanbebber - 1714 - "Milkum Island" - 1000 acres.

Augustine Herman - 1665 - "Mill Fall" - 100 acres.

Charles Rumsey - 1744 - "Mill Pond" - 70 acres. Certificate in the name of John Baldwin. [Note: Same entry in 1765].

Augustine Herman - 1671 - "Misfortune" - 1500 acres.

Augustine Herman - 1678 - "Misfortune" - 1339 acres.

Augustine Herman - 1682 - "Misfortune" - 1339 acres.

Robert Money - 1672 - "Money Worth" - 150 acres.

William Rumsey - 1732 - "Money Worth" - 66 acres. Certificate in the name of Col. Benjamin Pearce.

Ninian Dunlapp - 1714 - "Monin" - 100 acres.

Ephraim Augustine Harmon - 1716 - "Mons" - 379 acres.

Ephraim Augustine Herman - 1718 - "Mons" - 370 acres.

William Rumsey - 1769 - "Morass" - 4 3/4 acres.

John Browning and Henry Denton - 1688 - "Morelow" - 150 acres.

Phillip Calvert - 1659 - "Mannor of Morton" - 1000 acres.

Robert Mercer - 1742 - "Mounsefield Addition" - 26 acres.

Mouns Anderson - 1663 - "Mounsfield" - 150 acres.

Christopher Mouns - 1735 - "Mounsfield" - 243 acres.

Francis Mouldin - 1758 - "Mount Colliston" - 320 acres.

William Gillespie - 1760 - "Mount Gillespie" - 273 acres. Certificate of Survey in the name of William Willis.

Godfrey Harmer - 1658 - "Mount Harmer" - 200 acres.

James Murphy - 1684 - "Mount Hope" - 500 acres.

Mathias Vanbibber - 1716 - "Mount Hope" - 456 acres.

Thomas Johnson, Jr. - 1726 - "Mount Johnson" - 75 acres.

Rowland Chambers - 1723 - "Mount Joy" - 130 acres.

Abraham Collett - 1735 - "Mount Pisgah" - 80 acres.

Stephen Hollingsworth - 1713 - "Mount Pleasant" and "Hollowing Point" and a third unnamed tract - 300 acres.

Abraham Collet - 1725 - "Mount Pleasant" - 80 acres.

William Husband - 1752 - "Mount Pleasant" - 30 acres.

Vincent Lowe - 1683 - "Mount Pleasant" - 300 acres.

Stephen Hollingsworth - 1715 - "Mount Pleasant" - 250 acres.

Charles Quigly - 1688 - "Mount Quigly" - 300 acres.

Thomas Yerbury - 1685 - "Mulberry Dock" - 205 acres.

Thomas and Elizabeth Nichols - 1696 - "Mulberry Dock" - 205 acres. Certificate in the name of Thomas Yerbury.

John Ryland - 1721 - "Mulberry Month[?]" - 95 acres.

Bryan Omeely - 1664 - "Mulberry Mould" - 200 acres.

William Rumsey - 1726 - "Mulberry Mould" - 90 acres. Certificate in the name of James Baldwin.

Patrick Murphy - 1696 - "Murphy's Forrest" - 1000 acres.

Thomas Nash - 1753 - "Nash's Adventure" - 115 1/2 acres.

Benjamin A. Rumsey - 1763 - "Necessity" - 186 acres.

James Harris - 1695 - "Neglect" - 240 acres. Certificate in the name of Edward Jones.

James Harris - 1701 - "Neglect" - 240 acres.

James Harris - 1706 - "Neglect" - 300 acres.

William Ward - 1683 - "Neighbour's Grudge" - 175 acres.

John Brice, W. Harris, and D. Cheston - 1743 - "Neighbour's Joke" - 42 acres.

Thomas Etherington - 1743 - "Neighbour's Neglect" - 141 acres.

Peter Clawson - 1688 - "New Amster" - 200 acres.

Thomas Johnson - 1706 - "New Amster" - 164 acres.

Robert Dutton - 1713 - "New Cannaught" - 50 acres.

William Dare - 1687 - "New Castle Back Landing" - 400 acres.

George Talbot - 1683 - "New Connought Mannor" - 32000 acres. [Note: Tract formerly called "Susquehannough Mannor"].

Richard Mechary - 1687 - "New Coroborough" - 200 acres.

Rebecca Campbell - 1687 - "New Garden" - 190 acres.

John Stockton - 1747 - "New Garden" - 102 acres.

John Larkin - 1737 - "New Hall" - 485 acres.

Matthew Smith - 1701 - "New Intersection" - 159 acres.

Benjamin Pearce - 1744 - "New Intersection and Addition Vacancy" - 67 acres.

Nicholas Highland - 1715 - "New Kent" - 520 acres.

John Highland - 1728 - "New Kent" - 520 acres. Certificate in the name of Nicholas Highland.

Edmund O'Dwyer - 1686 - "New Munster" - 6000 acres.

Rees Jones - 1724 - "New Munster" - 200 acres.

William Dare - 1697 - "New Port" - 300 acres.

Thomas Sympers - 1723 - "New Spain" - 50 acres.

James Aston - 1724 - "New Turkey Point" - 300 acres.

Edward Nicholas -1739 - "Nicholas' Dear Purchase" - 70 acres.

Robert Croker and wife Rachel Croker - 1741 - "None So Good in Finland" - 525 acres.

Bartlett Hendrickson and Cornelius Peterson - 1665 - "None So Good in Finland" - 350 acres.

Rachel Crouch - 1725 - "Part of None So Good in Finland" - 158 acres. Certificate in the name of Thomas Crouch.

Edward Goodman - 1683 - "Norfolk" - 200 acres.

John Smallpiece - 1679 - "Norland" - 200 acres.

Robert Norrest - 1695 - "Norrest's Desire" - 18 acres.

William Husbands - 1745 - "North Addition to the Level" - 50 acres.

William Ward - 1687 - "North Levell" - 300 acres.

Stephen Onion - 1734 - "Nostrodamus" - 101 acres.

Benjamin Pearce - 1727 - "Octagon" - 60 acres.

George Oldfield - 1680 - "Oldfield's Lott" - 100 acres.

Edward Oldham - 1753 - "Oldham's Venture" - 55 acres.

George Talbot - 1683 - "Ormond" - 600 acres.

Orphans of John Vansant: Jacobus, Elizabeth, Ann, Rachel, and Cornelia Vansant - 1734 - "Orphans' Legacy" - 500 acres.

Thomas Paine - 1671 - "Paine's Lott" - 480 acres.

Ann Atkey - 1734 - "Pain's Lott" - 600 acres.

Nicholas Painter - 1678 - "Painter's Rest" - 1500 acres.

Thomas Bordley - 1724 - "Painter's Rest" - 1901 acres.

Henry Meese - 1658 - "Palmer's Island" - 200 acres at the mouth of the Sasquesahnow [Susquehannah] River.

Richard Bennett - 1723 - "Palmer's Island" - 125 acres. Certificate in the name of James Campbell.

John Cappon [Coppen] - 1735 - "Parcener" - ? acres.

William Rumsey - 1733 - "Parcener's Beginning" - 90 acres. Certificate in the name of John Coppen.

Richard Boyer and Francis Robinson - 1675 - "Partner's Addition" - 150 acres.

John England, Joshua Gee, Stephen Onion, John Rustin, William Russell, and Thomas Russell - 1724 - "Partnership" - 200 acres. Certificate in the name of Edward Griffith.

Enoch Storey - 1759 - "Partnership" - 237 1/2 acres.

Abram and Stephen Hollingsworth - 1724 - "First Part of Partner's Parcells" - 400 acres.

William Boone - 1696 - "Partness" ["Partners"?] - 321 acres.

John Banington - 1715 - "Part of Addition" - 100 acres.

Hugh Watson - 1730 - "Part of Banks" - 210 acres.

Joseph Gilpin - 1769 - "Part of Bevers Dam" - 338 acres.

John Stockton - 1771 - "Part of Brereton Resureyed" - 111 1/2 acres.

James Paul Heath - 1740 - "Part of Glass Go and Look" - 97 acres.

William Baxter and others - 1743 - "Part of His Lordship's Manor" - 20 acres.

Abraham Bondwell - 1680 - "Part of James' Forrest" - 100 acres.

Nicholas Hyland - 1761 - "Part of St. John's Manor" - 301 acres.

Edward Jones - 1688 - "Pasture Point" - 18 acres.

Henry Ward Pearce - 1762 - "Pearce's Beginning" - 78 acres.

Nathaniel Pearce - 1723 - "Pearce's Hope" - 155 acres.

Henry Ward Pearce - 1760 - "Pearce's Lane" - 45 acres.

Andrew and William Pearce - 1763 - "Pearce's Lot" - 8 acres.

Andrew Pearce - 1765 - "Pearce's Meadow" - 41 acres.

Henry Pennington - 1680 - "Pennyworth" - 71 acres.

Peregrine Frisby - 1754 - "Peregrine's Delight" - 1347 acres.

Elisha Perkins - 1731 - "Perkins' Delight" - 50 acres.

Stephen Onion - 1729 - "Perk's Island" - 61 acres. Certificate in the name of Edmund Perk.

John Bateman - 1659 - "Perry Neck" - 200 acres.

Benjamin Chew - 1736 - "Perry Neck" - 575 acres. Certificate in the name of John Perry, Jr. and George Perry.

D. Barren, John Perry, Jr., G. Perry, and A. Templer - 1728 - "Perry Point" - 840 acres.

Peter Jacobson - 1658 - "Peter's Fields" - 200 acres.

John James - 1684 - "Petton" - 50 acres.

Philip Stoops - 1752 - "Philip's Addition" - 5 1/2 acres.

Thomas Phillips - 1732 - "Phillips' Bottom" - 30 acres.

William Rumsey - 1732 - "Phillips' Neglect" - 69 acres. Certificate in the name of Edward Rumsey.

Henry Baker - 1763 - "Philips' Neglect" - 137 acres.

John Lewellin - 1684 - "Pickadilly" - 1000 acres.

William Rumsey - 1730 - "Pigg Point Landing" - 8 acres. Certificate in the name of John Baldwin.

Alexander White - 1723 - "Pleasant Mount" - 108 acres.

Jonas Chambers - 1763 - "Pleasant Mount" - 226 acres.

Thomas Simpers - 1773 - "Pleasant Range" - 37 acres.

Alexander White - 1724 - "Plum Point Fork" - 100 acres.

William Fisher - 1666 - "Poplar Neck" - 1400 acres. Deed to Henry Ward.

Henry Ward - 1674 - "Poplar Neck" - 1400 acres. Deed from William Fisher.

John Highland - 1738 - "Poplar Valley" - 100 acres.

Andrew Pouleson - 1663 - "Pouleson" - 50 acres.

William Ward - 1681 - "Powles' Corner" - 175 acres.

Matthew Rogers - 1714 - "Prevention" - 10 acres.

William Rumsey - 1735 - "Prevention" - 100 acres. Certificate in the name of Edward Rumsey.

William Price - 1687 - "Price's Forrest" - 150 acres.

Henry Rippen - 1741 - "Price's Intelligence" - 12 1/2 acres.

Thomas Severson - 1745 - "Price's Intelligence" - 115 acres.

Ephraim Price - 1767 - "Price's Luck" - 30 acres.

William Price - 1673 - "Price's Venture" - 250 acres.

William Harris - 1743 - "Prosperity" - 250 acres. Certificate in the name of Edward Jones.

John Briscoe - 1700 - "Providence" - 159 acres.

Abraham Hollingsworth - 1713 - "Providence" - 500 acres.

Samuel Robinett - 1732 - "Providence" - 350 acres.

Richard Pullin - 1681 - "Pullin's Refuge" - 500 acres.

James Robinson - 1706 - "Purchase" - 110 acres.

Vincent Lowe - 1683 - "Quigly's Grove" - 1000 acres.

Charles Quigley - 1688 - "Quigley's Lodge" - 108 acres.

Alexander White - 1723 - "Raccoon Point" - 150 acres.

Thomas Phillips - 1716 - "Rachoone Range" - 67 acres.

John Brice, William Harris, and Daniel Cheston - 1740 - "Ramble" - 62 acres.

William Ramsey - 1727 - "Ramsey's Patent" - 100 acres.

Thomas Medford - 1695 - "The Range" - 118 acres.

William Ward - 1672 - "Rattle Snake Point" - 100 acres.

John Read - 1755 - "Read's Addition" - 34 1/2 acres.

George Martin - 1735 - "Repensation" - 150 acres. Certificate in the name of John Baldwin.

William Blankestein - 1687 - "Requittal" - 400 acres.

Peter Hack - 1683 - "Resurvey" - 470 acres.

James Husband - 1723/4 - "Resurvey" - 140 acres.

Nathan Phillips - 1723 - "Resurvey" - 37 acres.

John Mackey - 1756 - "Resurvey Mackey Garden" - 152 1/2 acres.

Caspary Smith - 1730[?] - "Resurvey of Addition" - 360 acres.

Alexander Fulton - 1760 - "Resurvey of Amory's [Emory's] Satisfaction" - 107 acres.

Mathias Vanbibber - 1707 - "Resurvey Blankesteen Park" - 56 acres.

Thomas Bolden, Jr. and others - 1744 - "Resurvey on Bristole" - 500 acres.

Robert Patterson - 1756 - "Resurvey on Daughtery's Desire" - 122 acres.

Augustine Pasmore - 1768 - "Resurvey on Doe Hill and Bear Point" - 421 1/2 acres.

Robert Evans - 1759 - "Resurvey on Duck Neck" - 109 acres.

Benjamin Ward - 1750 - "Resurvey on Green Field" - 691 acres.

John Dempster - No Date - "Resurvey on Glaster" - ? acres.

John Davidson - 1766 - "Resurvey on High Park" - 220 acres.

Moses Davidson - 1773 - "Resurvey on High Park" - 255 acres.

William and Thomas Husbands - 1723 - "Resurvey on Hillington" - 142 acres.

John Roberts, Sr. - 1751 - "Resurvey on Hornes" - 64 acres.

Nicholas Hyland - 1766 - "Resurvey on Johnson's Adventure" - 222 acres.

Thomas Lloyd - 1762 - "Resurvey on Money Worth" - 26 acres.

Joseph Husband - 1769 - "Resurvey on Mount Pleasant" - 225 1/2 acres. Certificate in the name of William Husbands.

Joseph Gilpin - 1769 - "Resurvey on Part of Beaver Dam" - 338 acres.

Francis Moldin - 1756 - "Resurvey on Part of Colliston" - 320 acres.

Thomas Severson - 1748 - "Resurvey on Price's Intelligence and Severson's Point Plantation" - 115 acres.

John Holtham - 1753 - "Resurvey of Sutten's Forrest" - 205 acres.

Michael Earle - 1751 - "Resurvey on Swan Harbour" - 350 acres.

Robert Graham - 1764 - "Resurvey on Teague's Delight" - 208 acres.

Thomas Harris - 1756 - "Resurvey on Twelfth Point" - 216 acres.

Richard Bennett - 1749 - "Resurvey on The Grove and Hazelmore" - 1738[?] acres. Patented as "Bennett's Grove."

Roger Larramore - 1720 - "Resurvey of Two Branches" - 184 acres.

Peregrine Ward - 1754 - "Resurvey on Ward's Knowledge and Ward's Addition" - 647 acres.

Thomas Harris - 1756 - "Resurvey on Welsh Point" - 216 acres.

Richard Boulding - 1723 - "Richard's Chance" - 335 acres.

Lambert Willmore - 1707 - "Rich Level" - 840 acres.

Phillip Holeager - 1684 - "Rich Level" - 800 acres.

Sabina Rumsey - 1744 - "Rich Lott" - 17 acres. Certificate in the name of William Pearce.

Thomas Ricketts - 1773 - "Ricketts' Resurvey" - 396 1/4 acres.

John Ricketts - 1761 - "Ricketts' Triangle" - 59 acres.

William Smith - 1763 - "Rook and Pill" - 382 acres.

Francis Rock - 1765 - "Rock's Purchase" - 50 acres.

John Glover - 1676 - "Rooke and Pill" - 250 acres. Certificate in the name of Peter Jones.

John Browning - 1679 - "Rounds" - 500 acres.

William Pierce - 1704 - "Rounds" - 1000 acres.

John Wheeler - 1659 - "Round Stone" - 300 acres.

Robert Rowland - 1752 - "Rowland's Chance" - 53 acres.

Robert Rowland - 1752 - "Rowland's Venture" - 34 acres.

John Hyde - No date - "Royston's Purchase" - 350 acres.

Robert Carvile - 1684 - "Royston's Purchase" - 500 acres. Certificate in the name of Richard Royston.

Tobias Rudulph - 1769 - "Rudulph's Desire" - 514 acres.

John English - 1683 - "Rumford" - 200 acres.

William Rumsey - 1733 - "Rumsey's Double Parcell" - 300 acres. Certificate in the name of Edward Rumsey.

William Rumsey - 1754 - "Rumsey's Lott" - 1 acre.

William Rumsey - 1761 - "Rumsey's Negligence" - 32 acres.

Edward Rumsey - 1731 - "Rumsey's Ramble" - 300 acres.

William Rumsey - 1733 - "Rumsey's Range" - 300 acres.

William Rumsey - 1731 - "Rumsey's Retreat" - 100 acres. Certificate in the name of John Baldwin.

William Rumsey - 1733 - "Rumsey's Success" - 600 acres. Certificate in the name of Benjamin Pearce.

William Rumsey - 1733 - "Rumsey's Treble Parcel" - 150 acres. Certificate in the name of Edward Rumsey.

Stephen Onion - 1733 - "Russell Onion" [Union?] - 99 acres.

John Rutter - 1739 - "Rutter's Choice" - 100 acres.

John Rutter - 1746 - "Rutter's Purchase" - 97 acres.

John Rutter - No date - "Sanday [Sunday?] Point" - ? acres.

Will Rutter - 1773 - "Rutter's Resurvey" - 619 acres.

John Williams - 1736 - "Rycroft's Choice" - 284 acres.

John Rycroft - 1678/9 - "Rycroft's Choice" - 300 acres. Certificate in the name of John Bollen.

William Williamson - 1695 - "St. Albans" - 367 acres.

Thomas Mansell - 1706 - "Saint Haverins" - 458 acres.

James Heath - 1711 - "Saint Ignatius" - 100 acres.

John Carr - 1674 - "Saint John's Manor" - 3000 acres. Certificate in the name of John Pate.

Nathan Phillips - 1723 - "Part of St. John's Manor" - 200 acres.

Nathaniel Phillips - 1726 - "Part of St. John's Manor" - 97 acres.

Thomas Moore - 1720 - "St. John's Town" - 2 acres.

Thomas Moore - 1725 - "Saint Johnstown" - 100 acres.

James Heath - 1711 - "Saint Paul's" - 500 acres.

Vincent Lowe - 1684 - "Saint Vincent's" - 1000 acres.

Thomas Mansell - 1706 - "Saint Xavier's" - 378 acres.

Joshua George - 1759 - "Salem" - 318 acres.

Hugh Woodberry - 1671 - "Salem" - 300 acres.

John Reynolds - 1732 - "Sarah's Jointure" - 660 acres.

Richard Peacock - 1683 - "Sarah's Joynture" - 600 acres.

William Savin - 1680 - "Savin's Lott" - 50 acres.

William Savon - 1665 - "Savon's Rest" - 200 acres.

Andrew Wier - 1730 - "Scotland" - 179 acres.

William Rumsey - 1735 - "Scraps" - 12 1/2 acres. Certificate in the name of Edward Rumsey.

Samuel Seal - 1744 - "Seal's Lott" - 50 acres.

Abram and Stephen Hollingsworth - 1719 - "Second Part of Partner's Parcel" - 100 acres.

William Frisby - 1720 - "Security" - 134 acres.

Stephen Onion - 1722 - "Security" - 73 acres.

John Ruston - 1734 - "Security" - 133 acres.

Michael Turbutt - 1684 - "Sedgefield" - 500 acres.

Thomas Severson - 1741 - "Severson's Point" - 84 acres.

Thomas Severson - 1745 - "Severson's Point" - 115 acres.

John Severson - 1729 - "Severson's Delight" - 140 acres.

Nicholas Sewall - 1721 - "Sewall Mannor" - 4000 acres.

Samuel Sharpe - 1768 - "Sharpe's Trapezium" - 42 1/2 acres.

Thomas Sharp - No date - "Sharp's Industry" - ? acres.

William Rumsey - 1726 - "Shear Mould and Coulter" - 48 acres. Certificate in the name of Benjamin Pearce.

John Dowdell - 1716 - "Sheffield" - 500 acres.

Edward Jones - 1680 - "Shrewsbury" - 180 acres.

Pharloe Gleeb - 1698 - "Shrewsbury Pan" - 40 acres.

John Coppen - 1730 - "Silvania's Folly" - 240 acres.

William Rumsey - 1738 - "Silvania" - 20 acres. Certificate in the name of Edward Rumsey.

Henry Pennington - 1680 - "Silvanes Folly" - 100 acres.

John Simpers - 1751 - "Simpers' Forrest" - 110 acres.

John Simpers - 1761 - "Simpers' Meadow" - 376 acres.

John Simpson - 1751 - "Simpson's Meadow" - 241 acres.

John Simpus [Simpers] - 1753 - "Simpus' Chance" - 239 acres. Certificate in the name of Henry Baker.

Thomas Simpus [Simpers] - 1753 - "Simpus' Forest" - 110 acres. Certificate in the name of John Simpus.

John Simpus [Simpers] - 1752 - "Simpus' Meadows" - 400 acres.

Marmaduck Sims - 1687 - "Sims' Forrest" - 400 acres.

Dennis Inglish - 1678/9 - "Sinclair's Purchase" - 110 acres.

Francis Child - 1670 - "Sister's Dowry" - 200 acres.

Jacob and Bartholomew Jacobs - No date - "Part of Skeelton" - ? acres.

James Murphy - 1683 - "Skelton" - 500 acres.

Samuel Alexander - 1714 - "Sligoe" - 200 acres.

Ninian Dunlap - 1696 - "Sligoe" - 200 acres. Certificate in the name of Alexander Mullaney.

George Wilson - 1672 - "The Slipe" - 50 acres.

Thomas Wiley - 1720 - "Small Hope" - 5 acres.

Sampson George - 1688 - "Small Hope" - 8 acres.

William Rumsey - 1735 - "Small Hope" - 8 acres. Certificate in name of Edward Rumsey.

Augustine Herman - 1665 - "Small Hopes" - 1500 acres.

William Douglas - 1715 - "Smith's Addition" - 50 acres. Certificate in the name of Thomas Smith.

John Smith - 1719 - "Smith's Discovery" - 70 acres.

Caleb Ricketts - 1764 - "Smith's Discovery" - 111 acres.

Richard Smith - 1687 - "Smith's Fort" - 500 acres.

John Severson - 1724 - "Smokey Point" - 61 acres.

John Severson - 1731 - "Smokey Point als Severson's Delight" - 140 acres.

Jacob Divillard - 1683 - "Smoaking Point" - 50 acres.

Thomas Johnson - 1719 - "Snow Hill" - 100 acres.

Thomas Johnson - 1716 - "Snow Hill Addition" - 150 acres.

James Carroll - 1734 - "Society" - 2104 acres.

Jacob Reynolds - 1737 - "Southampton" - 303 acres.

Joseph Sparnon - 1676 - "Sparnon's Delight" - 250 acres.

Benjamin Pearce - 1725 - "Shear Mould and Coulter" - 48 acres.

Hugh Lawson - 1720 - "Speedwell" - 350 acres.

John Buck - 1741 - "Spencer's Harbour" - 1 1/2 acres. Certificate in the name of Thomas Spencer.

Samuel Willes [Willis?] - 1714 - "Spring Head" - 200 acres.

Fergus Smith - 1773 - "Spring Head" - 205 3/4 acres.

Oliver Sprye - 1658 - "Sprye's Hill" - 600 acres.

Henry Lowe - 1717 - "Spry's Hill" - 573 acres.

Philip Holeager - 1683 - "Stanaway" - 200 acres.

Thomas Johnson, Jr. - 1726 - "State Hill" - 225 acres.

John Hause Steelman - 1711 - "Steelman's Delight" - 200 acres.

John Steel - 1745 - "Steels" - 200 acres.

William Mansfield - 1688 - "Steele Head" - 40 acres.

Henry Baker - 1762 - "Steel's Head" - 150 acres.

John Gale - 1724 - "Stillington" - 142 acres. Certificate in the name of William and Thomas Husband.

Axel Still - 1673 - "Stillington" - 100 acres.

John Cockes [Cox] - "Stillington" - 160 acres.

Thomas Vaughan - 1683 - "Stockton" - 500 acres.

Richard Bennett - 1716 - "Stockton Addition" - 225 acres.

William Rumsey - 1739 - "Stoney Chase" - 1050 acres.

John Baldwin - 1732 - "Stoney Chase" - 400 acres.

Caleb Carman - 1744 - "Stoney Hill" - 88 acres.

Henry Baker - 1761 - "Stoney Hill" - 22 acres.

Hugh Nicholas - 1762 - "Stoney Point" - 5 acres.

Johannes Arrant, Michael Lum and Peter Boyer - 1752 - "Stoney Range" - 178 acres. Certificate in the name of Johannas Arrant, Michael Lum, Peter Boyer, Hance Rudulph, and William Bristow.

John Stoops - 1695 - "Stoop's Folly" - 100 acres.

Alexander Williamson and Isaac Benson - 1770 - "Stoop's Purchase With a Mortgage" - 58 1/2 acres.

Enock Storey - 1756 - "Storey's Meadow" - 578 acres.

George Gouldsmith - 1748 - "Strainge" - 500 acres.

Joshua George - 1738 - "Strange" - 476 acres. Certificate in the name of John Thompson.

Thomas Yerbury - 1684 - "Strawberry Bank" - 89 acres.

Thomas Mackenny - 1732 - "Struggle" - 89 acres. [Note: His name in the record book is written as Thomas Macklehenny].

John Reed - 1707 - "The Suburbs" - 100 acres.

John Hammond - 1734 - "Success" - 375 acres.

Thomas Lytfoot - 1683 - "Success" - 300 acres.

John Browning - 1678/9 - "Successor" - 500 acres.

John Hammond - 1733 - "Success Resurveyed" - 375 acres.

John Rutter - No date - "Sunday Point" - ? acres. [Note: Probably the same "Sanday Point" recorded earlier herein].

Benjamin Chew - 1735 - "Part of Susquehanna Manor" - 455 acres.

Richard Sedgwick - 1744 - "Part of Susquehanna Manor" - 190 acres.

Thomas Miller - 1744 - "Part of Susquehanna Manor" - 16 acres.

John Wallas - 1744 - "Part of Susquehanna Manor" - 100 acres.

William Elliott - 1752 - "Part of Susquehanna Manor" - 160 acres.

Thomas Archer - 1744 - "Part of Susquehanna Manor" - 62 acres.

Jeremiah Brown - 1747 - "Part of Susquehanna Manor" - 78 acres.

Andrew Alexander - 1748 - "Sutton's Forrest" - 205 acres.

Thomas Sutton - 1685 - "Sutton's Forrest" - 100 acres.

Phillip Calvert - 1659 - "Mannor of Swaile" - 1000 acres.

Stephen Hollingsworth - 1715 - "The Swamp" - 10 acres.

John Poole - 1669 - "Swan Harbor" - 450 acres.

Michael Earle - 1751 - "Resurvey of Swan Harbour" - 350 acres.

Olle Matthaison - 1665 - "Sweed Land" - 200 acres.

Angelica Coppen - 1734 - "Sylvania's Folly" - 240 acres. Certificate in the name of John Coppen.

Henry Pennington - 1695 - "Sylvan's Folly" - 100 acres.

Jeremiah Taylor - 1772 - "Taylor's Lot" - 5 1/2 acres.

William Teague - 1734 - "Teague's Choice" - 50 acres.

Robert Graham - 1754 - "Teague's Delight" - 208 acres. [Note: Originally granted to Edward Teague in 1695].

William Teague - 1734 - "Teague's Forrest" - 100 acres.

William Teague - 1734 - "Teague's Hopewell" - 50 acres.

William Teague - 1716 - "Teague's Endeavour" - 100 acres.

Edward Tegg [Teague] - "Tegg's [Teague's] Delight" - 130 acres.

Richard Edmonds - 1683 - "Thomas' Lott" - 200 acres.

John Thompson - 1715 - "Thompson's Inspection" - 200 acres.

George Thompson - 1659 - "Thompson's Town" - 500 acres.

William Bristow - 1714 - "Part of Thompson's Town" - 100 acres.

William Bristow - 1722 - "Part of Thompson's Town" - 90 acres.

William Bristow - 1733 - "Part of Thompson's Town" - 100 acres.

John Campbell - 1732 - "Thompson's Town" - 175 acres. Certificate in the name of Charles Carroll and Joshua George.

John Campbell - 1737 - "Thompson's Town" - 575 acres.

John Thompson - 1713 - "Thompson's Town Point" - 22 acres.

William Bristow - 1721 - "Thompson's Town Point" - 44 acres.

Adam Wallace - 1753 - "Thompson's Town Point" - 22 acres.

Thomas Jacobs - 1723 - "Three Partners" - 768 acres. Certificate in the name of Ephraim Augustine Herman.

Isaac Hawkins - 1718[?] - "Three Partner's Island" - ? acre.

Thomas Jacobs - 1720 - "Three Pastures" - 768 acres.

John Brice, Daniel Cheston, and William Harris - 1743 and 1747 - "Three Prongs" - 100 acres.

Rowland Chambers - 1739 - "Tilley Broome" - 100 acres.

Vincent Lowe - 1684 - "Timber Ridge" - 2700 acres.

Richard Peacock - 1683 - "Toes Purchase" - 400 acres.

James Heath - 1708 - "Toes Purchase" - 195 acres.

William Pierce - 1706 - "Tolchester" - 955 acres.

Thomas Gutterin - 1665 - "Town Point" - 800 acres.

Joseph Wood - 1749 - "Trancina" [Francina?] - 858 acres.

William Rumsey - 1731 - "Trebble Parcel" - 150 acres.

Rowland Williams - 1666 - "Trevollyon" - 100 acres.

John Hawkins - 1667 - "Triangle" - 150 acres.

Rees Hinton - 1723 - "Triangle" - 40 acres. Certificate in the name of Ariana Frisby.

John Collett and George Gouldsmith - 1665 - "Triumph" - 1000 acres.

John Hyland - 1684 - "Triumph" - 234 acres.

Anne Morgan - 1665/1771[?] - "True Game" - 150 acres.

John Veazey - 1747 - "True Game" - 710 acres.

John Veazey - 1749 - "True Game" - 240 acres.

Robert Hodgson - 1725 - "Tryall" - 100 acres.

Richard Bennett - 1722 - "Tryall" - 150 acres.

William Dare - 1718/9 - "Tryangle" - 150 acres.

John Altham - 1724 - "Tryangle" - 56 acres. Certificate in the name of Matthias Vanbebber.

Michael Tulley - 1746 - "Tulley's Lott" - 12 acres.

Sampson George - 1757 - "Turkey Harbour" - 101 acres. Certificate in the name of Nicholas Hyland.

Richard Bennett - 1738 - "Turkey Point" - 690 acres.

Nicholas Spencer and Richard Wright - 1659 - "Turkey Point" - 1000 acres. Certificate in the name of Richard Wright.

Nicholas Sporne - 1696 - "Tuskorora Plains" - 961 acres. Certificate in the name of Garret Murrey.

Thomas Maddox and Charles Vincent - 1670 - "Two Branches" - 250 acres.

John Pennington - 1725 - "Two Branches" - 184 acres. Certificate in the name of Roger Laramore.

John and Richard Collett [Collect?] - 1664 - "Two Necks" - 600 acres.

William Dare - 1684 - "Two Necks" - 600 acres.

William Dare - 1714 - "Two Necks" - 568 acres.

Eleanor and Mary Campbell - 1761 - "Two Sisters" - 264 acres.

Richard Booker - 1665 - "Uppermost" - 500 acres.

John Hiland - 1680 - "Upper Triumph" - 460 acres.

Niles Urinson - 1670 - "Urinson" - 150 acres.

Nathaniel Hynson [Urinson?] - 1721 - "Urinson" - 173 acres.

Matthias Vanbibber - 1720 - "Vanbibber's Forrest" - 850 acres.

Cornelius Vansant - 1724 - "Van's Hamlet" - 344 acres.

William Rumsey - 1762 - "Variation" - 19 1/2 acres.

John Veazey - 1753 - "Veazey's Lott" - 393 acres.

Edward Veazey - 1768 - "Veazey's Lot" - 4 1/2 acres.

Philip Cazier [Cozier?] - 1746 - "The Venter" - 7 1/2 acres.

William Rumsey - 1733 - "Virginity" - 50 acres. Certificate in the name of Col. Benjamin Pearce.

John Beedle - 1766 - "Vulcan's Choice" - 9 acres. Certificate in the name of William Beedle, Jr.

Thomas Smith - 1667 - "Vulcan's Rest" - 500 acres.

William Douglas - 1714 - "Vulcan's Rest" - 522 acres.

William Douglass - 1669 - "Addition to Vulcan's Rest" - 50 acres.

William Morgan - 1685 - "Wales" - 50 acres.

Matthew Wallace - 1737 - "Wallace's Scrawl" - 378 acres.

Francis Wallace - 1720 - "Wallace's Scrawl" - 378 acres.

William Borne - 1696 - "Walnut Thicket" - 200 acres.

Thomas Wamsley - 1721 - "Wamsley's Lott" - 50 acres.

John Ward - 1706 - "Ward's Addition" - 450 acres.

John Ward - 1766 - "Ward's Addition and Ward's Knowledge" - 647 acres.

John Ward - 1694 - "Ward's Knowledge" - 140 acres.

Alphonse Cosden - 1746 - "Warmust [Wormust?] and Hack's Addition" - 386 acres.

George Warner - 1688 - "Warner's Levell" - 276 acres.

Samuel Alexander - 1722 - "Warwick" - 55 acres.

Vachell Denton - 1719 - "Warren" - 454 acres. Certificate in the name of John Browning.

Thomas Sympers - 1723 - "Wasp Nest" - 50 acres.

John Simpers - 1762 - "Wasp's Nest" - 204 acres.

Isaac Miller and others - 1722 - "Webster" - 41 acres.

Rowland Williams - 1658 - "Welsh Point" - 100 acres.

Christopher Williams - 1725 - "Welsh Point" - 50 acres.

John Wheeler - 1658 - "Wheeler's Point" - 250 acres.
Thomas Ward - 1737 - "Wheeler's Point" - 250 acres.
Ann Wheeler - 1680 - "Wheeler's Purchase" - 100 acres.
Ann Wheeler - 1680 - "Wheeler's Warren" - 100 acres.
Alexander White - 1714 - "White's Folly" - 200 acres.
Moses Jones - 1752 - "White Marsh" - 297 acres. Certificate in the name of Henry Baker.
Stephen Hyland - 1772 - "White Marsh" - 564 acres.
James Alexander's Heirs - 1724 - "Widow's and Orphans' Portion" - 316 acres.
Hester Gough - 1679 - "Widow's Lott" - 800 acres.
Martin Wilcox - 1758 - "Wilcox Adventure" - 12 acres.
William Bowling - 1702 - "William's Chance" - 100 acres.
William Benson - 1680 - "William's Choice" - 100 acres.
Thomas Impey - 1684 - "Winfield" - 500 acres.
Samuel Withers - 1659 - "Withers" - 200 acres.
John Baldwin - 1730 - "Withers" - 145 acres.
David Makina - 1680/1 - "Woodbridge" - 200 acres.
Dennis Nowland - 1714 - "Woodbridge" - 200 acres.
Francis Child - 1665 - "World's End" - 500 acres.
Peter Hack - 1676 - "Wormust" - 450 acres. Certificate in the name of George Hack.
Peter Sayer - 1685 - "Worsell Mannor" - 1000 acres.
Thomas Ricketts - 1774 - "Worthless" - 28 1/2 acres.
Zebulon Hollingsworth - 1750 - "Worth Little" - 69 acres.
William Starkey - 1753 - "Worth Little" - 110 acres.
Thomas Hanker - 1681 - "Worton Meadows" - 200 acres.
Henry Wright - 1710 - "Wright's Lott" - 244 acres.
Thomas Wright - 1673 - "Wright's Rest" - 200 acres.
Daniel Garnell - 1679 - "Yorkeshire" - 500 acres.
Richard Bennett - 1738 - "Yorkshire" - 675 acres.
Jacob Young - 1658 - "Young's Neck" - 50 acres.
Zebulon Hollingsworth - 1733 - "Zebulon's Fancy" - 150 acres.
John Archer - No date - "The Zone" - ? acres.

Unpatented Certificates and Leases: Nathan Baker (1748), Samuel Arnett (1747), John Copson (1744), Garrett McKinsey (1751), Johann Arrant (1745), Richard Rutter (1746), Jane Grady (1743), John Allison (1752), Edward Veazey (1746), Tobias Ampokker (1744), Robert Anderson (1747), Richard Patten (1748), Thomas Ross (1751), John Rutter (1751), Edward Brumfield (1746), John Rutter (1746), James Baxter (1751), John Rutter (1739), John Meek (1744), Thomas Branion (1747), Samuel Seal (1744), James Buchanan (1747), Margaret Brumfield (1747), William Emmet (1744), Osgood Gee (1745), John Copson (1744), Thomas Cord (1771), David Creswell (1745), James Creswell (1745), William Creswell (1747), Benjamin Crocket (1751), John Clerk (1747), James Crage (1745), Mary Crocket

(1751), Benjamin Chew (1745), Benjamin Chew (1747), Benjamin Chew, Jr.
(1750), James Disney (1747), John Dempster (1749), Mary Dawety (1748),
Moses Ewings (1755), James Ewens (1753), John Underhill (1752), Samuel
Edmunston (1745), Alexander Ewings (1750), Samuel Gilpin (1747), Andrew
Gibson (1748), James Glasgow (1750), John Green (1745), John Glasgow
(1747), Mary George (1757), James Thompson (1750), William Graham
(1752), John Green (1757), Thomas Hartshorn (1744), Patrick Hambleton
(1752), William Hutchman (1748), Harman Husband (1750), Jonathan
Hartshorn (1745), James Paul Heath (1745), Henry Jackson (1747), Edward
Jackson (1744), Jacob Johnson (1744), Thomas Janney (1747), John
Kirkpatrick (1750), John Kirkpatrick (1755), Thomas Kerns (1746), William
Kelly (1747), Thomas Kennady (1742), Nicholas Kelly (1744), James Leeper
(1747), William Maffit (1749), Jane Mitchell (1747), John Murphy (1748),
Jane Martin (1747), Thomas Miller (1744), Edward Mitchell (1750), Oliver
Miller (1750), William McKown (1749), William Meek (1753), Thomas
Miller (1750), James McClure (1747), Francis Mabury (1744), Adam Meek
(1747), Robert Nicholas (1751), William Nelson (1753), Francis Owin (1747),
James Orr (1753), John Pasmore (1746), Samuel Piggott (1745), Joseph
Richardson (1746), Walter Rogger (1747), Elizabeth Steele (1746), William
Sherwood (1744), John Stump (1744), Henry Stump (1748), James Speer
(1748), Samuel Thomas, Jr. (1748), Samuel White (1745), John Welsh (1754),
William Watson (1744).

LOTHOLDERS IN 1702 IN THE TOWNSHIP OF NOTTINGHAM: Edward Beeson, Henry Reynolds, John Richardson, Ebenezer Empson, William Brown, Cornelius Empson, James Cooper, James Brown, Robert Dutton, Samuel Littler, Andrew Job, Randal Janney, John Richardson, Joel Bayley, John Churchman and John Bates. [Note: Cornelius Empson, John Richardson, Henry Reynolds, Ebenezer Empson and John Guest were mentioned in the 1701 warrant of survey but they never resided in Nottingham]. Additional information on early lotholders is available in "Early Settlers of the Nottingham Lots," by A. Day Bradley (National Genealogical Society Quarterly, Vol. 70, No. 4, December, 1982, pp. 282-294).

COMMISSIONERS EMPOWERED ON AUGUST 6, 1730 (to lay out a town on Broxen's Point [called Ceciltown] on the south side of Bohemia River): Col. Ephraim Augustine Herman, Col. Benjamin Pearce, Mr. Thomas Colvill, Mr. Stephen Knight, Mr. Nicholas Ridgely, Mr. Joshua George, and Mr. Alphonso Cosden. John Baldwin, Sheriff. Jurors: Nathan Hynson, John Coppen, John Veasey, John Price, Philip Barret, Isaac Caulk, John Pennington, George Childs, Daniel Benson, John Roberts, and John Bateman (all substantial freeholders).

COMMISSIONERS APPOINTED IN THE FALL OF 1742 (to carry out the act of incorporation of Charlestown, the town to be laid out at a place called Long Point on the west side of North East River): Thomas Colvill, Nicholas Hyland, Benjamin Pearce, William Alexander, Henry Baker, Zebulon Hollingsworth, and John Reed.

PETITION OF TENANTS OF SUSQUEHANNAH MANOR TO THE
GENERAL ASSEMBLY OF MARYLAND (SIGNED IN 1779 AND
REFERRING TO THEIR ANCESTORS IN 1680 AND 1744): "The petition of the inhabitants of Susquehannah Manor alias New Connaught
situated to the southward of the Temporary Line in Cecil County in behalf of
themselves and the other inhabitants of said Manor----Humbly sheweth that
the said Manor was first settled under a grant made by the Proprietor to
George Talbot about the year 1680 who parcelled it out on easy terms to the
first settlers; they and their posterity remained thereon peaceably and quietly
until about the year 1744 when the same was claimed by the Proprietor who
obtaining verdicts in ejectments against several of the inhabitants they were
obliged to take leases from him on such terms as was prescribed them; that
the said Manor has been cleared by the labour and industry of the said inhabitants and their ancestors who have expended large sums of money in
making valuable improvements on the same. They are therefore much alarm
at a certain Mark Alexander's attempting to escheat it, who, if he succeeds
will have it in his power to ruin numbers of said inhabitants and greatly dis-
tress them." [They asked the General Assembly of Maryland to pass a law to
avert this danger.] Petition signed on December 23, 1779 by: Samuel
Thomas, Richard Thomas, William Rowland, Samuel Miller, William Patten,
David Patten, Jonathan Hartshorn, William Glasgow, Andrew Walker, Ben-
jamin Foster, John Laygart, Robert Marquess, Samuel Marquess, Robert Fin-
ley, John Finley, Amos Ewing, John Cambell, John McHarey, Moses Ewing,
Andrew Wier, Robert Wier, James McLochlan, Thomas Russell, Thomas
Hughes, William Gibson, Daniel Corbett, James Millegan, John Millegan,
Jeremiah Baker, William Croshers, Jon. Cather, James Hegon, Stephen
Nevitt, Thomas Hartshorn, John Kirkpatrick, John Cameron, Thomas Mc-
Clenry, Edward Murphy, John Carswell, John McKewn, John Jack, William
Johnson, John Cothew, Edward Justice, John Alexander, Richard Abrams,
John Hall, James Rowland, John McCay, Hugh McCay, William Griffee,
Richard Griffee, Robert Lyon, Andrew Kidd, George Kidd, William
Hitchman, Robert Welsh, James Welsh, John Patterson, Robert Porter,
Robert McMaster, Samuel Gay, Francis Boyd, John Cunningham, William
Watson, George England, Joshua White, Daniel Sheredine, Nathaniel Litton,
John Blackburn, John Butterfield, John Butterfield, Jr., Thomas Conway,
Baruch Williams, William Currier, William Marnonscooo[sic], Joseph White,
James Campbell, James Creswell, John Pritchard, William Brumfield,
Patrick McComb, William Sanderson, Francis Brumfield, James Hasson, Wil-
liam Crookshank, John Robertson, John Brumfield, Patrick Hamilton, Jonas
Cooper, Edward Jackson, Nathan Norton, Samuel Crockett, Robert Mc-
Mullin, Mary Mitchell, John Bankhead, Henry Plaxco, Thomas Kelley, Ar-
thur Alexander, Sr., Andrew Barrett, Samuel McMullin, Samuel McMullin,
Jr., Moses Cannon, William Dickson, Charles Whitelock, John Murphy, Wil-
liam Currier, and James McMollon. (Ref: "Petition of Tenants of Susquehannah Manor for Titles in Fee of Their Respective Holdings," *Maryland
Historical Magazine*, Volume 5, pp. 58-60).

NATURALIZATIONS, 1660-1729
(Gleanings from *Colonial Maryland Naturalizations*, by Jeffrey A. Wyand and
Florence L. Wyand, Baltimore: Genealogical Publishing Co., 1986).

Denizations Granted by the Council: Augustine Herman, late of Manhatans,
marchant, naturalized January 14, 1660; Peter Meyor, Swedish, late of New
Amstel, naturalized July 22, 1661; Swedish, late of New Amstel, naturalized
July 29, 1661 - Andrew Clementson, Mathias Cornelison, Gothofrid Harmer,
Batholomew Hendrickson, Hendrick Hendrickson, Paule Johnson, Hendrick
Mathiason, Clment Micheelson, Peter Montson, Marcus Sipherson, Axell
Stille, Andrew Toreson, Cornelius Urinson, John Urinson and John Wheeler
[Ed. Note: John Wheeler was not Swedish, but was an Englishman; he mar-
ried a Swedish girl, however.]; Dutchmen, late of New Amstel, naturalized
July 30, 1661 - Jacob Clauson, Cornelius Comages, Jacob Micheelson and
Michaell Vandernote. Naturalizations Granted by Enactment of Private
Laws: Naturalized May 1, 1666 - Anna Hak, born in Amsterdam, Holland; '
Greorge Hak, son of Anna, born at Accomacke, Virginia; Peter Hak, son of
Anna, born at Accomacke, Virginia; Augustine Herman, born in Prag,
Bohemia; Anna Herman, daughter of Augustine Herman; Casparus Herman,
son of Augustine Herman; Ephraim Herman, son of Augustine Herman;
Francina Herman, daughter of Augustine Herman; Georgius Herman, son of
Augustine Herman; Judith Herman, daughter of Augustine Herman; Mar-
garita Herman, daughter of Augustine Herman; Naturalized May 8, 1669 -
Isaac DeBarrette, born in Harlem, Holland; Peter Johnson; Robert
Roelands, born in Brabant, Holland; Garrett Vanswaringen, born in
Reensterdwan, Holland; Barbarah DeBarette, born in Valenchene, in the
Low Countries when under Spanish control, and wife of Garrett Vanswarin-
gen; Elizabeth Vanswaringen, born in New Amstel, and daughter of Garrett
and Barbarah Vanswaringen; Zacharias Vanswaringen, born in New Amstel,
and son of Garrett and Barbarah Vanswaringen; Hans Hansun, born in
Delaware Bay of Swedish parents, naturalized October 20, 1671; Naturalized
June 6, 1674 - Mounts Anderson, Swedish; Cornelius Arenson, Dutch;
Andrew Clements, Swedish; Oliver Colke, Swedish; Henry Freeman,
Swedish; Henry Henderson, Swedish; Jeffrey Jacobson, Swedish; Cornelius
Johnson, born in Fiacina, Holland; John Nomers, Swedish; Cornelius Peter-
son, Swedish; Hans Peterson, Danish; Axell Stille, Swedish; Marcus Syferson,
Swedish; William Tick, born in Amsterdam, Holland; Naturalized November
6, 1683 - Peter Anleton, Simon Johnston, Mathias Peterson (and his
children), and Andrew Poulson alias Mullock; Naturalized April 26, 1684 -
Peter Bayard, Jasper Daunces, Peter Sleyter, Nicholas Verbrack; Mathias
Vanderheyden, naturalized June 9, 1692; Naturalized October 18, 1694 -
Jacob Sluiter, Jr., Hendrick Sluyter and Herman VanBurkelo; Mathias
Mathiason alias Freeman, naturalized May 22, 1695; John Hans Steelman
and John Hans Steelman, Jr., naturalized October 19, 1695; Naturalized May
9, 1700 - Michael Bellicane, Sr., born of Dutch parents; Michael Bellicane,
Jr., born of Dutch parents; Christopher Bellicane and James Bellicane, sons
of Michael Bellicane, Jr.; Christopher Mounts, born of Dutch parents;
Naturalized March 25, 1702 - Derrick Collickman, planter, of Dutch parents;
Hermann Schee, gentleman, of Dutch parents; Isaac Vanbiber, gentleman, of
Dutch parents; Mathias Vanbiber, merchant, of Dutch parents; Naturalized
May 3, 1704 - John Tawers, gentleman; Naturalized October 3, 174 - Otho

Othason, of Cecil County, born in Pennsylvania, of Dutch parents; Naturalized April 22, 1720 - Herman Kinkee (and his children), Dutch; Peter Manadoe (and his children), French; Christian Peters, a German, naturalized August 8, 1729. [Ed. Note: One should consult this reference for other Cecil Countians that may have been overlooked in this abstraction since all counties of residence were not given in the records].

PETITIONERS OF NEW MUNSTER CIRCA 1722 TO LORD BALTIMORE. [They stated their belief that Maryland was their proper place of residence, not Pennsylvania]: Joseph Alexander, James Alexander, David Alexander, James Alexander (farmer), James Alexander (tanner), Elias Alexander, Moses Alexander, Arthur Alexander, Mathew Wallace, Jane Wallace (widow), David Wallace, John Wallace, Mathew Wallace, Jr., Cornelius Vansant, George Vansant, James McLuse, Adam Rinkin, John Gemison, William Pendergrass, and James Tailor. (Ref: Calvert Papers, Maryland Historical Society, Manuscript Division, MS.174, Microfilm No. 6, Document No. 279).

RELIGIOUS OATHS TAKEN IN ST. MARY ANN'S P.E. CHURCH, 1742-1774: "I do declare that I do believe that there is not any trans-substantiation in The Sacrament of the Lord's Supper, or in the Elements of Bread and Wine at or after the Consecration thereof by any person whatsoever." Signed in 1742: Robert Whitaker, Garrett Mekinn [McKim?], Zeb. Hollingsworth, Peter Trytill, J. Hamilton, G. Rock, Randell Death, Nicholas George, Nathan Baker, Robert Williams, Peter Baker, William Currer. Signed in 1751: John Rutert [Rutter?], Nichs. Hyland, Michael Lum, Amos Fogg, Francis Mauldin, G. Bock, Edward Johnson, James Harrison, William Husband, Peter Boyer, Robert Williams, Anthony Smith, Richard Sedgwick, Robert Harte, Edward Taylor, Henry Baker, John Arrant, Thomas Forster, Zeb. Hollingsworth, Thomas Simpers, John Welsh, John Hyland (Warden), John Stump (Warden). Signed in 1752: Johannes Arrant, John Foster, Richard Sedgwick. Signed in 1753: William Hitchman, William Currer (Vestryman), Nathl. Baker, John Lewin. Signed in 1755: James Harrison (Vestryman), John Bailey (Warden), Thomas Simpers, William Brumfield, Nichs. George, Thomas Simpers, Andrew Barrett (Vestryman). Signed in 1763: John Brookins (Warden), Thomas Baker (Clerk), James Hart, Thomas Cord (Warden), Nathan Oldham. Signed in 1764: Francis Rock (Register), Thomas Whitaker, Robert Little, H. Hollingsworth, Will Baxter, (Vestryman), Isaac Crouch (Vestryman). Signed in 1765: Nich. Hyland Jr. (Warden), Isaac S. Watson (Warden), Charles Rumsey. Signed in 1766: Nic. Hyland (of John), Tobias Rudulph (Vestryman), John Stump (Vestryman), John Good (Warden). Signed in 1767: William Veazey, Frans. Keyes (Vestryman), Richard Oldham (Vestryman), George Hadrick (Warden). Signed in 1768: William Rutter (Warden), Murty "M" Mahon (Warden), Thomas Savin, Isaac VanBibber. Signed in 1769: Frans. Mauldin, Andrew Welsh, Richard Williams. Signed in 1770: Benjamin Mauldin (Warden), William Foster (Warden), Edward Dougherty (Vestryman), Moses Rutter (Vestry Clerk). Signed in 1771: George Johnson, William Rock, George Rock, Stephen Hyland. Signed in 1772: Richard Dobson, William Mauldin,

J. W. Pritchard, Abraham Cozier. Signed in 1774: Stephen Nevill (Warden), Sam Thomson.

PEW HOLDERS IN ST. STEPHEN'S P.E. CHURCH,MAY 12, 1747: 1 - Col. John Ward, Mr. Vanderheyden, Mr. Peregrine Ward; 2 - Mr. James Paul Heath, Mr. John Veazey, Mr. John Ward Jr.; 3 - Mrs. Mary Pearce, Benjamin Pearce, Nathaniel Hynson; 4 - Mr. John Baldwin, Mr. Edwd. Larramore, Mr. John Thompson; 5 - John Campbell, Mr. John McManus, George Veazey; 6 - John Ryland, Sr., William Freeman, Robert Thompson; 7 - Hugh Terry, Thomas Savin, Masterfree School; 8 - William Beadle, William Penington, Henry Penington; 9 - Susannah Ward, Thomas Ward, William Ward; 10 - Philip Cazier, John Poilloun, Richard Smith; 11 - Thomas Price, Philip Stoops, William Price; 12 - Robert Penington, William Beastin, John Ryland, Jr.; 13 - Peter Numbers, James Wroth, Robert Walmsley; 14 - John Beadle, John Penington, John Lusby; 15 - Alphonso Cosden, Henry Rippon, Francis Banner; 16 - Thomas Jones, James Husbands, Widow Warner; 17 - John Bateman, Rosamon Terry, William Savin, Sr.; 18 - Henry Penington, Jr., Thomas Davis, Fouch Davis; 19 - Thomas Mercer, Sr., Robert Mercer, John Mercer; 20 - Simon Wilmore, Capt.Mills, Capt.Spencer, Peregrine Frisby; 21 - Otho Othoson, Garriot Othoson, Kinvin Wroth; 22 - Mary Freeman, John Tree, John Cox, Sr.; 23 - John Roberts, Sr., James Morgan, Sr., Benjamin Childs; 24 - Peter Overstock, Widow Mounce, Ann Atkey; 25 - Robert Penington, Jr., John Ozier, Barnet Vanhorn; 26 - Isaac Caulk, Thomas Beard, William Mercer; 27 - Robert Money, Sr., John Coxsell, Michl. Manycousens; 28 - John Price, Joseph Price, John Morgan; 29 - Nicholas Dorrell, John Cooper, John Morris; 30 - John Bavington, John Keyes, Benjamin Terry; 31 - Robert Crocker, John Penington, Jr., William Bateman; 32 - John Winterbury, Michael Ruly, Elizabeth Kimber; 33 - Daniel Gears, John Fillingam, John Cox, Jr.; 34 - Jonathan Hynes, Thomas Eathrington, Henry Hendrickson; 35 - Robert Porter, John Price, Thomas Peirce; 36 - William Price, Jr., Andrew Price, George Holten; 37 - Thomas Burnham, William Abbiott, Richard Houghton; 38 - Ann Clements, John Severson, Jessey Holten; A - Mrs. Jennings and her daughters; B - Col. Herman, Col. Colvill, Mr. George, Dr. Bradford, and Mr. Rumsey.

UNLAWFUL COHABITATIONS IN ST. MARY ANN'S P.E. PARISH, 1749-1776

John Key (Keyes) and Mary Skurry (Scurry) ordered to appear before the Vestry to show cause why they are unlawfully cohabiting together (May, 1749). [He appeared in May, 1750 and was admonished by Rev. Hugh Jones. She did not appear. Later, John Keyes and Mary Scurry, wife of Thomas Scurry, did appear and both were legally admonished in November, 1751. In March, 1752 they were still unlawfully cohabiting together]. John Howard and Alice Walley were ordered to appear before the Vestry on suspicion of unlawfully cohabiting (July, 1750). Alexander McIntosh and Alice Howard were ordered to appear before the Vestry for unlawfully cohabiting together (December, 1752) and George Thornberry was summoned as evidence. [Neither appeared but George said he had seen them in bed together in January, 1753]. Thomas Beetle and Sylvia Jones ordered to appear to show cause why they unlawfully cohabit together, and Ann Crouch to appear as evidence. [Beetle appeared in November, but the other two did not; ordered again to appear by the vestry. Thomas Beetle and Sylvia Jones appeared in December and were admonished by Rev. Hamilton and the matter to be dealt with according to law in March Court. They failed to appear and by September, 1766, still had not appeared]. Samuel Faris and Elizabeth White ordered to show cause why they unlawfully lived together and not being married (November, 1765) and Robert Nesbitt ordered to appear as evidence (in March, 1766). [They appeared and were reported married]. John Magruder and Elizabeth Jackson ordered to show cause why they unlawfully cohabit together (November, 1765) in March, 1766. [Subsequently reported that "John Magrager is gone out of the county"]. Charles Brookins and Margaret Gordon ordered to appear to show cause why they unlawfully cohabited together and do not marry (September, 1766). Jacob Johnson and Rebecca Hewkin ordered to appear as to why they are cohabiting and not married (September, 1766). James Wareham and Sabina McDowell (widow) ordered to appear as to why they cohabit unlawfully (June 1767). [They appeared in August and were admonished by Rev. Hamilton]. Mordecai Cloud and Elizabeth Connolly ordered to show cause why they cohabit unlawfully (October, 1767). Alexander Butler and Hester Hughes ordered to show cause why they cohabit unlawfully (October, 1767). Edward Bryan and Lydia Wells ordered to show cause why they cohabit unlawfully (August, 1768). [They appeared and were admonished by Rev. Hamilton and the vestry]. Edward Welden and Mary Campbell ordered to show cause why they cohabit unlawfully (October, 1768). James Orrick produced the following certificate of marriage: "These are to certifie all concerned that Mr. James Orrick and Miss Eve Baker were some considerable time agoe married by me by virtue of a license from his Excellency Robert Eden Governor of Maryland. Given under my hand this September 2, 1770. Signed, John Beard" (presented to the vestry September 4, 1770). Edward McVinish (McVinchie) and Sarah Noland (Nowldham) ordered to appear to show cause why they cohabit unlawfully (April, 1771). [They appeared in August and were admonished by Rev. Hamilton and desired to separate by the vestry]. Samuel Logan and Jane Bing were ordered to appear regarding their unlawful cohabitation, but were reported to have left the county (June, 1771). William McCullough and Susannah Connoly were ordered to appear regarding their unlawful cohabitation (December, 1774).

SUNDRY PERSONS MENTIONED IN ST. MARY ANN'S P.E. CHURCH VESTRY PROCEEDINGS, 1754-1774

Henry Baker, 1 Oct 1754; Amos Fogg, 1 Oct 1754; Thomas Forster, 1 Oct 1754; Joseph Young, 1 Oct 1754; Col. Nicholas Hyland, 26 Jun 1758; William Hedges, Sheriff, 26 Jun 1758; Martha Hyland, admx. of Capt. John Hyland, 9 Oct 1758; George Milligan, Sheriff, 1759; Nicholas Hyland, Junior, 6 Sep 1760; Francis Rock, 23 Mar 1761; John Neal, money due him as Sexton, July, 1759; William Currer, for wine to the Common Table, 5 Feb 1760; Rev. John Hamilton, for fees concerning Glebe land, 1760; John Neal, money due him as Sexton, 4 Nov 1760; John Baily, for bread and wine, 4 Nov 1760; Nicholas Hyland, Junior, Register, 12 Apr 1762; James Baxter, Sheriff, 2 Nov 1762; William Baxter, Sheriff, 6 Dec 1763; Richard Thomas, 6 Dec 1763; Thomas Whitacar, for bread and wine, 14 Jul 1761; John Neal, money due him as Sexton, 12 Apr 1762; Francis Rock, for washing the surplice, 12 Apr 1762; Berry Rose, for hinges to hand the pews, 2 Nov 1762; Henry Miller, for scantling, 5 Apr 1763; William Baxter, late Sheriff, 1764; Richard Thomas, late Sheriff, 2 Jun 1767; Edward Mitchell, Esq., 4 Aug 1767; Mr. Mitchell, Sheriff, 1768/1770; Mary Rock, for washing the surplice, 4 Apr 1763; William Adair, for the dial post, 1 Nov 1763; John Neal (Nealey?), money due him as Sexton, 5 Jun 1764; Mary Rock, for washing the surplice, 1 May 1770; Francis Rock, for his salary, 1769 and 16 Apr 1770; John Neal (Neele?), money due him as Sexton, 8 Oct 1768; David Trew, for bolts and hinges, 3 Aug 1772; William Currer, for one cord of wood, 3 Aug 1772; George Callah, for painting the church doors, 6 Oct 1772; John Neal (Neele?), money due him as Sexton, 1772; Richard Thomas, Sheriff, 23 Apr 1763; Thomas Baker, late Register, year's salary, 23 Apr 1764; Thomas Savin, Sep 1764; Andrew Barrott, Sep 1764 and Nov 1766; William Veazey, 1771; Moses Rutter, 1771; Mr. Nelson and Mr. Crockett, 6 Aug 1771; George Rock, for hooks and hinges, 6 Apr 1772; William Key, 2 Jun 1772; William Rock, 2 Jun 1772; Stephen Hyland, 4 Aug 1772; Thomas Hughes, 10 Nov 1772; George Cullah, for painting the church, 10 Nov 1772; John Wakefield, 5 Mar 1765; Nathaniel Simpson, 5 Mar 1765; Edward Mitchell, Sheriff, 1767; James Campbell, 28 Apr 1770; John Hamilton, Sheriff, 1772; Rev. Mr. William Thomson, 4 Jan 1774; John Neal, for one pewter bason, 1 Mar 1774; George Rock, for one lock to the press, 1 Mar 1774; Nathan Baker, for expenses, 4 Apr 1774; William Currer, for wood, 4 Apr 1774; Samuel Thomson, 4 Apr 1774; John Veazey, Apr 1774; Robert Armstrong, for surveying the Glebe in April, 1774.

UNLAWFUL COHABITATIONS IN ST. MARY ANN'S P.E. PARISH, AUGUST, 1756: Lewis Lee and Rebecca Childs -- both appeared and were strictly admonished by Rev. Thomas Thornton. [They were still cohabitating together unlawfully in March, 1757]. Charles Ragon and the Widow Death -- both appeared and produced a certificate signed by Mr. William Lindsay, Minister living in Pennsylvania. John Gardener and Ann Hughey....[nothing further recorded].

UNLAWFUL COHABITATIONS IN ST. MARY ANN'S P.E. PARISH, MARCH 5, 1759: Jonas Cooper of Charles Town, cordwainer, and Elizabeth Jackson ordered to appear, but Rev. John Hamilton informed the vestry that he has since married them. Walter Rodgers and Martha his supposed wife ordered to appear, but Rev. John Hamilton informed the vestry that they were married.

BATCHELOR TAX LIST IN ST. MARY ANN'S P.E. PARISH, JULY 10, 1759. William Thornton, Charles Town, 300 lbs.; Thomas Norton, ditto; Joseph Ellot, ditto, 100 lbs.; John Wallice, marchant, North Elk, 300 lbs.; Sampson Currer, ditto; Nathaniel Simpas, ditto, 100 lbs.; Richard Claiton, South Milford, 300 lbs.; Isaac Grist, millright, ditto, 100 lbs.; Joseph Gilpin, North Milford, 300 lbs.; Doctor Peter Evins, ditto, 100 lbs.; Jesse Hollingsworth, ditto, 100 lbs.; Doctor John Caldwell, ditto, 300 lbs.; William Mackervee, ditto; David John, ditto, 100 lbs.; Andrew Barnett, ditto; Mark Alexander, ditto; James Smith, North Susquahana, ditto; John Blackburn, ditto; John Morgain, ditto; James Hunter, ditto; Aquilla Johns, ditto; Isaac

Janney, South Susquahana, 300 lbs.; Arthur Alexander, ditto, 100 lbs.; Thomas Janney, ditto; Zebulon Oldham, ditto; Samuel Gilespie, Octorara, 300 lbs.; Bennit Chew, ditto; Thomas Savin, Jr., ditto, 100 lbs.; John Foster, Jr., ditto. John Blackborn appeared and stated he was not yet age 25. Henry Baker testified that James Smith was taxed as a batchelor but he was then married. Doctor Peter Evings stated he was not yet 25 when taxed.

BATCHELOR TAX LIST IN ST. MARY ANN'S P.E. PARISH, JULY 8, 1760. William Thornton, Charles Town, 300 lbs.; Thomas Norton, ditto; Nathan Norton, ditto; Joseph Ellot, 100 lbs.; Benjamin Nelson, ditto; John Wallace, Elk Hundred, 400 lbs.; Sampson Currer, ditto, 300 lbs.; John Foster, Jr., ditto, 100 lbs.; Bennet Chew, ditto, 300 lbs.; Thomas Savin, ditto, 100 lbs.; Benjamin Rumsey, ditto, 300 lbs.; Richard Clayton, South Milford, 300 lbs.; Samuel Gilpin, Jr., ditto, 100 lbs.; Joseph Gilpin, North Milford, 300 lbs.; Doctor John Colwell, ditto; David John, ditto, 100 lbs.; Andrew Barnett, ditto; Mark Alexander, ditto; John Blackborne, North Susqueannah, 100 lbs.; John Morgan, ditto; James Hunter, ditto; Joseph Orr, ditto; Joseph Rotherford, ditto; Thomas Jenny, South Susqueannah, 300 lbs.; Samuel Taggart, Jr., North Susqueannah, 100 lbs.; Samuel Gallasbie, Octoraro, 300 lbs.; William Porter, son of James, ditto, 100 lbs.; Robert Porter, son of Andrew, ditto; Lawson Beard, North Milford, 100 lbs.; William Grymes, Octoraro, 100 lbs.; John Crosewell, North Susqueannah, lbs.; and, John Keirnes, ditto. Thomas Jenney, being one of those people called Quakers, affirmed that at the time the vestry ataxed him as a Batchelor he had not a real or personal estate to the amount of 300 lbs. and acknowledged he is worth 100 lbs.

BATCHELOR TAX LIST IN ST. MARY ANN'S P.E. PARISH, JULY 7, 1761. Charles Town: William Thornton, 1 lb.; Thomas Norton, 1 lb.; Benjamin Nelson, 1 lb.; John Wallace, 1 lb.; Nathan Norton, 5 sh.; Joseph Ellot, 5 sh.; Doctor James Spavold, 5 sh. Elk Hundred: Sampson Currer, 1 lb.; Benjamin Rumsey, 1 lb.; Thomas Savin, 1 lb.; James Orrick, 5 sh.; Jacob Johnson, 5 sh. South Milford: Richard Clayton, 1 lb.; Samuel Gilpin, Jr., 5 sh.; Lawson Beaird, 5 sh. North Milford: Joseph Gilpin, 1 lb.; Doctor John Caldwell, 1 lb.; David John, 5 sh.; Andrew Barnett, 5 sh.; John Morgan, 1 lb.; James Hunter, 5 sh.; Joseph Rutherford, 5 sh.; John Cresswell, 5 sh.; John Kearns, 5 sh.; Zebulon Hollingsworth, Jr., 5 sh. South Susquahanah: Thomas Jenny, 5 sh.; John Brookins, 1 lb.; Robert Hill, 5 sh.; James McKeown, 5 sh. Octarara Hundred: Samuel Gillespie, 1 lb.; Joseph Husbands, 1 lb.

UNLAWFUL COHABITATIONS IN ST. MARY ANN'S P.E. PARISH IN 1761: William Lashell and Elizabeth Ryan ordered to appear, and they did on 9 November 1761, and were ordered to produce a marriage certificate by next Easter. Ralph Rutter, of Charles Town, and Liddy Wells (widow), she being with child, were ordered to appear and show cause why they live together being not married. [They appeared and were admonished by Rev. John Hamilton and the rest of the vestrymen]. Joseph Ellot of Charles Town and Sarah Brumfield (Brumfeld), she big with child, ordered to appear and show cause why they cohabit together. William Merchant and Jane Armstrong ordered to appear and show cause why they live together not being legally married. [They were reported to have moved out of the province].

BATCHELOR TAX LIST IN ST. MARY ANN'S P.E. PARISH, JULY 13, 1762. William Thornton, Charles Town, 300 lbs.; Thomas Norton, Charles Town, 300 lbs.; Benjamin Nelson, Charles Town, 300 lbs.; John Wallice, North Milford, 300 lbs.; Joseph Ellot, Charles Town, 100 lbs.; Sampson Currer, Elk Hundred, 300 lbs.; Benjamin Rumsey, Charles Town, 300 lbs.; Thomas Savin, Jr., Charles Town, 300 lbs.; James Orrick, Charles Town, 100 lbs.; Richard Claiton, South Milford, 300 lbs.; Samuel Gilpin, Jr., South Miilford, 300 lbs.; Lawson Beard, South Milford, 100 lbs.; Joseph Gilpin, North Milford, 300 lbs.; Doctor John Caldwell, North Milford, 300 lbs.; David Johns, North Milford, 100 lbs.; Andrew Barnet, North Milford, 100 lbs.; Zebulon Hollingsworth, Jr., North Milford, 300 lbs.; Jacob Johnson, North Milford, 100 lbs.; Joseph Rutherford, North Susquahannah, 100 lbs.; John Creswell, North Susquahannah, 100 lbs.; John Kearns, North Susquahannah, 300 lbs.; John Brooking, South Susquahannah, 300 lbs.; Samuel Gillespie, Octoraro Hundred, 300 lbs.; Charles Brooking, South Susquahannah, 300 lbs.; John Read, South Milford, 300 lbs.; David Ricketts, North Milford, 300 lbs.; William Baxter, South Susquahannah, 300 lbs.; Richard Dobson, South Milford, 100 lbs.; Thomas Baker, South Susquahannah, 100 lbs.; Samuel Patterson, North Susquahannah, 300 lbs.; James Grimes, Octoraro Hundred, 300 lbs.; Thomas Currer, Elk Hundred, 100 lbs.; Isaac Vanbebber, Charles Town, 100 lbs. "Vestry certified that through a mistake they had returned one James Grimes as a Batchelor above 25 years of age and having an estate valued to 300 lbs. and they are since well informed that they mistook his Christian name which put it our of the sheriff's power to collect the same, as was best by the vestry." Dated April 4, 1763.

BATCHELOR TAX LIST IN ST. MARY ANN'S P.E. PARISH, JULY 12, 1763. (Name, Residence, Value, Tax): Thomas Norton, Charles Town, 300 lbs., 1 lb.; Benj. Rumsey, do.; Benj. Nelson, do.; Isaac Vanbebber, do.; Joseph Bouchell, do., swore of [sic]; Thomas Savin, Elk Hundred, 300 lbs., 1 lb.; Nicholas George, do., swore of [sic]; James Orrack, do., 100 lbs., 5 sh.; Nicholas Hyland, Jr.; do.; Thomas Currer, do.; Joseph Gilpen, North Milford, 300 lbs., 1 lb.; Dr. John Caldwell, do.; David Johns, do., 100 lbs., 5 sh.; Andrew Barnett, do.; Zabulon Hollingsworth, Jr., do., 300 lbs., 1 lb.; Jonathan Booth, do.; Henry Hollingsworth, do., 100 lbs., 5 sh.; John Fagen, do.; David Rickatts, do., 300 lbs., 1 lb.; Daniel Alexander, do.; Samuel Gilpin, Jr., South Milford, 300 lbs., 1 lb.; Richard Clating, do.; John Reed, do.; Richard Dobtson, do., 100 lbs., 5 sh.; Jacob Johnson, do.; James Frazer, do., 300 lbs., 1 lb.; William Pasmore, do., 100 lbs., 5 sh.; Joseph Rutherfoard, North Susquahannah, 300 lbs., 1 lb.; Samuel Patterson, do.; William Baxter, South Susquahannah, 300 lbs, 1 lb.; Charles Brookins, do.; John Brookins, do.; Thomas Baker, do., 100 lbs., 5 sh.; John Creswall, do.; Samuel Gellaspy, Octa14raro Hundred, 300 lbs., 1 lb.; William Porter, do., 100 lbs., 5 sh.

BATCHELOR TAX LIST IN ST. STEPHEN'S P.E. PARISH, JULY 10, 1763. ("List of Batchelors age 25 and older"): James Coppin, North Sassafras Hundred; John McDuff, West Sassafras Hundred; John Coppin, ditto;

Thomas Williams, ditto; John Loftis, ditto; Nicklas Dorrell, ditto; Thomas
Beard, Jr., North Sassafras Hundred; Rev. Mr. Manners, ditto; Rev. Mr. Wil-
liams, ditto; Sylvester Ryland, ditto; Dominick McDermond, ditto; William
Pearce, ditto; Andrew Pearce, ditto; William Savin, Bohemia Hundred; John
Spalding, ditto, at Wm. Ward's; Alexander McClouds, ditto, at John Wards;
Richard Savin, North Sassafras Hundred; John Winterberry, Bohemia
Hundred, at B. Price's; John Ward, surveyor, Bohemia Hundred; James
Hughs, Jr., North Sassafras Hundred; Elisha Terry, ditto; Joseph Phelps,
Bohemia Hundred; Benjamin Price, ditto; and, Richard Caulk, ditto.

BATCHELOR TAX LIST IN ST. MARY ANN'S P.E. PARISH, JULY 11,
1765. Richard Claton, North Milford, 300 lbs.; Joseph Gilpin, South Milford,
300 lbs.; Thomas Norton, Charles Town, 300 lbs.; Nathan Norton, ditto;
Sampson Currer, North Elk, 300 lbs.; John Colvell, doctor, North Milford,
300 lbs.; William Muckilve, ditto; Thomas Hartshorn, North Susquahanah,
300 lbs.; David Johns, North Milford, 100 lbs.; James Smith, North
Susquahanah, 100 lbs.; Francis Humphris, North Elk, 300 lbs.; Andrew Barnett, North Milford, 100 lbs.; John Morgan, South Susquahanah, 100 lbs.;
Nathaniel Simpass, North Elk, ditto; Joseph Ellot, tailor, Charles Town, 100
lbs.; Hugh McCrea, North Milford, 100 lbs.; Forgus Smith, ditto; Isaac Jenney, South Susquahanah, 300 lbs.; Thomas Jenney, ditto, 100 lbs.; Arthor
Alexander, ditto, 300 lbs.; Samuel Glaspey, Octoraro, 300 lbs.; Thomas Husbands, ditto, 100 lbs.; Isaac Grist, mill rite, South Milford, 100 lbs.; James
Hunter, South Susquahanah, 100 lbs.; Mark Alexander, North Milford, 100
lbs.; William Thornton, Charles Town, 300 lbs.; John Wallice, marchant,
North Elk, 300 lbs.; John Blackborn, South Susquahanah, 100 lbs.; and,
Zebulon Holdham, ditto. On September 5, 1758, John Blackhorn appeared
and stated he was not yet 25 years of age. Arthur Alexander declared he was
not worth the sum of 300 lbs. and asked to be taxed as being only worth 100
lbs. It was done.

BATCHELOR TAX LIST IN ST. MARY ANN'S P.E. PARISH, AUGUST
7, 1765. (List of Batchelors age 25 and older): Elihu Hall, Octoraror
Hundred, 1000 lbs.; Richard Cleaton, Milford Hundred, 500 lbs.; Joseph Gil-
pin, North Milford Hundred, 400 lbs.; Thomas Norton of Charlestown, 400
lbs.; Nathan Norton of Charlestown, 300 lbs.; Sampson Currer of Elk
Hundred, 300 lbs.; John Colwell of North Milford, doctor, 300 lbs.; Charles
Brooking, South Susquahanah, 300 lbs.; John Courier, Elk Hundred, 300 lbs.;
William Muckilive, North Milford, 300 lbs.; Lewis Lee, North Susquahanah,
300 lbs.; Thomas Hartshorn, North Susquahanah, 300 lbs.; David Johns,
North Milford Hundred, 200 lbs.; Joseph Mauldin, Elk Hundred, 100 lbs.;
James Smith, North Susquahanah, 100 lbs.; Francis Umphfrey, South
Susqahanah Hundred, 200 lbs.; John McCluer, South Susquahanah
Hundred, 100 lbs.; Thomas Whitaker, South Milford Hundred, 200 lbs.;
James Frayshure, South Milford Hundred, 150 lbs.; Andrew Barnett, North
Milford Hundred, 100 lbs.; Henry Miller, South Milford Hundred, 100 lbs.;
John Morgan, South Susquahanah Hundred, 100 lbs.; Nathanel Simpers, Elk
Hundred, 100 lbs.; Joseph Allit, Charlestown, 100 lbs.; Joseph Ruthiarford,
North Susquahanah Hundred, 100 lbs.; John Kirkpatrick, North Milford
Hundred, 100 lbs.; Samuel Kirkpatrick, ditto; James Cochran, ditto; James

McSwane, ditto; Hugh McCrea, ditto; Forgus Smith, ditto; William Harvey, ditto; Isaac Jennay, South Susquahanah Hundred, 300 lbs.; Thomas Jeney, ditto, 100 lbs.; Arthur Alexander, ditto, 200 lbs.; John McCoy, North Susquahanah Hundred, 300 lbs.; William Elliss, ditto, 100 lbs.; Samuel Gallaspey, Octorarer Hundred, 100 lbs.; Thomas Husband, ditto; Isaac Grise, Mill Right, 100 lbs.; David Henry, black smith, Milford Hundred, 100 lbs.; Hugh Walker of Milford Hundred, 100 lbs.; James Hunter, South Susquahanah, 100 lbs.; Jonathan Williams, Milford Hundred, pedler, 100 lbs.; and, Mark Alexander, Milford Hundred, 100 lbs.

CECIL COUNTY TAX LIST OF AUGUST, 1761.

(Ref: Original Lists in Manuscript MS.1929 at the Maryland Historical Society):

TAXABLES IN 1761 IN BOHEMIA MANOR HUNDRED: Anthony Linch, Georg Linch, Negroes Solomon and Phillis; Anthony Noones; Ann Hooper, Abraham Douglas; Absolem Bouing [Boring?]; Alexander Kirk; Andrew Laronson, Negro Nan; Andrew Crow; Alexander Clark; Andrew Rider; Benjamin Moody, Esq., Negroes Jack, Tom, Bob and Nan; Barnit Lockman; Benjamin Husbands, Richard Hukil, security; Benjamin Beaston, John Price, security; Benjamin Sluyter, Peter Sluyter, Negroes Daw, Jin, Nan and Sall; Charles Ford, Negroes Harey, Georg, Burdock, Cate and Poll; Charles Pearsce; Cristopher Parkeson; Edward McGonagal; Ephraram Beaston; Fredrick Stern; Farel McCormack; Fredrick Elsburey, Negroes Sip and Jude; Gilder Hukil, Spensor Halthom, security; Georg Beaston; Georg Hall, Negroes Toney and Jude; Georg Lewis; Highland Pennington, John Getey, security; Henery Nail, Negro Poldore; Hugh Johnson, John Seegwell Robeson, security; Henery Sluyter, Negroes Diddo and Lonnon; John Veazey, Jr., Negroes Tom, Manuel, Will, Phillis, Patt and Hanah; Jeremiah Poulson, John Veazey, Jr., security; John Getey; John Smith; John Carty; John Mullon, Sr., Jacob Hamm, Negroes Dine, Sall, Jone, and apprentice Zebulon Beaston; John Linch; James Hukil; John Obryan, Negroes Cudjo, Ned and Bess; Dr. John Holland, John Holland, Jr., Isaac Douglas, and Negro Nuss; John Latham, Negroes Harey, Murr and Dine; James Wroth, Jr.; John Bayard, James Wroth, Jr., security; Joseph Burnom; Joseph Taylor; John Crow; James Bryson; Jonas Jones, Andrew Jones; John Kirk; John Goloher; John Pennington, Andrew Laranson, security; John Murphy; John Elwood, Andrew Hughs; James Moody; Joseph Rider; James Robeson, John Zelefro, Negroes Harey and Beck; John Douglas, Edward Rumsey, Jr., security; John Groves; John Price; James Cage, Robert McCurdy, security; John Mullon, Jr., Jacob Ozer, Negroes Jack, Charles, Britan and Nann; John Neide; John Riggs, William Kleinhoff, security; Joseph Neide, Negro Moze; John Larance, Fredrick Brooghar, Joseph Neide, security; Joseph Cocheron, Sr., Joseph Cocheron, Jr., Negroes Wench Name Refused; John Seegwell Robeson; Isaack Brin, William Kleinhoff, security; Judith Biggs, Nathneil Biggs; Johnathan Hodgson, Negroes Jacob, Rachel, Jin, Flora and Ann; Dr. James Ashton Bayard, Negroes Tom, Bobb, Tomboy, Wilk, Sarah and Raney; James Boyls, Negroes Will, Sambo, Phillis and Candiss; Mary Van-

bebber, John Seeders, Negroes Dave, Tom, Marea and Marea [sic]; Mark
Cuningham; Martain Conn[?] [soiled page]; Mathew Deney; Manasa Logue,
Isaac Logue, Negroes Jo and Sall; Moses Cocheron, Joseph Cocheron;
Nicholas Wood, Sr., Nicholas Wood, Jr., William Wood; Neal Danily;
Philimon Noble; Peter Wingate; Perugrain Vandergrift, John Latham; Peter
Rider, William Crage, Jr., Robert McClure, Negro Pheeb; Patrick Fageings;
Peter Gullat, Thomas Bouchel, security; Peter Kleinhoff, Thomas Forden,
Thomas Hoogings, William Caroll, Abraham Vanbebber, William Lewis;
Peter Lawson, Michal Bassett, Alexander Rice, Negroes Andrew Rany,
Nann and Doll; Peter Bayard, Negroes Old Jack, Voll, Jackboy, Will, Ben,
Lonn and Sarah; Robert Veazey, Sr., Negroes Nedd, Will and Pegg; Robert
Veazey, Jr., Richard Elwood; Richard Price, James Price, Highland Price;
Rebecca McCoy, Negro Hanah; Richard Hukil (farmer); Richard Bouing
(Boving?); Robert McCrudy; Richard Canter; Robert Mansfeild, John
Mansfeild, Samuel Galbreth, Negroes Cook and Bridget; Richard Ford,
John[?] Ford, Edward Ford; Richard Smith; Samuel McConecah; Solomon
Hersey; Samuel McClarey; Samuel Bayard, Sr., Samuel Bayard, Jr., Negroes
Tom, Dan, Nan, Phillis and Sall; Sarah Hughes, James Crage; Thomas
Sumers, Jacob Hamm, security; Timothy Campaign; Thomas Cronwall;
Thomas Hooker; Thomas Bouchel; Thomas Beaston; Thomas Wallace,
Negro Will, Dave and Betey; Thomas Pankit, Jr., Thomas Pankit, Sr.,
security; Volentine Jump; William Baker; William Crage; William Taylor;
Negroes Jerey and Jude; William Kleinhoff; Wolter Jackson; William Willkn
[sic]; William Peaklin, Peter Kleinhoff, security; William Plunket; Epharim
Pennington; James Dickson; John Jones (miller); Samuel Simons; Samuel
Taylor; Spenser Holtham; Michal Morison, John Getey, security; Thomas
Moore; John Hukil; Robert Husbands, Georg Lewis, security; Daneil Hukil;
Cornelious Hukil; "Vacance for Straglers" - Adam Scott, Michael Morison,
security. "A List of Chace Wheels in said Hundred" - Dr. James Ashton
Bayard (pair); Dr. John Holland (pair); Col. Peter Bayard (pair); Capt. John
Veazey (pair); Mr. Charles Ford (pair); and Mr. Peter Kleinhoff (pair). Mr.
rrancis Key, Clerk of the County, and William Kleinhoff, Constable.

TAXABLES IN 1761 IN NORTH SUSQUAHANNAH HUNDRED:
James Carson; John Carson; William Jorns[?]; William Callendar, Benjamin
Aranart; John Bleak; Alexander Cocheren, Samuel Mullen, Alexander
Cochran, Jr.; John Ash, Robert Ash, Slave Filles; John Kerns; James Afreall
[Asreall?]; Andrew Friland; William Meek; William Devall; Patrick Mcjerity
[Mgerity?]; John Smith; Edward Murphey; James Anderson, Samuel Ander-
son; John Ricketts; John Murphy; Amos Evins, and slave; Hendry Tuchston,
Cornailes Lashly[?]; Charls Porter; James Tagart; Samuel Tagart; Robert
Marguas[?]; John Priene[?]; Hendry Good, John Good; Benjamen Chew, Jr.,
Joshua Yall[?], Salves Joseph, Brigget and Namy; Benjamin Chew, Sr.,
Phinas Chew, and slaves (10 unnamed); John Wellch, Andrew Wellch; James
Hunter; Aquila Joans, Jr., Slaves Andrew, Sipo, Tom, Jeny, Gorg, Jack, Will,
Joe, Johana and Abelow; Hendry Bowers, Aquila Joans, surety; Nicolas Al-
lender; Edward Doughrtey, John Drinker; John Taylor; John Anderson;
John Mculagh [sic]; Jonathan Hartshorn; John Carson; William Glashow;
William Beankhad [Bankhead?]; James Buhanen; Cristian Bowers; Gorge
Anerom; John Smith, Slaves Charls and Sembo; John Crisswell, Slave Bett;
Joseph Oar; Gorge Johnston, Slaves Mingo, Robin and Jack; Robert Little,

Sr., John Riddel; Andrew Barratt, Slaves Judy, Simon, Fill, Jin and Pender; James Busbey; Benjamin Furgison; James Hunter; Charls Bonar, William Bonar; William Murphy; John Woods; Andrew Tutchston; James Whittock; Joseph Corlet; Thomas Coard; Samuel Arnet, Samuel Arnet, Jr., Edward Arnet; Patrick Kelly, John Kelly; Theopheles Morise; Olifer Miller; William Willson; Moses Ewing; Adam Smith; William Curier; James Harison, Slaves Bram, Charls, Sera and Ester; Isaac Wattson; John Bleak, Sr.; William Wattson, and slave; Richard Thomas, Slaves Cara, Jacob, Flora and Ives; John Callendar, Sr.; James Spear; Murty Mahon, and two slaves; John Tutchston; Joseph Rutherford; Cornailes Balife; Alexander Lang; David Pettrson; John Pettrson, Slaves Will and Jen; John Stump, Richard Hall, Slaves Dobin and Jame; James Mgerety [sic]; Arthur Alexander, John McWreth; John Kidd, Andrew Kidd, James Kidd; Fidilis Foster; James Grahams; Charls Reagan[?]; Tobias Lang; James Breeding; Adam Meek, Slave Bett; John Vance; Thomas Miller; Slaves Valentin and Rose; John Marguas; John Harrise; John McVinshey; William Givians; Samuel Miller, Slaves Gorg and Bett; David Pettrson, Jr.; Thomas Tagart; David Hendry; William Hitchman, Slave Mingo; John Lion, Robert Lion; Samuel Carr; Robert Little; James Elder; Robert Conn; John Walker; John Laughlin; Charls Orrick, Slaves Arah, Pompy, Dina and Sue; Robert Pettrson, Samuel Pettrson, Slaves Primus and Pesthina; Jacob Dath, Petrson surety; William Roulands; Joseph Bass, Slaves Jack, Chance, Moll and Arrer; Thomas Bowin; Robert Findley; Samuel Thomas, Slaves Juba, Jack, Ned, Jacob, Jane, Sera, Pegy, Poly, and Moriah; Samuel Crocket; Thomas Alaway; Nathan Johns; John Mcoy [sic]; Lewis Lee; Samuel Ewing; William Willson; John Ewing; John Campble; Robert Campble; Richard Sedgwick, Slaves Mingo, Bess and Prisila; Samuel Allison; John Kirkpatrick; Gilbirt Donihue; William Deal; James Evans, and slave; Robert Miller; William Corbit; David Dinon. James Corbit, Constable.

TAXABLES IN 1761 IN SOUTH SUSQUAHANNAH HUNDRED: William Barns; John Neal; William Howell, security for John Howell, Benjamin Lee, John Clark; John Wallter; Walter Baker, Thomas Baker, Negroes Dancer, Dinah and Johannah; Perry Rose; Francis Maybury; Robert Lesslie, William Lesslie; John Stevenson; Francis Lesslie; Thomas Willey; Martin Willcox; Samuel McCollagh; William McKeown, William McKeown, Jr., Samuel McKeown; Archable McCollagh; John Alexander; Richard Bennett; Isaac Johnson, Jethro Baker, security; John Clark, William Clark; Samuel Clark, security for David Hill; Thomas Jannay; Isaac Janney, Mikel Dougherty; Robert Smith; Robert Nellson; Joseph McNealy; James Glasgow, William Glasgow; Andrew Gibson, Negro Dick; Enious McCoy; John Reynolds; Benjamin Moor; Thomas Murphy; Charles Carty; John McDade; William Lee; John Hall; Morgan Sweney; John Baker; John Green; John Green, Jr.; Pheven Willcox; James Willson; James McMullin; Henry Baker, Jethro Baker, Jeremiah Baker, Robert Campbell, Negroes Sam, Jack, Lincon, George, Nancy, Hannah and Peg; Peter Justis, security for John Thomson; Peter Justis, Edward Justis; Nicholas Kelley; Robert Hill; Andrew Frazier; William Harvey; James Orr; James Hewet; William Moor; James McCollagh, Artha Alexander; Robert Nickels, John Nickels; William Carothers; John Griffy; William Ford; William Crookshank, William Crookshank, Jr.; Samuel McKeown, William McKeowen [sic]; James Garner; John Willson; John Golloher; Alexander Nuckel; Matthew Logan, Matthew Logan, Jr.; John Cunningham; John Jack; Alexander Ewning [sic]; Robert Williams, Richard Williams; John McCabe; Daniell Feagen; John Bruckings, Negro Silve; George Hedrick; Joseph Penington; Matthew Reily; William Welsh; William Shawswood; Whttn [sic] Rutter; Thomas Foster; William. Whitley [Whilley?]; Robert Thackrey; Daniel Brumfill; William Brumfill; George Philipe; William McCollagh; John McVegh; Henry Miller; David McCracking; Zebulon Oldham; William Willson; William Kelley, John Kellev: William McClure, Negro Nan; Samuel Yeamans; William Cather; Richard Kidd; Francis Henderson, security for James Meek; William Marshell; Alexander Moor; John Glasgow; David Louremor[?]; Samuel Kilpatrick; James Stevenson; John Cather; Thomas Hartshorn, security for Andrew Marshell; Stephen Niewell, Joshua Niewell; Thomas Mehaffy; William Campbell; Hugh Dougherty; Aaron Grase, Negro Samson; Richard Cazier; John Smith; William Boyd; James Cunningham; Negroes Bob, Peter and Joe, "to be charged to Francis Key"; Ephrem Johnson; Alexander Arnett; Roger Domigan, security for John Shannahan; James Lightfoot, William Howel[?], security; Col. James Baxter's taxables - Charles Coatts, Samuel Mills, and Negroes Harry, Sue, Bess, Frank, Dick, Tom, Manta, Will, Phillis and Nan; taxables belonging to Sr. Nicholas Carew and Company at North East Forge - James Baxter, Thomas Hughes, and Negroes Dick, Prince, London, Emanuel, Jack, Harry, Dancer, Catto, Boson, Ben, Charles, Pompey, Will, Ned and Phillis. Zebulon Oldham, Constable.

TAXABLES IN 1761 IN NORTH MILFORD HUNDRED: George Catto, Esq., William Shea, Patrick Melody, Negroes Stirling, George, Adam, Tom, Mary, Jeny, Peg and Patt; John Macky, Esq., David Macky, Negroes Jo and Hager; Zebulon Holensworth, Henery Holensworth, Joseph[?] Holensworth, Zebulon Holensworth, Jr., John Bowhaman[?], Negroes Santo, Sipo and Jan; Tobias Rudolf, William Scogant, Negro Nell; Thomas Jacobs, Negroes Hick, Jill, Bigs, Sue and Sam; Moses Alexander, John Simontown[?], Dan Alexander, William Fryer; William Whan, Samuel Whan; John McCay, James McCay, Negro Hanah; William Gillespy, James McElheney, Samuel Marchel; James Fryer; Abraham Emet; James Ritche; Robert Flemen; Abraham Holms, James Holms, John Holms, Abraham Holms, Jr.; Andrew Rears [Bears?], James Fryer, Jr., James Killgore; George Lason, John Lason; John Strobridge; Henery Williams; Petter Balldon; William Bently; Nicolos Hoy; William Longwill; Daniel McClain; Daniel Balleys; Hugh Longwill; Thomas Killgore, William Killgore; William Davison; Thomas Chesnot; Forgas Smith, William Armstrong; Moses Andrews, Thomas Nobel; Andrew Harvey; William Harvey; Robert Evens, John Giant, Negroes Sip, Geck and Bet; John Smith; Jesse Holensworth, Hans Hakabough; Jonathan Booth; James Dougan; John Smith (mariner), Daniel Obrine; Thomas Weir; Edward Weir, Thomas Weir, Jr.; James McCarey, William McCarey, James McCarey, Jr.; Edward Taylor; Ritchard Bradly, Neal Bradly; David Hendry; Samuel Sheperd, Joseph Johnston; James Hemphill; Samuel Stephenson, Samuel William [sic]; Zekiel Chambers; Mary Rickels [Rickets?], widow, "one tax James Anderson"; Alexander Chesnot; Joseph Gillpin, William Stanop, Cristfor Thomas, Thomas Broak, Emor Stanop; Joshua Brown; Thomas Mason, Benjamin Mason; Robert Hugins, David Hugins, Negro Phillis; Samel Barr; Andrew Means, John Armstrong, William Marchant; John

Carry, John Carry, Jr.; Andrew Barnet; Robert Campbel, Samuel Moore; John Ash; Dorety Cochran, widow, "one taxabel Andrew Cochran"; Franses McClintock; James McClintock; Phenieas Hodson, Abel Hodson; John Hodson; Thomas Wallace, Nathaniel McDowel; John Hutchison; Amos Alexander, Joseph Canon, Negro Gif; James Alexander, Negroes Pompy, Jeson, Hannah, Moriah, Jula; Joseph Dason [sic]; Widow Broom, "two taxabel Harmon Gavet and Negro Ratchel"; Thomas Rickets, Negro Hanah; David Rickets; Edward Crow; William Thomson; Thomas Batty, John Batty; William Davis, James Kelley; William Chambers; David John, Jonas Chambers; John Gillis, Thomas Gillis; Franses Carithers, John Steel; Samuel Cumins; Archibald Armstrong, Negro Jack; John Simpos; Samuel Peak; Rev. James Finley, Negro Sam; John S. Cott [Scoot?]; Robert Hibits; Thomas Simpors, Negroes Ben, Pompy and Phillis; Samuel McCutchen; James Cochran; Alexander Loagan; Robert Breckenridge; Robert Barr, Joseph Rankin; Joseph Wallace, John Hyst, Franses Eliot, Negroes Nade, Babe and Aries[?]; William Robison; John Shanon; John Moor, George Haslet, John Makitrick, John Forker; John Alexander; Adam Willson, Robert Willson; Samuel Hill; Robert Loagan; James McCrakan, John McCrakan; Robert Rowland, Dr. John Caldwell, Negroes Will, Solomon and Moriah; David Elder, William Prise; Adam Teale; Daniel Turner; Patrick Hart; Fredrick Maremer[?]; Theophilis Alexander, Joseph Moor, Negro Aky; Walter Carr; Patrick Dinis; William Wallace; Benjamin Alet. Thomas Mason, Constable.

TAXABLES IN 1761 IN SOUTH MILFORD HUNDRED: Adam Dobson, Richard Dobson, Phillip Hissar; Adam Short, Jr.; Allen Stuart; Augustine Passmore, George Passmore, Bartley Leere, Slave Bess; Benjamin McVe [sic], William Passmore; Bryan McMurry; Bryan McCauley; Benjamin Lowry; Charles Rumsey, Slaves Tom, Pero and Flora; David Owens; David Morrow; David Moore, Sr., Hugh Moore, Joseph Moore; David Moore, Jr.; Edward Oldham, Richard Oldham, Slaves Amos and Fillis; Edward Harding; Edward Wilson; Ezekiel Denneston, Robert Denneston; George Skipton; George Black, William Black; George Allison, Thomas Allison, William Allison; Henry Miller; Hugh Brown, Hugh Nickles, Henry Lenard; Jacob Johnson; John Short; John Richardson; John Baily; John Bing, George Bing, John Nowland; John Miller; Joseph Thompson; John Griffith; John Todd, William Todd; John Little; James Finley, William Finley; John Passmore, Slave Will; James Bradford; John Fultown, William Fultown, David Mackey; James Coffey; James Morgan; James Frazier; Joseph Hickman; John Beard; John Campbel; John Read; John Buttrum; John Anderson; James Mackey, William Mackey, Michael Law, Slave Bob; John Scoals; John Tusey; John Welsh; Lawson Biard; Matthew Thompson; Matthew Hart, John Hart; Michael Wallace, Daniel Mullen, Slaves Dolly, Kate and Dinah; Mathias Johnson; Matthew Taylor, Henry Taylor; Nicholas White; Robert Smith; Ralph Whitaker; Robert Boulton; Robert Jones; Richard Hall, William Foster; Richard Clayton, Obediah King; Robert Lutten, John Lutten; Ratchson Duffield; Simon Johnson; Samuel Thompson; Samuel Gilpen, Sr., Samuel Gilpen, Jr., George Sayer, William Johnson, and Slave Keto; Samuel Passmore; Samuel Bond, Richard Bond, Thomas Phillips, and Slave Quarto; Thomas Underhill; Thomas Turner; Thomas Whitaker; Thomas McCrery, Sr., Thomas McCrery, Jr.; Thomas Huston; William Maffit, Thomas Maffit,

Samuel Maffit, and Slave Cesar; William Kar, Hugh McCrea; William Hull; William Smith; William Adare; William Tallowfield. Matthew Taylor, Constable.

TAXABLES IN 1761 IN ELK HUNDRED: Johannes Arrents; Benedicktus Averain, Henry Averain; Willam Bristow, Negroes Gabril and Vilt; Petter Boyer, Negroes Ben and Nan; Joseph Burnham; Samson Currer, Negro Hery; Jaas[sic] Crouch, John Readman; Willam Currer, Negroes Prince, Joe and Bess; Willam Cox; Thomas Crouch, Sr., Thomas Crouch, Jr.; Willam Crouch; Elaxander Dudgen; Charls Emanselbager; John Foster, Sr., John Foster, Jr.; Willam Foster; Ritcherd Feddry, Joseph Thomas, surety; Niclus Geer, Willam Johnes, Negroes Mingo and Din; Willam Grace; Ritcherd Greedey; Mathew Grues, Frainces Mauldin, surety; Lazers Graner, Ritcherd Greedey, surety; John Hyland, Negroes Jame and Simon; Martha Hyland, widow, Niclis Hyland, Negroes Petter, Ben, Archabel, Groll, Jonas and Coock; Col. Niclus Hyland, Jaas[sic] Hyland, Negroes Pompy, Nance, Jack and Herrey; Niclus Hyland, Jr., Negroes Ned and Dina; Robert Hart, James Byard, Negroes Georg, Nead, Petter and Bess; James Hart, Negroes Joseph, David and Dina; Thomas Hart; Thomas Hidgcock; Thomas John [John Thomas?] Hidgcock; Moses Johnes, Aron Johnes; Moses Johnes, Jr., Thomas Beattle, Jr., surety; John Keittley, Sr., John Keittley, Jr.; Philip Keittley, Henry Keittley; Harman Kankey, Negroes Shery and Pompy; John Kankey; James Lowery; Mary Lume [Lum?], widow, Negroes Dick and Suck; John Lewis; William Lashels; Joseph Loman[?], Negroes Polle and Dafney; John Moodey; Thomas Murphe [sic]; John Mainley; William Mainley; Robert Mills; Samuel Mekeaney; Robert Milborn, Benjamin Garish, William Garish; Ann Mauldin, widow, Negroes Sqasabe[?] and Philis; James Madowell, William Orton, Negroes David and Moll; John Madowell, Willam Fan; Frainces Mauldin, Benjamin Mauldin, Negroes Jam, Nat, Seaser, Bess, Dina and Gudy; John Nevill, Edward Nevill, surety; Thomas Nevill; Willam Nevill; Willam Newill, Mary Carman, widow, surety; John Orsborn; Danel Orton; James Orrick, Negroes Phill, Tom, Jack, Daniel, Jam, Graner, Rosse, Rachel, Moll, Sue and Hanner; Samuel Philips, Sr., Joseph Philips; Samuel Philips, Jr.; Moses Rutter; Johathan [sic] Readman; John Ritckets; Jacob Rudolph; Willam Randels; James Rock; Thomas Rose; Andrew Ryon; James Readman; Sabina Reidgbey, widow, John Rumsey, Negroes Pero, Bob, Abner, Mattila, Bette and Flora; Benjamin Rumsey; James Rundels, John Worckfeald, surety; Hance Rudolph, Negro Bistow; Frainces Rock; John Stalcap; Patrick Shurkey, John Toulson, Sr., surety; John Smith (caler?); Ritcherd Simpus; Nathanel Simpus, William Rutter, Negro Sam; Henry Sewill; Mickel Smith, John Kankey, surety; Thomas Savin; Henry Steidham; Joseph Thomas; John Toulson, Sr.; John Toulson, Jr.; James Veazey, Sr., Thomas Holins, Negro Petter; Thomas Veazey, James Veazey, Jr.; Willam Veazey; Lewis Veanlkor[?], John Mainley, surety; John Weickfeild. Henry Steidham, Constable.

TAXABLES IN 1761 IN OCTORARA HUNDRED: Robert Brotherton, William Brotherton; Hanse Baker; Simon Cosier; William Clerk; Samuel Caldwell; Henry Dougharty; Patrick Doil; Patt: Ewing, Samuel Ewing, Slaves Bet and Sezar; Hugh Edmiston, Slaves Phillis and David; William Ewing, Jr.;

William Ewing from Virginia; Samuel Fulton, Alexander Fulton, James Fulton, William Snodgrass; Stephen Fisser; Francis Flood; James Fraiser; Richard Gay, John Gay, Richard Gay; William Graham; John Gallaway; Samuel Gillespie, Robert Gillespie, Slaves London, Phillis and Bet; William Gillespie, Jr.; William Gillespie, Sr., Samuel Gillespie; Elihu Hall, Esq., Slaves Jefry, Sezar, Roben, Morea, Hector, Jenny and Effy; Ruth Hall, Slaves Thom, Cuff, Roben, Jack, Dover, Flora, Hager, Sue, Judah and Jack; William Husband, Joseph Husband, Slaves Jim, Sezar, Sam, Bob, Pegg, Bess and Jeff; Joseph Jacob, Slave Ned; Christopher Jones, John Jones; Thomas Love; Samuel Love; Thomas McDowel; William Mitchell, James Mitchell; Kenneth McKinzie; Daniel McGuire; John Morrow; James Porter, William Porter, Robert Porter; Andrew Porter, John Porter, James Porter; Luke Peacock, Slaves Phill and Jerry; James Reed; John Sconnell; James Skilleien[?]; Nicholas Troy; Nicholas Ulrich, John Ulna; John Wasson, Sr., James Wasson; John Widdowfield; Robert Walker. William Gillespie, Constable.

TAXABLES IN 1761 IN BACK CREEK HUNDRED: Richard Thompson, Jr., Abraham Thompson, Slaves Tom and Hannah; Richard Boulden, Slave Ben; David Demster; William Richardson; William Boulden; Jeremiah Taylor; John Armstrong; William Beetle; Noble Beetle; Edward Armstrong, William Foster, William White; William White, James White, Joseph White; Daniel Golder; Alexander Scott, Abraham Scott; James Wallace, John McDowel, Samuel McDowel; William Seares; Cornelius Conley; ---- Vanculan[?]; John Nash; Abraham Thompson; Susannah Alexander, James[?] Alexander, Aaron Alexander, Jessy[?] Alexander, Amos Alexander, Slave Permelia; Moses Alexander; Thomas Nash; William Padgett; David Faris; Benjamin Bravard, John Maxfield; James Foster; Samuel Halor; Thomas Burnam; Nicholas Night; Thomas Moody; Robert McCoy, Slaves Sasse, Moll, Sara, Tom, Will, Gabriel, Prince, Martilla, Vitt[?]; William Prine, Slaves Burch, Jim, James and Bobb; Thomas Prine, James Prine, Veazey Prine, Slaves Frank, Cate and Bett; Richard Beetle, Dominick Beetle, Slaves Jeff, Norgie[?] and Till; Richard Hukill, Henry Hukill, Christopher Picklan; Griffith Williams, Evan Bell, Micael Kinsals; Arther Cortney; John Ford, Richard Ford; John Bavington, Slave Nan; Samuell Adair, Slave Harry; Richard Ellis, Slave Sall; James Boulden, Jessy Boulden, Slaves Mingo, Hagar and Cate; Thomas Meloan, Jeremiah Franklin; George Ford, Hanse Atthebough[?]; Benjamin Whittiam, Isaac Parker; John Hall; David Alexander, Thomas Mereen; Edward McDermott; John Calvert; William Chick, John Check [sic]; Natthaniel Chick; ---- [page torn], Alexander[?] Hutchesson, Samuel Hutchesson, Slaves Will and Megg; Benjamin Thomas, Slave Nan; Elijah Brown, Thomas Brown; Andrew McCinney; Andrew Miller, Thomas Craton, John Erwin, Slave Thaime; Menassah Ohorley[?]; Andrew Wallace; Samuel Bonfield[?]; Bartholomew Johnson; Pady McCafferty; Thomas Morgan; Abraham Miller, Benjamin Miller, Slave Harry; William Miller; James Miller; Peter Hood; Widow Hallett, John Hallett; John Beard; Samuel Sharp; John Larrance; David Bayland; Thomas Bettle, John Tillton; Jos.[Jas.?] Thomas; Eloner Cambell, John Chambers, Slave Nan; William Buckhannon, Robert Buckhannon; David Clark, Dennes Doyle, Slave Jem; William Clark, William Stewart, Slaves Ned, Dick, Little Dick and Sue; Thomas Stewart, James Crumbwell; James Cuningham; James Smith, James

Samson, Slave George; Thomas Ogle, Hugh McGinnis, Abraham Ayres; Micael McGillion; John McCarty; Ephraim Thompson, Ephraim Logue; Robert Thompson, Slaves Flint and Steel; Richard Thompson, Sr., Jonathan Meloan, Slaves Dave, Hagar, Betty, Hannah, and a two wheel chair; Alexander Smith; Francis Reynolds, William Clark; Thomas Boulden, William Smith, John Cowan, Slave Cuff; Adam Wallace; William Brown; Thomas Bravard, Thomas Patton; Eli Alexander; John Thompson; Neal Donnelly; Moses Scott. Thomas Boulden, Constable.

TAXABLES IN 1761 IN WEST SASSAFRAS HUNDRED: Thomas Savin, Sr., Richard Savin, John Savin, Augustine Savin, Negroes Jack, Charming, Sarah, Rachel and Harp; John Geers, Negro Limus; Robert Briant; John Moulster; Peter Waren; John Coppen; James Simmonds, Isaac Chambers, William Man; Daniel Bridge, Briant McDermot, security; Elisha Terry, Vatchel Terry, Negro Boson; Thomas Ryland, Sr., Aldrige Ryland; Michael Standly; Daniel Pearce; William Starling; Andrew Crocker; John Stoops, Negroes Will, Flora and Sall, and a chair; William Smith, Negroes Harry, James and Mime; Nicholas Dorrel; William Hawkins, Mary Bavington, security; James Frisby; John Graham, Negroes Ned, Charles, Charles, Charles, Ben, Nace, Clayton, Joe, Jervis, Janey, Janey, Philis, Pegg, Sam, Peter, Sam, Lucy, Ned, Bob, David, Tom, Bess, Nan, Cate, and one coraile[?], Peter Hendrickson, Nehemiah Vansandt; Andrew Pearce, Negroes Bob, Stephen, Abner, Betty and Silvia; William Pearce; John Cooper; Charles Hutson, Thomas Cooper, Negroes Quash, Sampson and Silvia, one chair, and Daniel Gears; Mary Ricketts, James Ricketts, Negro Black, Tom and Bina; William Abiot, Negroes Major and Rose; William Bateman, Sr., John Bateman, Christopher Bateman, Andrew Bateman; William Bateman, Jr., Negroes Judge and Rose; Robert Porter, Jr., James White, Negro Jem; Briant McDermott; Philip Stoops, Jeremiah Coerin[?], Negroes Ben and Hanah, and a chair; Andrew Ball, and a chair; James Chetham Ward, Negroes Pegg, Sarah and Philis; Dominick McDermott; James Hughes, Sr., Negro John; Jacob Jones, Sr., Negroes Marget and Cuff; Thomas Pearce, Richard Pearce, Negro Jack; John Pearce; Gavin Hutchinson; Thomas Ryland, Jr.; Thomas Williams, Thomas Charles Williams, and one chair; Thelwell Loftis; Robert Porter, Sr., William Porter, Negro Frank; James Langworthy; John McDowell[?], James Hughs, Jr.; James Colvill; Moses Frampton; Matthis Hendrickson, Negro Dick; William Davis, Morris Davis, Benjamin Davis; James Kemp; John Artigee; Major George Milligan, Abraham Hynes, Robert French, Negroes Bob, Ned, Toby, Stephen, Glasgow, George, Benjamin, Cezar, Peter, Phill, Moll, Nell, Joan, Joan, Ruth, Sue, Nan, Nan, and one chaire; Nathan Dobson; Ebenezer Penington, Negroes Jem and Sam';Benjamin Cox; John Barneyby; Charles Gorden; George Cuningham, Negroes Tim, Jem, Nace, Jack, Micke, Joe, Plymoth, Cuff, Bob, Nan, Moll and Rainey; Thomas Loyd, Negroes Sam and Teny, and one chair; Samuel Roberts; Jacob Jones, Jr., John Jones, David Woods, Negroes Cuggoe and Nico; Widow Mary Penington's Negro Cuff; Isaac Penington; Stephen Ryland; Hugh Gribbin; Robert Young; John Loftis; John Martin; Benjamin Benson, Iaac [sic] Benson, Negroes Jem and Lidia; Henry Penington, Andrew Monsone, Negroes Bob, Monk and Maria; Capt. John Brown, John Stoops, John Shepard, Negroes Jacob, Peter, Bett, Mosepo, Hague, Jen and Hanah, and one chair; James Logue; Owen McKelvy; Dr. John Jackson, Gilbert Jackson; William

Jackson; Drake Penington; John Ryland, Sr., Negroes Jem, Moll and Lucy; Silvester Ryland; George Porter, Charles Whitehead, Robert Clear; Michael Earle, James Ervin, Jeremiah Cronney, James Morris, Negroes Charles, John, Jack, Tom, Boston, Hannah, Bett, and one coraile; Benjamin Vansandt; Akey Penington; John Colvill, James Cooper security; Joseph Cowden, John Ryland, security; John Beastin, Isaac Penington, security; Williiam Silavan, Elenor Brown, security. Elisha Terry, Constable.

TAXABLES IN 1761 IN MIDDLE NECK HUNDRED: James McKay, Negroes Tony and Rack[?]; William Smith; James Cunningham, Thomas Steuart[?], security; John Weiley, Negroes Vilett and Bette; Edward Rumsey; William Weathers, John York, Negroes Katt and Jem; James Morrason; Edward Rumsey, Jr., James Rien; Sebbelen[?] Weathers; Dennis Kelley; Michael Megowen; Thomas Meetage (Mectage?); Ann Pennington, Abraham Pennington, John Hollens; Thomas Reynolds, Patrick Duffe; Ephram Mecay; John Scott (miller); William Rumsey, Negroes Ben, Noco[?], Leah, Sarah, and one chare; Patrick Doughetty; John Driscol; John Scott (millwright); Johnathan Hollens; William P---- [illegible]; Brian Garrity; John Potts, Negro Doblen; Danniel Meclan, John Meclan, Negroes Pristean[?], Luse and Kadner; Peter Cowardin, Ambrose Cowardin, Negroes Robbin, Nose, Nan and Moll; James Hasset[?]; Sidney George, Benjamin Elsberry, Negroes Tom, Adam, Jacob, Lucy, Sall, Sander, Bob, Tom, Ned, Sarah, and Sarah; John Elsberry, Negroes Charles and Jack; John Dobin, James Willey, Negroes Will, Jem, Charles and Judey; Catterin Scott, Negroes Bob, Will, Jem and Moll; Robbert Marcer; Charles Scott, William Scott, William Cradock, Negroes Jack, Dina and Rachel; Thomas Savin, Jr., James Waidlicoff[?], Negroes Jack, Will, Kitt and Sarah; William Marcer, Jr.; James Reynolds, Jerremiah Reynolds, James Reynolds, Jr.; Jacob Evertson, Negroes Jem, Harre and Peg; Antony Vortade[?]; Burthallume Jacobs, Negroes Coffe and Rachel; Benjamin Elsberry; James Harper, William Whight; John Ozer, John Meklrey[?], Negroes Bob and Nan; Richard Flintham[?]; Ellicksander Macfarling[?]; Elizabeth Evertson, Negroes Jans and one chare; Richard Brown, Elizebeth Evertson, security; John Fillinggam, John Fillinggam, Jr.; Benjaman Hull, James Tapper[?]; John Ferrel, William Smith; Michael Mennecossens, Negroes Tom and Jen; James Mennecossens; John Hance; Justis Gonce; Radalf Gonce; Michael Earl, John Thomas, Negroes Will, Ben, Charles, Nan and Dely; Barnet Vanhorn; Patrick Nugen; James Clark; William Mecbride, James Clark, security; Mary Knarsborough, Michael Knarsborough, Negro Toney; John Carnan, William[?] Carnan, Negroes Bob, Jack, James, Silve and one chare; John Rien; Jacob Harper; John Harper, Negro Frank; John Bohannon; William Laller[?]; Sarah Rumsey, William Cox, Negroes Tom and Sue; Elias Elieson, Elias Elieson, Jr., Negroes Will and Jem; John Elieson, Negro Hannah; Cornelous Elieson; Richard Reynolds; Ellicksander Stuart, Nicholas Harres, Negro Jim; James Vance; Isaack Vandick; James Stele; John Scott (farmer); Ellicksander Pars[?]; John Rien, Jr.; John Cazier, Negroes Antheny, Bet, Nan, and one chare; Micheal Arrenoha[?], melatto; Joseph Hattery[?]; ---- ---abuck[?], Negro Dick; James Smith; John Williams; John Cunninggem; Samuel Stuart, James Forster; William Paul, Adam Cornish [Cornesal?]; John Awl [Aul?],

James Awl [Aul?]; John Paul, William Paul, security; Nicholas Leeds. John
Cazier, Constable.

TAXABLES IN 1761 IN NORTH SASSAFRAS HUNDRED: Sylvester
Nowland, Negroes Jack and Dunkin; Charles Heath; William Jones; John Sil-
lack[?]; John Donnohoe, James Donnohoe, Negro Dick; Henry Gilaspy; Cor-
nelius Augustine Savin; James Mahnny [sic]; ---- Carsan; ---- Humberstone,
---- Humberstone, ---- Humberstone [several names torn off page, followed
by names of negroes, names partly missing]; Elizabeth Patterson, Thomas
Patterson; Thomas Beard, Sr., Thomas Beard, Jr., James Beard, Negroes
Tom, Isaac, Pompy and Dino; James Coppin[?], Negroes Will, Dino and Sal;
Charles ----[page soiled]; Thomas Robi---[?]; John We----[?]; Richard Lock-
wood; James Barthlmore [sic]; Jacob Jacobs; Edward Ferrener, John
Creasour[?], Negroe Peter, and two wheel chare; George Douglas, William
Douglas; William Mordo; Clem Lynard; Neal Go---oner [page torn]; Daniel
Jackson and two wheel cheer; James[?] Chetten [Chelten?]; John Sampson;
James Hepding[?]; John Brown, Sr., John Brown, Jr., Richard Brown, David
Fitzgar----[soiled page]; William Marcer, Samuel Marcer, John Marcer;
Stephen Biddle, Augustine Biddle, Negroes Majer and Vilet; Isaac Gibbs
and two wheel cheer; John Hood[?], Thomas Robartson, Negro Seser; ----[?]
Snow, ---- ---ckson[?], ---- [soiled page]; ----[?] Vancleave, ---- Waltham[?], ---
- Richards [soiled page]; William Gudgeon; Thomas Marr, Joseph ----
bens[?]; Isaac Blakiston[?]; Mary H----[?], James ----[?], Benjamin ----[?],
Henry Home---[?], Martain H----[?]; Lewis Beard[?]; John N----[?], Negroes
Isaac and Sophie; William ----[?]; John Ward[?], Sr., John ----[?], George
Vansandt; three illegible names ending in "---ngton"[?]; Garret Vansandt;
Daniel Nowland, Benjamin Nowland, Ephrim Nowland, Richard Orman,
John Harling; John Huston, Charles Huston; Murter[?] Shay, Negro Nan;
Hearthlley Sappington, Banjamin Sappington, George Scott, Abraham
Parker; Benjamin Body, Peter Body, James Rue--[?]; Isaac ---[page torn;
several names missing]; Nathaniel Bow---[?], Nicholas Vanhorne, Jr., Negroe
Hafer[?]; Nathan Newland, John Hawkins; Walter Bourk, Patrick Carney,
Negro Nan; Tobias Bourk, Thomas Bourk; Bryan O'Danabey[?], William
Base; James Mullon; William Hedges, Daniel Heath; seven names illegible
[soiled page]; Lawrence Blanchfield; James O'Neal, Patrick Dagney; John
Crawsby; Nicholis Vanhorne, Sr.; ---- ---awson [soiled page]; Dr.[?] Hugh
Matthews, Owen Matthews, Negroes Will, Rafe, Bob, Tom, Jeffry, James,
Grace and Moll; Thomas Hynson; seven names illegible [soiled page]; Bar-
tholome Anderson; Rev. John Lewis, Rev. Mathias Mennen, Thomas
Banester, Negroes Raff, Nanncy, Dick, Mary, Jack, Charles, Tom Dick,
Hary, Fill, Peter, David, Hannah, and several others illegible; Mary War--[?],
John ----[?], John ----[?], and several negroes [soiled page]. Thomas Savin,
Jr., Constable.

COLONIAL MILITIA OF CECIL COUNTY IN 1740

Reference: *Maryland Historical Magazine*, Vol. 6, pp. 44-51, published 1911. It should be noted that there are signicant differences in this and the publication of the same source in *Citizens of the Eastern Shore of Maryland, 1659-1750*, published by Family Line Publications. The original lists are held by the Maryland State Archives, Box 1, Folder 4.

TROOPS UNDER COMMAND OF CAPT. JOHN BALDWIN IN 1740: George Veazey, Lieutenant; Thomas Davis, Cornett; John Lusby, Quartermaster; William Creaston, Corporal; John Pennington, Corporal. Privates: Robert Porter, Phillip Hooper, Hugh Terry, John Betle, Walter Scott, Jr., Charles Scott, William Pearce, John Davage, Richard Houghton, John Pennington, Jacob Everton, Evert Everton, Jr., Jacob Hozier, William Ellis, William Savin, James Hughes, Richard Pennington, Anthony Lynch, Barthow. Smith, John Ryland, Jr., John Mercer, Robert Wamsley, and John Beetle, Jr.

FOOT COMPANY UNDER COMMAND OF CAPT. EDWARD JACKSON IN 1740: Robert Story, Lieutenant; Henry Jackson, Ensign; Neall Carmichall, Sergeant; William Ewing, Sergeant; Thomas Miller, Corporal; John Read, Corporal; Tobias Long, Corporal; Chris. Tuchstone, Corporal. Privates: John Johnson, Edward Brimfield, John McLaughlin, William Devall, John McTear, Reed ----[?] Hunter, Richard Titbald, John Osburn, Joseph Young, Benjamin Dickson, James Coulter, James Green, Anthony Dickson, William McKewen, Thomas Neall, Adam Armstrong, Charles Pigeon, Patrick Kelly, James Walker, Richard Harrison, James Harrison, Joseph Crosswell, Samuell Crosswell, James Bread, John Callwell, William Orre, James Finley, James Kennedy, Marty Machen, John McFadden, John Young, James Campble, Archibald Campble, John Currier, Randall Marshall, Robert Patten, Peter Justice, Thomas Tenney, John Clark, Roger Perryman, William Brown, John McClelen, Thomas Hartshorn, Robert Lashley, John McKenney, Enoch Enouchson, Benjamin Collner, William McDowall, Nathan Beye, Jedediah Alexander, Robert Morgan, Samuel Crawford, William Crawford, John Manery, Hugh McAlaster, Samuell Calwell, James Crennay, and Nathaniel Ewing.

TROOPERS UNDER COMMAND OF CAPT. THOMAS JOHNSON (DECEASED) IN 1740: Nicholas Hyland, Lieutenant; James Alexander, Cornett; Edward Johnson, Quartermaster; John Hankey [Kankey?], Corporal; William Barry, Corporal; Robert Holey, Corporal. Privates: James Veazey, Peter Boyer, Michael Lunn [Lum?], William Wallis, Samuel Jones, John Ricketts, Thomas Edwards, William Maffat, Samuel Bond, Michael Wallace, Hugh Lawson, Alexander McConil, John Alexander, Joseph Alexander, Theops. Alexander, David Patterson, Richard Foster, John Ferrel, Robert Patterson, William Danniel, and John Barry.

FOOT COMPANY UNDER COMMAND OF CAPT. JOHN VEAZEY IN 1740: John Pennington, Lieutenant; Thomas Ward, Ensign; Valentine Silcok [Silock?], Sergeant; Michael Riely, Sergeant; Benjamin Childs, Corporal; Edward Morann, Corporal; John Roberts, Jr., Corporal; Joshua Meakins, Corporal; William Morgan, Corporal; James Price, Corporal. Privates: Alphonso Cosden, John Wagoner, Thomas Turk, John Brown, Thomas Mercer, Jr., Robert McCleary, James Navell, Mounts Justice, Joseph Ritherford, Samuel Davis, Richard Davis, William Kelly, Joseph Clift, Nathaniel Childs, George Childs, Thomas Ethrington, Henry Hendrixson, Robert Roberts, Alexander Thompson, Thomas Wallace, Dennis McNanny, Samuel Savin, Mathew Phippes, John Clark, Thomas Scurry, John Campbell, Jr., Richard Parsley, Robert Scurry, Joshua Campble, Anthony Lynch, Charles Leach, Henry Fowler, William Price, Jr., Joseph Price, Nathaniel Alexander, Edward Morgan, Bartholomew Parsley, Thomas Severson, Jr., Thomas Severson, James Morgan, William Cole, Mathew Bulley, William Pickard, Edward Murfey, John Urin, George Robertson, Thomas Cox, John Kimber, Henry Cox, Peter Numbers, Otho Otherson, John Wood, John Wallace, Barthw. Edrin, Andrew Price, John Money, James Cetch, David Cole, Joseph Ryley, and Dennis Sullivane.

FOOT COMPANY IN 1740: Officers Unknown (Original Defective): Privates: John Archbald, David Crosswell, John Mitchell, George Lashley, James Bond, William Callwell, Joshua Ewing, Nathan Baker, Henry Baker, John Starrot, Moses Latham, William Nelson, Robert Williams, Robert Dickson, Jacob Johnson, Randell Death, Edward Death, James Death, John Death, Thomas Hennry, William Jones, Jonathan Hartshorn, Jr., Benjamin Hartshorn, William Dixon, Moses Andrews, William Bristow, Jr., William Price, Robert Price, John Golet, James McFarrel, James See, William Whittom, Thomas Crisp, Thomas Sanders, Charles Huston, and John Childs.

FOOT COMPANY UNDER COMMAND OF CAPT. ZEBULON HOLLINGSWORTH IN 1740: Andrew Barry, Lieutenant ("refuses to serve"); Moses Alexander, Ensign; William Currer, Sergeant; John Jones, Sergeant; George Bristow, Sergeant; Walter Sharp, Sergeant; Jacobus Doulson, Corporal; Simon Johnson, Jr., Corporal; John Phillips, Corporal; Thomas Phillips, Corporal. Privates: Thomas Wallace, Mathew Hodgson, Richard Nowland, John Alexander, Andrew Alexander, William Queatt, John Irvin, James Haswell, James Nowland, Andrew Hall, John Ritchie, James Ritchie, Robert Ritchie, Mathew Hopkins, William Henry, Nathaniel Moore, John Null, Robert Null, David Slone, Thomas Killgore, Robert Evans, Mathew Wallace, John Hodghead, John Wallace, David McKendley, William Balley, John Meke, George Welch, Gaven Clubege, William Irvin, James Armstrong, Oliver Johnson, Peter Johnson, Thomas Rite, John Were, David Leech, James Stewart, Edward Clark, Charles Stewart, John Surgen, John Gray, Patrick Milton, John Hartness, John Sith, Edward Patterson, Irvin Patterson, John Gardner, James Smith, George Thompson, George Sair, William Hoddge, John McMaster, James Burns, Robert Edmundson, Benjamin Winsley, John Mills, Nathaniel Dawson, Joseph Thompson, William Young, Hugh Ross, James Carter, Adam Short, David Pain, David Rees, Francis Gardner, Richard Lewis, Hugh Morgan, David Hampton, Peter Brown, John Parker, Robert Carlile, John Carlile, Uria Anderson, William Daniel, John McArter, Samuel Jackson, Peter Campble, William Phillips, Rubin Phillips, William Manson, Archibald Armstrong, William Hall, Phenies Hodgson, Archibald

Jackson, John Rutter, John Rutter, Jr., Samuel Whitton, Francis Milburn, Benjamin Mauldin, Jacob Johnson, Jr., Nicholas George, John Wescote, John Corsine, Edward Veazey, Thomas Ricketts, Thomas Hitchcock, Thomas Parkerson, Joseph More, John Hitchcock, Samuel Brown, Samuel Philips, James Nox, Mathew Arthur, William Caughthran, Abraham Homes, John Stinson, James Kees, John Hambleton, Robert McKey, James McKey, Anthony Ross, Robert Miller, Thomas Roberson, Robert Morrison, Mathew Irvin, William Mont, David Care, William Wood, Robert Gorden, William Armstrong, Thomas Armstrong, William Boyd, John Burns, John McCune, Hugh Were, John Vancaslin, James Anderson, Peter Poulson, Powel Johnson, Thomas Veazey, John Mitchel, Edward Condon, Isaac Foster, Elias Everson, James Leake, Mathias Seal, William McCluer, Lazerus Grainger, William Jemson, John Jones, Thomas Crouch, Richard Parsley, John Care, Richard Roach, John Midleton, Peter Peco, John Hiteley, John Winsley, Nathan Pickles, John Littles, William Gilletson, Martin McHaffey, Richard Foster, John Mainly, Jacob Johnson, William Sluby, Benjamin Taylor, Philip Hitely, James Orton, Jeffery Beasly, and James Pearce.

TROOPS UNDER COMMAND OF CAPT. WILLIAM RUMSEY IN 1740: William Knight, Lieutenant; Benjamin Slyter, Cornett; John Holland, Corporal; Peter Bushell, Corporal; Andrew Zelifrow, Corporal; William Price, Corporal. Privates: Alexander Armstrong, Enock Jenkings, Abraham Allman, John Tilton, Thomas Beaston, Thomas Bolding, Richard Taylor, Lawrence Lawrenceson, John Harmon, Peter Poulson, Mana---[?] Logan, Thomas Beetle, Richard Boulden, John Oltham, Thomas Price, Andrew Alexander, Thomas Ebthorp, Edward Rumsey, Thomas Stewart, Adam Van-Bebber, Cornelias Eliason, Jr., Richard Foord, John Bravard, Jr., Peter Lawson, John Husband, William Chick, Henry McCoy, William Harper, John Segar, Jr., Joseph Alman, Joseph Leeman, and Francis Ozier.

FOOT COMPANY UNDER COMMAND OF CAPT. PETER BAYARD IN 1740 (part of the list is defective with some names obliterated): James Bayard, Lieutenant; Samuel Bayard, Ensign; Jermiah Larkins, Sergeant; Thomas Reynolds, Sergeant; Jacob Harper, Sergeant; Robert Patton, Sergeant; Nicholas Wood, Corporal; Richard Reynolds, Corporal; Jacob Hann, Corporal; John Wood, Corporal; John Lathem, Corporal; Steven Julien, Corporal; Samuel McClery, Corporal; John Oglsby, Corporal. Privates: Richard Franklin, William ----, John ----, James ----, M-- ----, Dan-- ----, William ----, Thomas ----, Samuel ----, Thomas Foster, Abraham Hughes, John Ford, William Bowen, James Lyon, Thomas ----, William ----, Thomas ----, Thomas ---- , William ----, Francis ----, Richard Elwood, Edward Clark, George Hampton, William Crow, James Craige, William Craige, Andrew Rider, Nicholas Vandergrift, Alexander ----, James Read, Henry Miller, Mathias Tetlow, Thomas Bird, Edward Armstrong, Joseph Chick, John Barnabym James McKitterick, John Killpatrick, David Mierick, John Hunter, John Veazey, James Taylor, John McCrery, Richard Stevens, Ruben Roads, John Wood, John Hunter, Thomas Stewart, William Cook, Sr., Cornelius Wooliston, Abraham Anderson, James Custro, John Chick, Philip Lancaster, John Whitehead, James Hattery, Patrick Harris, Frederick Elberry, John Barron, Enoch Jenkins, Jr., John Oglesby, William Oglesby, Richard Bowen, Thomas

Moore, Aron Moore, Philip Elwood, Richard Hukill, Richard Elwood, Sr., John Jenkins, Andrew ----, John Gullick, Robert Glenn, Hance Patton, William Pitch, Hugh Guttery, Alexander Belding [Bolding?], James Smith, James Foster, Thomas Norman, Jacob Alexander, Charles Haltham, Alexander Scott, James McCurrey, John Nash, Samuel Nash, Isaac Gray, James Cowadon, Thomas Morrane, Elias Eliason, Stephen Julien, Alexander Waddle, John ----, Jo-- ----, Jo-- ----, Ch-- ----, Don-- ----, John ----, James ---- Benjamin Lancaster, Samuel Seagar, Samuel Hughes, Charles Ford, William Moore, John Wood, Hugh Wood, Marten Alexander, William Menus, Jonathan Melone, Henry Simmons, Aron Latham, George Oglesby, James Ford, Robert Wood, John McHan--, John Rey--, Robert ----, Samuel ----, George ----, John ----, Thomas ----, Isaac ----, John Harper, Thomas McCollough, and William Bedle.

MEN WITHOUT COMMANDING OFFICERS IN 1740, SASSAFRAS HUNDRED (part of the list is defective with some names obliterated): John Welch, John Welch, Jr., Robert Welding, James Welding, Charles Welding, John Ranzer, James Porter, James Jones, William Pennington, Henry Cox, Thomas Pennington, John Cooper, Jr., Alexander Black, David Ricketts, William Ricketts, Benjamin Benson, Edward ----, William Davis, Jeremiah Grisley, Richard Pennington, Manuel Blashford, Charles Mahany, Thomas Bean, Richard Smith, John Arnold, John Calk, John Christopher, John Coxill, Robert Pennington, Jr., John Pennington, William Catch, Richard Chandler, Matthew ----, Jacob Pen----, William Starling, William Penningon, Alexander Galaspy, Mathew Stul, Mathew Dunahoe, John Ashford, William Ridge, Benjamin Ridge, James Ridge, Joseph Gray, Nathaniel Sapping, Harky Sapping, Cornelius Vanhorn, James Poor, James ----, Tho-- ----, John ----, Jona-- ----, M-- ----, Wi-- ----, Isaac ----, William ----, Daniel ----, H-- ----, John ----, William ----, Robert Croker, Henry Pennington, Daniel Maclean, Thomas Owen, John Maclean, John Fane, John Jones, David Jones, John Loftus, John Coppin, John Price, John Artige, Nicholas Dorrell, Daniel Gears, Jr., James Pen----, Benjamin ----, John ----, Edward ----, John Cham--- William Cham----, John Chambers, Jr., John Shelley, William Bateman, Abraham Hollings, Patrick Tool, George Holton, William Richardson, William Mercer, Cornelius Vansant, John Bellarman, Nathaniel Bohannon, John Yorkson, William Sanders, William Marten, Richard McCarq[?], Charles Johnson, B-- ----, Peter ----, John ----, Ph-- ----, Joseph ----, Thomas Ryland, Evert Evertson, John Hendrickson, John Jones, John Samson, John Dun, Walter Hill, Bryan Cradock, William Willson, Henry Ball, John Trase, George Rees, George Lewis, John Ball, William Smith, Barnet Vanhorn, William Burgess, and Jno. Webb.

LISTS OF FINES DUE THE LORD PROPRIETARY, 1746-1774. [Note: All were charged with assault unless indicated otherwise.] (Ref: Original documents in Maryland Historical Society, Manuscripts Division, MS.231]: FINED IN 1746 - Richard Boulding, Anthony Hern, Philip Roach, Matthew Bonner, and William Cummings. FINED IN 1747 - Thomas Millar (John Smith, sheriff), and Peter Jones. FINED IN 1748 - William Beetle, Thomas Marr, Benedict Penington, James Poer, Augustin Penington, Peregrine Ward, John Ogg (John Sampson, security), Robert Love (Henry Baker, security), and William McKonky (George Ford, security). FINED IN 1749 - William Penington (Michael Earle, sheriff), Thomas Beaston, and Thomas Beard. FINED IN 1750 - Capt. Peregrine Ward (Michael Earle, sheriff), Henry Ward, John Price, John Stump, Cornelius Keef (James O'Bryan, security), and George Milligan (Michael Earle, sheriff). FINED IN 1751 - Peter Jones (Edward Veazey, sheriff), James Patterson, George Ford, Richard Beedle, and John Dare. FINED IN 1755 - Andrew Wallace (for concealing a taxable), Samuel Idair [Adair?] (for concealing a taxable), Margarett Dooling (William Hedges, sheriff), John Kinzey (John Rutter, Susqa., security), John Ward (John Veazey, sub-sheriff), Joseph Thompson (for concealing a taxable, Nathan Baker, Esq., security), George McNear (for concealing two taxables), Thomas Marr (William Hedges, sheriff), Robert Good (for concealing a taxable), and Henry VanBebber, Sr. Matthias Bordley, Clerk. FINED IN 1756 - Elizabeth Parsley (wife of Richard Parsley), Dr. John Caldwell (John Ricketts, sub-sheriff), Benjamin Thomas, and William Jones, Sassa. (Peter Lawson and William Terry, securities). Francis Key, Clerk. FINED IN 1757 - Michael Nesbarry (William Savin, sub-sheriff), Henry Ward Pearce (William Hedges, sheriff), Henry Baker, James Oliver (Thomas Savin, sub-sheriff), Catherine Oliver, William Jones, Sassafras (Benjamin Benson, security), Mary Snow (Nathaniel Cleave and Prince Snow, securities), Hugh Robertson, Robert Patterson (for concealing a taxable), and Lewis Lee (for marrying without publication or license (one moiety). FINED IN 1758 - William Maccleure (George Milligan, sheriff), Patrick Flin, Benjamin Rumsey (John Veazey, sub-sheriff), Mulatto Hannah (Thomas Savin, sub-sheriff), John Haing (Ewing) [sic], James Ward, Isaac Gibbs, and Henry Baker (for contempt and abuse of a magistrate in the execution of his office - fined twice). FINED IN 1759 - Robert Clear (Charles Whitehead, security), William Bouldin (Thomas Savin, sub-sheriff), William Bavington (George Milligan, sheriff), William Meek (Robert Neilson, security), William Meek (Thomas Savin, sub-sheriff), Rachael Beedle, and Mary Flinn (George Milligan, sheriff). Francis Key, Clerk. FINED IN 1760 - Ezekiel Denesin and wife (George Milligan, sheriff), William Murphy (Benjamin Chew, Sr., security), Margaret Cunningham (Mark Cunningham, security), John Carty (Thomas Savin, sub-sheriff), Phineas Hodgson (for concealing two taxables), Dr. Hugh Matthews, and John Brown (John Veazey, Jr., sub-sheriff). FINED IN 1761 - Rebecca Berry, John Pennington, Sr., Eleanor Campbell, Rosanna Hannah, Benjamin Daws, Robert Mills, Benjamin Benson, William Jackson, and John Campbell (Benjamin Chew, Sr., security). James Baxter, Sheriff. FINED IN 1762 - Anthony Fortack (for dealing with Negroes), Samuel Thomas, Elizabeth Marr, Charles Carty, Daniel Charles Heath, Thomas Marr (fined twice), Samuel McConkey, John McCoy, Susqa. (for assaulting Elihu Hall in the execution of his office as a magistrate - fined twice), John Stump (for not attending as a juryman), and Jonathan Hartshorn and James Glasgow (for not attending as jurymen). FINED IN 1763 - John Scott (miller), John Cunningham (John Hall, Susqa., security), Robert and Mary Sutton, John Gordon, Joseph Pew, and Alexander Doyle (precognisance in 10 lbs. currency forfeited). Richard Thomas, Sheriff. FINED IN 1764 - Bryan O'Donel, John Lawrence, Isaac Gibbs (Charles Gordon, security), William Porter, and William Ewing, Sr. FINED IN 1765 - Isaac Gibbs, Matts. Hendricksen, Charles Pearcey (Peter Reiter, security), and Hannah Johnson. FINED IN 1766 - Archibald Armstrong, Daniel

Heath, Abraham Poor, John McCown [Note: A second list gave his name as John McKown], Samuel Campbell (committed for fine), Henry Haise, John Cowen, John Hunter (Andrew Barratt, security), and Manassa Henley [Note: A second list gave his name as Mannassa Harly]. FINED IN 1767 - James Cunningham (William Brumfield, security), John Wilson (William Brumfield, security), Samuel Wilson (William Brumfield, security), Samuel Arnett, Thomas Elliott (Francis Rock, security), Samuel McClarey (Daniel Turner, sub-sheriff), David Alexander (for beating his servant too much), and Andrew Lawrenson (Thomas Savin, sub-sheriff). FINED IN 1768 - Richard Dicks (Edward Mitchel, sheriff), John Stump, Sr., James Spear (John McCoy, Susquahanna, surety), John Scott (innholder - fined thrice), Garritta Murphy, William Hawkins (Nicholas Dorrell, surety), and John Elliott. FINED IN 1769 - James Whitelock (James Orrick, sub-sheriff), William Hitchcock (William Veazey, sub-sheriff), Thomas Stil (Hyland Price, security), Owen Mathews (Edward Mitchell, sheriff), Thomas Ogle (Robert Thompson, security), William Mears (fined twice - Henry Miller, security), Bartholomew Etherington, Jr. (Samuel Veazey, sub-sheriff), and Robert Alexander. FINED IN 1770 - John Stoops (William Veazey, sub-sheriff), William Carty (Richard Thomas, sheriff), Raymond Beedle, William Crocker (James Orrick, sub-sheriff), Samuel Miller (Henry Pennington, sub-sheriff), Daniel Charles Heath (fined twice), Robert Porter, William Allender (for abusing a magistrate in the duty of his office - William Baxter, security), Thomas Williams, John McMahan, Thomas Bradley (Edward Mitchell, late sheriff amerced), Negro Aleck (Samuel Veazey, sub-sheriff), John Lowry (fined twice - Samuel Hill, security), James Heath, Richard Ellis, and Arthur Alexander. FINED IN 1771 - Henry Beedle, Manassa Harley (fined thrice - Alexander Scott, security), Richard Ellis, Samuel Miller, Christopher Peters, Mathew Alexander, John Armstrong (Henry Allen, sub-sheriff), William Arnet, Michael Trainer, and Joseph Davis. FINED IN 1772 - John McCoy, Thomas Baker, John Getty, and James Trainer. John Hamilton, Jr., Sheriff, and Benjamin Young, Clerk. FINED IN 1773 - John Ward Penington, James Day, Bartholomew Ethrington, Jr., Mary Cox (wife of John Cox), James Young, Negro Ned (property of Robert Hart), Jacob Annuells[?], Samuel Gillespie (for trespass), Prudence Hall, Lydia Gale, Mary Pew (wife of Joseph), Mathias Hendricksen, Jr., Jacob Johnson, William Hollis (for trespass), William Hollis (for assault), James Dunahoe, Thomas Doxen[?], and Mathew Alexander. FINED IN 1774 - Henry Staulkup, Thomas Savin, David Trew [Frew?], Andrew Mullan, Daniel McClean, Jr., John Crosby, Dr. Robert Johnson (Barthw. Etherington, Jr., late sheriff), William Cochran, Dr. Robert Mackey, and James Spear.

LISTS OF ORDINARY (TAVERN) LICENSES GRANTED, 1759-1774. [Ref: Original documents in Maryland Historical Society, Manuscripts Division, MS.231]. Tavernkeepers in 1759 - William Terry, Andrew Coulter, Thomas Wroth, John Lewis, Zebulon Hollingsworth, Susannah Loftus, Hanse Rudulph, Sarah Flinn, Eleanor Brown, Michael Tully, William Longwell, Mary Cowarding, James Harrison, Edward Furroner, Richard Thompson, George Lewis, Prince Snow, Harman Kankey, Peter Lawson. Tavernkeepers in 1760 - Thomas Elliott, Susanna Loftis, Willian Bentley, John Strawbridge, William Longwell, Zebulon Hollingsworth, William Currer, James Harrison, Eleanor Brown, Andrew Coulter, Hanse Rudulph,

George Johnson, Thomas Slicer, Edward Furroner, Richard Thompson, Peter Lawson, James Worth, John Barnaby, Henry Nail, Susanna McLaughlin, and Hermon Kankey. Tavernkeepers in 1769 - Henry Hollingsworth, Nathan Baker, Michael Stietz, George Johnson, Thomas Frisby Henderson, William Currer, John Strawbridge, Andrew Coulter, Thomas Elliott, William Gray, Francis Rock, Richard Ellis, William Douglass, Thomas Slicer, Philimon Noble, Jesse Boldin, Mary Harrison, and Edward Furroner. Tavernkeepers in 1770 - William Currer, Thomas Elliott, Francis Rock, Jacob Hollingsworth, John Strawbridge, William Longwill, Philemon Noble, Thomas Frisby Henderson, Nathan Baker, Andrew Coulter, Hannah Slicer, Edward Furroner, and Mary Harrison. Tavernkeepers in 1771 - William Longwill, Thomas Frisby Henderson, John Gray, William Bristow, John Strawbridge, Thomas Davis, Edward Furroner, Jacob Hollingsworth, Henry Jones, Jesse Bouldin, Thomas Elliott, Andrew Coulter, Richard Ellis, Nathan Baker, and Mary Harrison. Tavernkeepers in 1773 - Jacob Hollingsworth, John Justice, Joshua Donoho, John Gray, William Stevenson, Empson Bird, Andrew Coulter, Nathan Baker, Thomas Palmer, Andrew Miller, John Carr, William Bristow, and Benjamin Dutton.

INSOLVENTS IN ST. STEPHEN'S PARISH IN 1755: Sassafras Hundred - Isaac Alvinckle, Sr., very poor; Isaac Alvinckle, Jr., gone to Kent; Samuel Akey, ---- soldier; Francis Aaron, gone to Kent; Cornelius Coo---[worm holes in paper], not known; James Douglas, in Baltimore goal; James Gooding, gone to Kent; Barnet Grimes, dead and no effects; John Pennell, in Kent County; Sarah Penington, she is twice in levy list; William Robison, got out of goal by letter of license; Charles Welden, in Kent County; William White, dead and no effects; George Watson, dead and no effects. Bohemia Hundred - Henry Bozworth, in goal; Dennis Dullin, dead and no effects; Joseph Gray, runaway; John Lusby, can get nothing; Thomas Owens, runaway; Andrew Price, Sr., can get nothing; Thomas Robison, dead and no effects.

INSOLVENTS IN AUGUSTINE PARISH IN 1755: Manor Hundred - Brian Buckworth, Col. Bayard says dead and no effects; Daniel Carlington, runaway; Telly Cole, not known; William Hogg, this man is twice in levy list; John McIntire, dead and no effects; John McCordey, dead and no effects; Francis Ozier, runaway. Middle Neck Hundred - Archibald Hassell, not known; John O'Bryan, can't find him; Samuel Piper, runaway; William Smith, Sr., runaway. Back Creek Hundred - Andrew Alexander, runaway; John Clark (smith), gone away; [one name missing due to worm holes in paper]; and, Michael Standley, in Kent County.

SUNDRY INSOLVENTS IN 1756: Andrew Price, Sr., hath nothing; John Lusby, can get nothing; John Gallaher, can't find him; William Maclehenny, this man was taken by the constables of the Manor and Middle Neck Hundreds, he paid one levy and there is byt one of that name in the county; Isaac Alexander, gone to Pensilvania; [one name missing due to decayed paper]; St. Mary Ann's Parish - Patrick Gooding, no such man by that name; William Grace, this man is releast by the assembly; John Jones (Elk), dead and no effects; Mannadoe Philips, runaway; Nathan Worley, dead and no effects; and, Samuel Wiggins, dead and no effects.

INSOLVENTS IN ST. MARY ANN'S PARISH IN 1756: Octararo Hundred - John Alexander, gone away; William Carmichael, gone away; Dennis Mc-Fadding, gone away; Jared Neilson, in goal; Hanse Martin Pickeleny[?], runaway; Thomas Porter, runaway; Andrew Sloan, runaway; Moses Walker, dead and no effects; John Whin, runaway. North Susquehanna Hundred - Hugh Black, runaway; Samuel Breeden, runaway; Hugh Brawley, not known; Moses Bellaugh, in Pensilvania; Brian Lafferty, not known; Robert Millar, in Pensilvania; William Wilson, runaway. South Susquehanna Hundred - Joseph Brodley, runaway; Thomas Butler, runaway; William Clark, not known; Thomas Craig, not known; Samuel Cante[?], not known; John Davis, runaway; Charles Donalson, not known; Roger Dunnigan, runaway; William Elliot, runaway; Richard Fitzgerald, runaway; Edward Gideons, runaway; George Hamilton, runaway; John Holloway, runaway; Joseph Moore, in Baltimore; John Negal, runaway; Jacob Neal, dead and no effects; David Porter, in Pensilvania; ---s.[?] Richeson (ship carpenter), in Baltimore; George Spear, runaway; Henry Spence, runaway; John Smith (jobber), not known. North Milford Hundred - Margaret Evans, in Pensilvania; Alexander Elliott, runaway; Andrew McDowell, in Pensilvania; Alexander Maclure, not found; Hugh Martin, runaway; William Michael, runaway; Jacob Pool, runaway. South Milford Hundred - Samuel Cummings, runaway; Richard Duffield, runaway; John Donly, not known; ---- McCle---? [name gone due to decayed page], not known; Richard Nowland, in Pensilvania; David Owen, in goal; Adam Short, Sr., in goal. Elk Hundred - William Brown, runaway; Allen Barber, runaway; John Elliot, dead and no effects; William Grace, releast by assembly; Mannado Philips, runaway; John Tussey, not found; John Wachob[?], runaway. Charles Town - Michael Agulf, not known; Constantine Bull, releast by assembly; Edmund Burns, dead and no effects; James Cuningham, not known; William Cloud, runaway; John Clark, in Baltimore; Mathew McClintock, in ---- [page torn]; Arthur McMorris, not known; John Henry Presler, runaway; John Springs, runaway.

LIST OF AMERCIAMENTS (PERSONS OWING COURT COSTS) IN 1755: [Ref: Original documents in Maryland Historical Society, Manuscript Division, MS.231]. Persons Amerced in March, 1755 - Michael Earle, John Lackey, Peter Meekings, Benjamin Gibbs, William Kendry (not in the county), Thomas Mills, John Wells (not in the county), John Baldwin (not in the county), Hugh Kirkpatrick (not in the county), John Rickets, David Owen (in goal), Thomas McLaughlin, George Vickers, Moses Whitelock (not in the county), John Wells (not in the county), Isaac Daws (in Baltimore), John Tree, Dr. John Jackson, Isaac Ham, and Samuel Stoss (not in the county). Persons Amerced in June, 1755 - Thomas Knock (not in the county), John Hayes (releast by act of assembly), Richard Barnaby, Alexander Lunan, Henry VanBebber and Matts. VanBebber, Henry VanBebber, Jr., Francis Maybury, James Douglas (in Baltimore goal), John Price, Sr., Thomas Price, John Husband, Humphry Humphrys, Matthias Johnson, Peter Bayard, Doctor Bouchelle, George Vickers, Frederick Boem, John Dempster (in goal), Thomas Stewart and John Scott, The Revd. John Hamilton, George Lewis,

Peter Bouchelle, Dr. John Holland, Thomas Pryor, Joseph Wood, Prince
Snow, Henry Baker, William Rumsey, shoemaker (in Pensilvania), James
Schees, Henry VanBebber, Jr., and John Bryan. Persons Amerced in August,
1755 - Andrew Ryan, John Wallace (Kent County), Dr. Benjamin Bradford,
John Hays (releast by act of assembly), Capt. Moses Rankin (not in the coun-
ty), Francis Maybury, James Mainly, Francis Maybury, Conrade Raffier,
Jacob Giles (in Baltimore County), Samuel McCutcheon, James Alexander,
John Smith (sadler), Nathan Baker, Edward Casteloe (not in the county),
John Latham, Henry VanBebber (sadler), James Schee, Henry Bosworth (in
goal), William Cunningham, George Sewall Douglas, William Robison (hath
a letter of license), Thomas Robison (dead and no effects), George Hamilton
(runaway), Cornelius Augtn. Savin, Thomas Wethersbie (runaway), Andrew
Alexander (runaway), Thomas Richardson (Kent County), Bartholomew
Hayden (not in the county), Dr. John Jackson, David Rickets, Otho Othoson,
Andrew Alexander (runaway), James Burns, William Beaston, Joseph Holt,
Joseph Kimsey, John Hayes (releast by act of assembly), James O'Neal,
Hanse Rudulph, Benjamin Cox, Nathaniel Ward, Nicholas Carney (in Kent
County), Walter Kerr, Benjamin Bradford, Benjamin Rumsey, John Steel
(not in the county), Robert Evans, John Brown (runaway), Francis Ozier
(runaway), Adam Short, Jr., John Nash, Hanse Rudulph, Henry Spence
(runaway), Andrew Alexander (runaway), Hanse Rudulph, John McCue,
Ann Delaney, Moses Rankin (not in the county), and John Mereday
(runaway). [Note: The amount of each Amerciament varied from 30 to 60
pounds of tobacco].

LIST OF AMERCIAMENTS (PERSONS OWING COURT COSTS) IN
1767: [Ref: Original documents in Maryland Historical Society, Manuscripts
Division, MS.231]. Persons Amerced - John Hukill, Henry VanBebber (New
Castle), Robert Clair (not in county), George Porter (not in county), John
Demming (Baltimore), Robert Porter (released by assembly), Thomas Ogle,
Jr., John Lawrence (pensioner), Patrick Cairney (not in county), Andrew
Ball (not in county), Eleanor Campbell (denied), Daniel Jackson (in goal),
Peter Wingate (not in county), William Cox, Benjamin Etherington (denies),
Joseph Lowman (Baltimore), Andrew Ball (not in county), Thomas Green-
land (not in county), John Cestie, John Latham, James Gantley, Nathan
Baker, John Ward (Warwick) denied, William Douglass, George Ankram,
Eleanor Brown, Robert Lusby, Thomas Long (not in county), Robert Lewis
(Philadelphia), George Porter (not in county), Peter Wingate (not in county),
Moses McCay (not in county), JohnBrockson, John York, James Douglass
(not in county), Francis Richard Reynolds, George Rhea, Philimon
Lecompte (not in county), Benjamin Noxon (not in county), Samuel Roberts,
Elisha Terry, Catharine Keeve (not in county), Benjamin Chew, George
Lewis, Thomas Underhill, John Bayard, Bartholomew Etherington, James
Wroth, Jr., Thomas Chandler, John Latham, William Boyer Pennington and
Benjamin Etherington, Bartholomew Etherington, Benjamin Etherington,
Michal McGowen (not in county), Daniel Pearce, Thomas Baker, John Smith
and W. Gillespie (not in county), Richard Meekins (Pennsylvania), Joseph
Burnham, Ann Cowarding, Isaac Chambers, John Lebo [Sebo?] not in coun-
ty, Edward Pryce Wilmer (Kent), William Rumsey (denied), John Ryan
(dead and no effects), Joseph Maybury (not in county), Christopher Jones,

Samuel Clark, James Orr, Prince Snow, Roger Domagin and W. Walker, Ephraim Pennington, Thomas Ryland, Robert Bolton, Francis Reynolds and Richard Reynolds, Moses Jones, William Douglass, Robert Porter (released by assembly), John Gollaher, William Clark (run), Andrew Price, Francis Maybury and W. Baker, Andrew Means, Thomas Price, Francis Reynolds, Benjamin Chew, John Jack, John Armstrong (not in county), Francis McCortney (run), James Wroth, Jr., Robert Alison, Henry Baker, Matthew Logan, Jr. (listed twice), David Patterson, Morris Davis, Daniel McClann, John Alexander, Jonathan Guy (run), William Clark and wife [no name given] listed thrice, William Clark, Robert Porter, Jr. (listed twice - released by assembly), Jacob Jones, Jr., Michael Morrison (not in county), Lazarus Bartley (run), John Hunter and wife [no name given] not in county, John Hunter (not in county), Robert Porter (listed twice - released by assembly), William Withers, Hugh Nicklis (run), James Huit, Samuel Boude[?], James Lee (not in county), Cornelius Hukill, William Carnan and James McCay, John Jack and William Carnan, John Scott, Henry Touchstone, Benjamin Vansant, Daniel Jackson (in goal), John Hunter (not in county), John Ward, Rachford Duffield (not in county), Thomas Baker, William Cumming, Zachariah Kirk, Daniel Gears, Mary Foard, Mary Crow (nothing to be get), Matthew Logan, William Boyer Pennington, Lazarus Barkley (run), Robert Porter (released by assembly), Henry Touchstone, Richard Green and James Crummell, Richard Blackburn Jackson (listed twice - released by assembly), William Clark, James Mckeown (not in county), Benjamin Etherington and Thomas Etherington, Thomas Bruce (not in county), Andrew Coulter, Pere. Rose, Anthony Lynch, Andrew Touchstone, Thomas Davis (released by assembly), Moses Jones, W. Withers and Ed. Armstrong, John Thompson (not in county), Elias Owens, William Warner, Andrew Coulter, Hilent Benson, Bartholomew Etherington, Jr., James Mercer, and John Cowen (not in county).

OVERSEERS OF ROADS APPOINTED IN 1766 AND 1767: North and West Sassafras Hundred - John Cooper (James Coppen in 1767), John Ozier (Charles Heath in 1767), Benjamin Nowland (William Mercer in 1767), Edward Furroner, Thomas Etherington (Henry Hayes in 1767), Robert Thompson (John Dockery Thompson in 1767), and William Walmsley (William Savin in 1767). Bohemia Hundred - Thomas Price (tanner). Middle Neck Hundred - Ephraim McCoy (Charles Scott in 1767). Back Creek Hundred - William Clark (Alexander Smith in 1767), James Wallace, and Abraham Miller. Bohemia Manor - Frederick Elsberry (James McCoy in 1767), Solomon Hearsey, and Richard Foard (Joshua Donoho in 1767). North Susquahanna Hundred - William Husband, Richard Griffee, Andrew Porter, William Rowland, George Ankrim, Samuel McCullough (Thomas Jenney in 1767), James Whitelock, James Stinson, Richard Thomas (Phineas Chew in 1767), and George Hedrick (Robert Thackery in 1767). South Susquahanna Hundred - Samuel Miller (Charles Brookins in 1767), Thomas Sheer, William Baxter, and Augustine Passmore. North Milford Hundred - Daniel Bailey, Michael Wallace, Samuel Hill (Robert Rowland in 1767), and Archibald Armstrong. South Milford Hundred - Matthias Johnson (Andrew Frazier in 1767), Robert Smith, and Captain Catto (Jacob Rudulph in 1767). Elk Hundred - James Roach, Andrew Ryan (William Currer in 1767),

Robert Hart, David Ricketts, Peter Bouyer, and Robert Ewing (Francis Fulton in 1767).

CONSTABLES APPOINTED IN 1766 AND 1767: John Hood, North Sassafras (Lewis Beard in 1767); James Cheltham Ward, West Sassafras (Nicholas Dorrell in 1767); Otho Othoson, Bohemia (Thomas Parsley in 1767); William Chick, Middle Neck (John Wiley in 1767); Peter Sluyter, Bohemia Manor (Andrew Lawrenson in 1767); Edward Armstrong, Back Creek; Francis Carithers, North Milford (Andrew Cochran in 1767); John Anderson, South Milford (Jacob Johnson in 1767); William McClure, North Susquahanna (John Lion in 1767); Samuel McKown, Sr., South Susquahanna (John Glasgow, tanner, in 1767); Francis Mauldin, Elk (Sampson Currer in 1767); Jonas Cooper, Charles Town (Edward Beasley in 1767); and, Richard Guy, Octoraro (John McCrery in 1767). Pressmasters in 1766 and 1767: Henry Hollingsworth, North Elk District, and John McDuff, South Elk District. Francis Key, Clerk. Edward Mitchell, Sheriff.

LIST OF AMERCIAMENTS (PERSONS OWING COURT COSTS) IN 1771: [Ref: Original documents in Maryland Historical Society, Manuscript Division, MS.231]. Persons Amerced - Ephraim Pennington, James Scott, James Haughet, John Sprowl, David Patterson, Andrew Ryan and Alexander Dugan, Elizabeth Lynch the Younger, John Donoho, John Kirkpatrick, Guy Snow, John Adams, Sluyter Bouchelle, John Bing, Henry Touchstone, Jacob Harper and William Withers, Daniel McClan, John Adams, John Cavender, Henry Touchstone, George Rice, James Moore, John Morgan, James Cazier, William Withers, Patrick McGarity, John Holland, John Thomas Hitchcock, Adam Vance, Thomas Thompson, James Cunningham, William Sears, James Baythorn, Nathaniel Chick, Jr., William Withers, Cornelius Vansandt, William Pollatt and Mary Wightwick and William Russell and Thomas Russell and Charles Wright, John Getty, Peter Rider, John Thomas, Thomas Reynolds, John McDuff, William Withers, Peter Rider, Charles Heath, John Latham, John Ward, William Walmsley, Andrew Mears, William Lears [Sears?], Joseph Rutherford, John Carnan, Edward Dougherty, Cornelius Augustine Savin, James Wroth the Younger, John Touchstone, Benjamin Etherington, Isaac Johnson, William Griffey, Samuel M. Kennedy [McKennedy?], George Rice, Thomas Price, Thomas Davis, William Lesslie, John Nicholas, William Hitchman, Thomas Piggott, Benjamin Etherington, Hugh Brown, John Getty and Anthony Lynch, James Martin, Garison Weylie, William Walmsley, Cornelius Augustine Savin, John York, John Porter, Eleanor Brown, Alexander Kirk, Thomas Boyd, William Rowland, Edward Furroner, Allen Stewart, Andrew McMillan, George Grant, James Finley, Mosses Brown, John Read, Mary Crow, Francis Baker, John Kirkpatrick, James Mercer, James Martin, David Lewis, Robert Rouse, Cornelius Lesslie, William Clark, Jr., John Brown, John Gofton [Goston?], William McClure, William Cox, Henry Hayes, Sarah Ward and Henry Hayes, William Cox, John Ward (Warwick), Henry Gun and Joseph Ensor, William Lynch (listed twice), Robert Alison and William Stevenson, John Veazey, Jr., William Gilkey, Richard Thompson, Jr., James James, Ebenezer Penington, -- -- Glasgow [page soiled], Hugh Price and Sinclair Lancaster, William Stoops, Thomas Marr, James Coppen, Joseph Phelps, John Donave[?], Benjamin

McVey, James Scott, Thomas Underhill, Henry Hetherington
[Etherington?], Benjamin McVey, John Getty and John Latham, John
Donohoe, Joseph Mayberry, John Cesti, Thomas Boyd [Lloyd?], Benjamin
Etherington, Thomas Piggott, Francis Baker and Jeremiah Baker, Jacob Har-
per, Peregrine Rose, Thomas Underhill, John Gollaher, Andrew Barratt,
Jacob Jones, Thomas Piggott, Sarah Nowland (listed twice), Henry Miller
(listed twice), Edward Pryce Wilmer, and John Leddrun[?].

LIST OF AMERCIAMENTS (PERSONS OWING COURT COSTS) IN
1772: [Ref: Original documents in Maryland Historical Society, Manuscript
Division, MS.231]. Persons Amerced - Michael Peacock, John Ellsbury, Cor-
nelius Eliason, John Hall (weaver), John Hodgson, Samuel Thompson, Bar-
tholomew Etherington, John Donawe (listed twice), George Rice, Thomas
Price and John Ward, Ralph Whitaker, William Clark (cooper), Thomas
Etherington, Sr., George Lynch, Richard Blackburn Jackson, Robert Alison,
Joseph Elliott, Edward Bryan and Lydia Wells, John Nicholas, Adam Vance,
Joseph McNeely and Robert Lyon, Thomas Elliot, John Rankin, John Read,
Nathan Baker, James Boyles, Adam Vance, Thomas Stewart, Elizabeth
Lynch, William Craig, Robert Welsh, William Headlestone, --os.[?] Pryce,
Henry Miller, Samuel Thompson, Robert Lyon, Joseph McNeely, Nathan
Baker, Noble Needle, Henry Allen, Joseph Rutherford, Moses Cochran,
Robert Evans, Richard Reynolds, John Donave, William Walmsley,
Hezekiah Wingate, Henry Ward Pearce, and Bartholomew Etherington.

LIST OF AMERCIAMENTS (PERSONS OWING COURT COSTS) IN
1773 [Ref: Original documents in Maryland Historical Society, Manuscript
Division, MS.231]. Persons Amerced - David Poa, John Mahon, Daniel Mc-
Clann, Archibald McCullough, Daniel McClann, Jr., Edward Bryan, Joseph
Corbett, John Thompson, David Poa, Robert Welsh, Burnit Richards, Peter
Creswell, Margaret Atwood, Samuel Anderson, William Little, Michael
Montgomery, John Baker, John Thomas Hitchcock (listed twice), Thomas
Hitchcock (listed twice), Joshua Donoho, Edward Dougherty, John
Cavender, Margaret Cox, William Kleinhoff, John Cox the Younger, Roger
Donagan, William Richards, John Dockery Thompson and Robert
Thompson, Joseph Ensor, James James, William Corbitt, John Rankin and
James Hamilton, WIlliam Sinco, Henry Hayes, Benjamin Young, Francis
Baker, John Alexander, Samuel Reynolds, Joseph Felps, Bartholomew
Etherington, Robert Porter (son of Robert), Amos Garrett, William Gilkey,
Neal Donnally, Anthony Lynch, Daniel McClann, James Tigner, John Taylor,
John Holland, Robert Porter the Younger, George Price, Henry Hayes, Wil-
liam Lynch, William Withers, Henry Miller, John Cochran, Samuel McNear,
John Pickett, Bartholomew Etherington, Jr., James Hessey, William Mc-
Neeely, John Taylor, William Clark (cooper), John Wilson and William Mc-
Cullough, Thomas Hill, Benjamin Dutton, Daniel McClan, Sr. and Daniel
McClan, Jr., Roger Domagan, James Stevenson, John Holland, Robert
Roberts, Nathan Nowlan [Newlan?], Hezekiah Wingate, Peter Creswell
(listed twice), and Bartholomew Etherington, Jr.

LIST OF AMERCIAMENTS (PERSONS OWING COURT COSTS) IN
1774: [Ref: Original documents in Maryland Historical Society, Manuscripts

Division, MS.231]. Persons Amerced - Charles Brookins (listed twice), Sarah Cuningham, Samuel Anderson, William Rowland, Robert Cochran, Ann Arnold Key, Ralph Whitaker, Thomas Savin, Mathews Logan, Edward Beasley, William Howell, Andrew Barratt, Daniel Kenly, Daniel McClane, Sr., Robert Evans, Samuel Crockett, James Eliott, Thomas Price, William Jackson, Ann Arnold Key, Roger Domagan, Adam Dallam, Joseph Corlett, Capt. Garrett Brown, Ralph Whitaker, Richard Cazier, Samuel Roberts (painter), Henry Beedle and Mary his wife, James Young, Thomas Price, Edward Dougherty, John Alexander, Roger Domagan, Joseph Corlett, John Getty, William Kleinhoff, John Alexander, George Rhea and David Poa, Joseph Elliott, Patrick Hamilton, Francis Baker, Eleanor Brown, John Kirkpatrick, John Alexander, Richard Dicks, Benjamin Warner, John Rankin, Fredus Ryland, William Lesslie, Rudulph Gonce and Abraham Gonce, Benjamin Ellsbury and Rudulph Gonce, David Poa, John Beard, Rudulph Gonce (listed thrice), Edward Holeman, John Bing and George Bing, James Calhoon, Justice Gonce, Robert Bolton, William Lesslie, Fredus Ryland, Corenlius Vansandt (listed twice), Richard Bennett, David Hill, Joseph Cooper, Robert Glasgow, James Stevenson, Jr., Joseph Ensor, Edward Walden, James Ennis, Thomas Underhill, John Hall (gentleman), William Lesslie, John Holland, John Cox the Younger, Samuel Taylor and wife [no name given], Daniel Gears, Christian Gwither[?], William McClure, Thomas Baker, John Alexander, Mathias Hendrickson, John Getty and Anthony Lynch, John Touchstone, William Beck [Beek?], John Irwin, and Edward Bryan.

LIST OF JURORS IN APRIL, 1768. [Ref: Original document in Maryland Historical Society Manuscripts Division, MS.231]. George Cato, Joseph Gilpin, Nicholas Hyland, Jr., William Ewing, Samuel Gelaspie, Andrew Barrett, William McClure, John Rumsey, William Glasco, Francis Mauldin, Thomas Savin, John Mackie, John Alexander, Moses Andrews, Samuel Ewing, Robert Evans, James Boyles, Andrew Crow, Richard Thompson, Jr., William Withers, Thomas Bouldin, Alexander Stuart, Spencer Holtham, Ephraim Thompson, William Craig, Barrett Vanhorne, John Latham, Henry Sluyter, Henry Pennington, John Stockton, James Coppin, John Stoops, Samuel Pennington, John Roberts, William Walmsley, John Money, William Bavington, Hezekiah Wingate, William Rumsey, Charles Rumsey, Robert Walmsley, and William Lynch. William Thomas, Clerk.

PETITION FOR A ROAD FROM FULTON'S FERRY (OR BALL FRYAR) IN 1766: [Part of petition is missing. Original document is in Maryland Historical Society Manuscript Division, MS.231]. James Porter, William Ewing, Sr., Samuel Ewing, Pat. Ewing, Robert Porter, Robert Ewing, Thomas Love, Jno. Middefeild, Richard Gay, Wm. Ewing, Samuel Gillespie, Nat. Gillespie, Will Gillespie, John Ewing, Charles Regan, Jas. Graham, Jas. Buchanan, John McCay, Luck Packock, John Porter, Jno.[?] Gillespie, Daniel McCay, John Bralley, Char. Simy[?], Ralph Sime[?], and Andrew Rogan.

PETITION OF ROBERT LESSLIE, OVERSEER OF THE ROAD TO CHARLES TOWN IN 1766. Signed by: William Howell, Jon. Walter, John Neal, James Wilson, Thos, Beaty, James McMullan, Jon. Green, Jr., John Crookshanks, James Macullagh, Robert Whitley, John Steenson, Thomas Willey, Samuel Makeown, John Maboa, James Oar, Benjimin Maboa, and Archabald Macullagh.

LIST OF WORSHIPFUL GENTLEMEN JUSTICES FOR CECIL COUNTY IN 1768: Colonel Hyland, Captain Catto, Major Pearce, WIlliam Rumsey, Esq., Capt. Mackey, Jno. Read, Esq., Jos. Gilpin, Esq., Elihu Hall, Esq., Wm. Baxter, Esq., Sidney George, Esq., Geo. Milligan, Esq., and Jno. Hall, Esq.

OVERSEERS OF ROADS APPOINTED IN 1760: Philip Stoops, Prince Snow, William Savin, Sr., Isaac Gibbs, Thomas Etherington, Capt. John Brown, William Price, Thomas Severson, John McCoy, Sidney George, Robert Thompson, William Boulding, Abraham Miller, Joseph Neide, Thomas Wallace, Charles Ford, William Husband, Robert Finley, John Ewing, William Rowland, John McCullough, William McKeown, Andrew Touchstone, John Glasgow, Murhty Mahon, George Hedrick, James Buchannan, Joseph McNeely, Robert Lesslie, Samuel Gilpin, Samuel Bond, Robert Thackrey, John Alexander, John Passmore, Robert Rowland, Thomas Ricketts, Samuel Shepherd, Joseph Gilpin, Charles Quigley, John Alexander, William Manley, Harman Kankey, Robert Hart, William Bristow, Hanse Rudulph, John McVey, Samuel McKeown, and Archibald McCullough.

CONSTABLES APPOINTED IN 1760: Thomas Savin, Jr., Elisha Terry, Otho Othoson, John Cazier, William Kleinhoff, Thomas Bouldin, Thomas Mason, Matthew Taylor, James Corbit, Zebulon Oldham, Henry Stidham, John Hedrick, and William Gillespie (tanner). Pressmasters: John Read (North Side of Elk River) and Jacob Hamm (South Side of Elk River).

OVERSEERS OF ROADS APPOINTED IN 1765: Henry Pennington, Richard Flintham, Sylvester Nowland, Edward Furroner, Thomas Etherington, James Hughes, Jr., William Walmsley, Thomas Price (tanner), John Davidge, James Smith, James Wallace, Abraham Miller, William Craig, Robert Mansfield, Richard Ford, William Husband, Richard Griffee, Andrew Porter, William Rowland, George Ankrim, Samuel McCulloh, James Whitelock, James Stinson, Richard Thomas, Esq., William Welsh, Matw. Logan, Joseph McNealy, William Baxter, Esq., Richard Bond, John Alexander, William Pasmore, Samuel Hill, John McDowell, Jona. Booth, Robert Smith, Benjamin Thomas, John Rumsey, John Wakefield, Robert Hart, and Joseph Thomas.

CONSTABLES APPOINTED IN 1765: James Coppin (North Sassafras), Henry Pennington (West Sassafras), Otho Othoson (Bohemia), John Cazier (Middle Neck), Peregrine Vandergriff (Bohemia Manor), Edward Armstrong (Back Creek), Fergus Smith (North Milford), Samuel Maffitt (South Milford), Patk. McGavity (North Susquehanna), Robert Lasley

(South Susquehanna), Nicholas George (Elk), Samuel Kilpatrick (Charles Town), and Samuel Ewing (Octoraro). Pressmasters: Henry Hollingsworth and John McDuff.

OVERSEERS OF ROADS APPOINTED IN 1770: Alexander Williamson, Charles Heath, Lewis Beard, Daniel Charles Heath, WIlliam Walmsley, Hartley Sappington, John Roberts, Benjamin Price, John Ward (Warwick), Nathaniel Chick, James Wallace, Abraham Miller, William Withers, Andrew Gordon, George Beaston, George Ewing, Samuel Patterson, Samuel Ewing, WIlliam Rowland, Joseph Rutherford, Thomas Jenney, Robert Lytle[?], James Stinson, Phineas Chew, Robert Thackery, Charles Brookins, Nicholas Kelly, Ralph Whitacre, Jacob Rudulph, Michael Wallace, Francis Caruthers, Andrew Harvey, Jonathan Booth, Robert Smith, Benjamin Thomas, Benjamin Mauldin, Thomas Savin, Robert Hart, David Ricketts, William Phillips, David Price, Thomas May, and Thomas Smith.

CONSTABLES APPOINTED IN 1770: Benjamin Woodland (North Sassafras), William Crocker (West Sassafras), Augustine Hendrickson (Bohemia), James Scott (Middle Neck), Richard Hukill (Bohemia Manor), Elie Alexander (Back Creek), Abel Hodgson (North Milford), Robert Sutton (South Milford), John Good (North Susquehanna), Thomas Williams (South Susquehanna), Alexander Gray (Elk), Christian Guither (Charles Town), and John Craig (Octoraro). Pressmasters: Henry Hollingsworth (North Elk District) and John McDuff (South Elk District).

CONSTABLES LISTS OF WHEEL CARRIAGES (PERSONS CHARGEABLE) IN 1757: North Sassafras Hundred - Mr. Peregrine Ward, Mr. James Reed. West Sassafras Hundred - John Stoops, Thomas Williams, John Cooper, Michael Tully, Mary Ricketts, Patrick Flinn, John Brown, George Miligan, Michael Earle, James Frisby. Bohemia Hundred - Rev. Hugh Jones, Col. John Veazey, Robert Marcer, John Hall, Henry Ward, Thomas Wroth, Benjamin Maulding. Middle Neck Hundred - Charles Gordon, William Rumsey, Evard Evardson. Bohemia Manor - Col. Peter Byard, Slyter Boshell [Bouchell], Capt. John Veazey, Charles Ford, Peter Kleinhoff, Ms. Mary VanBebber (widow). South Susquehanna Hundred- James Baxter, Nathan Baker. Charles Town - Edward Mitchell, Francis Key, Edward Dougharty, John Smith.

CONSTABLE ANDREW PEARCE'S LIST OF PERSONS PAID FOR SQUIRREL SCALPS AND CROWS HEADS BURNT IN NOVEMBER, 1761: John Beedle, Sr., Stephen Beedle, Jonathan Hollings, William Rumsey, Charles Scott, Elizabeth Evertson, John Dobin, Hartley Sapington, Owen McCalvey, Thomas Beard, Silvester Nowland, John Artage, James Kemp, Elisha Terry, Isaac Penington, John Beaston, James Simons, Nathan Dobson, Benjamin Cox, Benjamin Money, John Ward (near Warwick), Nathaniel Hynson, James Frisby, Mrs. Mary Ward (Sassafras Hundred), Thomas Ryland, Sr., James Cosdin, Stephen Ryland, William Pearce (cow?), Benjamin Elsberry, James Manycozens, Michael Manycozens, William Bavington, Daniel Pearce, Andrew Pearce, William Bordley, George Sewal Douglas, Hugh

Gribben, William Sterling, William Hawkins, Samuel Beedle, William Davis, James Loag[?], James Penington, William Bateman, Sr., , Michael Earle, Henry Ward Pearce, Robert Porter, Benjamin Smith, Hyland Price, Mary Penington (Sassafras Hundred), Lewis Beard, Thomas Carson, Thomas Pearce, and John Pearce.

CONSTABLE NICHOLAS HYLAND'S LIST OF PERSONS PAID FOR SQUIRREL SCALPS AND CROWS HEADS DESTROYED IN NOVEM-BER, 1761: Thomas Crouch, William Crouch, Joseph Bass (Susquahannah), Daniel Orton, James Veazey, ---- Hyland, ---- Readman, Edward Gready, James Orrick, Mathew Driver Gleaves, Thomas Hart, Edward Nevill, Sr., Subina Riggbe, Thomas Veazey, John Mainly, Samuell Phillips, Jr., ---al[?] Smith, James Bouldin (Back Crick), William Price, John White, Thomas Moody, Thomas Boulden, Nathan Chick, John Bavington, John Ricketts, Harmon Kanky, Charles Emandor Badger, William Cox, William Mainly, Isaac Crouch, Moses Jones, Lazors Grainger, Nicholas Hyland, Jr., Robert Hart, Nicholas George, William Nevill, John Foster, Robert Milborn, Mary Lum, William Bristow, Joseph Burnam, John Medowell, Martha Hyland, Francies Mauldin, Ann Mauldin, Joseph Loman, James McDowell, John Stalcop, James Roach, Nicholas Hyland, Sr., James Hart, Sampson Currer, Benjaman Rumsey, William Veazey, Samuell Mekeney, John Byard, John Kanky, and Robert Hart.

CONSTABLE WILLIAM BORDLEY'S LIST OF PERSONS PAID FOR SQUIRREL SCALPS BURNT IN NOVEMBER, 1761 [Note: Original list is defective with some names obliterated and/or torn off]: --therine Scott, ---- Savin, Sr., ---as Savin, Jr., ---- Bohannan, ---wd. Furroner, ---n. Body, ---m. Ryce, ---cks. Banhorne, Sr., --hn Hawkins (cooper), ---- Jackson, Jr., ---- O'-Donald, ---as Hessy, ---id Fitzgerald, ---nl. McClan, --orge Douglas, ---m Vansandt, --orge Vansandt, --hn Mercer, ---a Hall, ---mas Frisby, ---s. Vansandt, ---- Hood, ---- Nowland, ---s. Augt. Savan, --mes Chattin, ---na. Pennington, --oses Frampton, ---n Guy, ---ry Galaspy, ---hd. Lockwood, ---- Mercer, ---ret Vansandt, ---- Jacobs, ---- Dawson, Richard Flintham, James Harper, Antony Fatado, George Humberstone, Peter Clinhofe, Ben: Alsburry, Murty Shee, James Reynolds, Charles Heath, William Jones, John Ferrel, William Murdo, Sarah Penington, John Huston, Robert Mercer, Jr., John Potts, Bryon Harrity, Jacob Evardson, John Ryland, Jr., Patrick Carny, Walter Burk, John Donaho, Tobias Burk, Thomas Hynson, Jacob Jones, Sr., James Chatm. Ward, James Langworthy, Barnett Vanhorn, Jacob Jacobs, and William Bordley.

CONSTABLE ELIHU HALL'S LIST OF PERSONS PAID FOR SQUIRREL SCALPS DESTROYED IN NOVEMBER, 1761: Robert Conn, Thomas Bowings, Robert Finley, William Husband, Ruth Hall, Hance Baker, Robert Markess, John Markess, Charles Porter, Vedelis Harster, John Kidd, James Kidd, Richard Kidd, Andrew Kidd, John Ewings, Kenith McKinzie, John Hamon Dorsey, Andrew Porter, Samuel Ewings (N. Susq. Hundred), Adam Meeks, John Vance, John Harris, William Ewings, Richard Gay, Henry Daugharty, Robert Walker, Nicholis Tray, William Galasbie, Sr., William Galasbie, Jr., John Morrow, Patrick Ewings, John Walker, Charles Orrick, Jacob Death, Richard Griffith, James Porter, John Widdowfield, James Shilbren[?], James Grahms, John Nelson, David Patterson, James Brading, Elihu Hall, John Lyon, Robert Little, James Alder, and Peter Bower (Elk Hundred).

CONSTABLE GEORGE CATTO'S LIST OF PERSONS PAID FOR SQUIRREL SCALPS BURNT IN THE YEAR 1761: William Harvey, Joseph Peew[?], Zeb. Hollingsworth, Elijah Harris, Thomas Welty, Samuell Sharp, Theophelas Alexander, Hance Black, Samuel Anderson, Samuel Shipard, Abraham Thompson, Edward Croe, James Wallace, Adam Wallace, William Dawson, Abrm. Miller, William Miller, James Miller, Andrew Miller, Andrew Wallace, Andrew Harvey, James Frazer, Robert Campble, John Wallace (marcht.), James Donnely, Robert Hugguns, Thomas Chesnot, Robert Smith, Jesse Hollingsworth, Tob. Rudulph, Thomas Killgour, William Thompson, Samuel Barr, John Giles, David John, William Challmers, James Eliot, Benjamin Thomas, Patrick McCaffity, William David, William Allison, Bruyon McColley, Thomas Rickets, David Rickets, Thomas Bettle, Jr., Charles Quigley, Thomas Burnhm [sic], Samuell Cummings, Peter Flood, William Read, John Carrey, Alexr. Chesnot, George Nash, Elenor Campble, William Brown, David Henrey, John Smith (Head Elk), Thomas Price, Thomas Melon, James Smith, Jeremiah Franklin, Thomas Breverd, Benjamin Breverd, James Foster, William White, Hanah Hollet, William Smith, John Fulton, Thomas McCrery, James Braford, Robert Bolton, Samuel Adear, William Richardson, John Armstrong, Manaseth Harley, Cornelias Connely, William Buchannon, William Ceak, William Sears, Joseph Gilpin, Adam Dobson, Barthelomew Jonston, Samuel Nash, William Bettle, William Crath, Andrew Means, Patrick Dinnes, Zekiel Dennston, Nickolas Knigh [Knight?], George Foard, Edward Armstrong, Jonathon Booth, John Armstrong, Alexr. Scot, Andrew Barnet, Sushana Alexander, Mosses Alexander, David Alexander, Eli Alexander, Richard Bouldin, Thomas Bouldin, William Willson, Daniel McClean, James McCrurey, John Hall, Griffeth Williams, William Bouldin, John Culley, Archbald Armstrong, Robert Frier, George Catto, and Joseph Thomas ("E:H").

CONSTABLE BENJAMIN MOODY'S LIST OF PERSONS PAID FOR SQUIRREL SCALPS BURNT IN NOVEMBER, 1761: Richard Thompson, Jr., Jonathan Hodgson, Gorge Hall, Sr.[?], Richard Thompson, Sr., James Sampson (shoemaker), Col. Peter Bayard, Richard Smith, Samuel McClary, Morton Conn, Robert Veazey, Sr., John McCartney, Michael McGillion, Michael Morrison, Adam Scott, Richard Price, Thomas Savin, Sr., Samuel McCunneghy, John Eliason, Cornelias Eliason, Joseph Hattery, Sarah Rumsey, John Harper (farmer), Elias Eliason, Walter Jackson, Absolam Bowen, John Cartey, Joseph Rider, John Golaher, Edward Rumsey, Sr., Capt. John Veazey, Thomas Bouchell, Philemon Noble, Frederick Starn, Henry Sluytor, Benjamin Sluytor, William Kleinhoff, Mary Knaresbrough, James Boyle, John Rigs, John Hartness, Alexander Stewart, Richard Reynolds, John Bonhonnon, William Taylor, Benjamin Frankling, Peter Kleinhoff, Nicholas Wood, James Morrison, Isaac Brind, Anthony Noones, John Sedgwell, Jacob Ozer, John Neide, John Elwood, Timothy Camper, Richard Beedle, Peter Gullet, Peregrine Vandegrift, William Baker, Manassah Loge, David Clark,

Thomas Stewart, Dennis Doyle, Thomas Hooker, Vollentine Jump, James Robertson, Thomas Malone, Robert Thompson, Edward McDormond, Jacob Attabough, Nicholas Leeds, John Cunningham, John Scott, Samuel Bayard, Sr., Dr. James Bayard, Richard Ford, Alexander Kirk, John Kirk, Jonas Jones, Andrew Jones, Cristopher Parkerson, Anthony Linch, John Linch, Samuel Taylor, Samuel Simmons, James Brison, Judah Bigs, Richard Bowen, John Hukell, William Crage, John Lawrence Frederick Burger, Abraham Hooper, John Price, Solomon Hearser, James Cromel, Dennis Kelley, Joseph Cochran, Andrew Lawrenson, John Dennington, Thomas Beeston, George Beeston, Ephraim Beeston, Benjamin Beeston, George Lewis, Richard Elwood, Thomas Reynolds, William Lawler, Cornelius Hukell, Daniel Hukell, Richard Hukell (smith), John Aull[?], John McCoy, Ephraim McCoy, Johannas Arrance, John Lewis, John Gettey, James Wroth, Jr., John Potts, Spencer Holtham, Thomas Frankel, Jr., Griffeth Pue, Anthony Ruley, Benjamin Pennington, Sarah Ruley, William Mercer, Jr., John Mullen, Sr., Jeremiah Frankling, Benjamin Frankling, Phillip Stoops, Hesekiah Winget, Peter Rider, John Mullen, Jr., Robert McCurdey, John McCurdey, James Cage, Ephraim Thompson, James Sampson, William Savin, Jr., Joseph Taylor, Richard Meekens, Richard Hukell, James Hukell, Jacob Hamm, Thomas Summers, James Vance, Dr. John Holland, Richard Ellice, David Dempster, George Porter, John Sutton, Freed Ryland, Benjamin Moody, and Thomas Wallace.

CONSTABLE JOHN HALL'S LIST OF PERSONS PAID FOR SQUIRREL SCALPS DESTROYED IN NOVEMBER, 1761: William Lynch, William Price, Jr., John Davige, John Stockton, William Price (boson), Andrew Price (son of Andrew), William Brice (minor), James Wroth, Sr., William Walmsley, Jacob McDowal, James Beard, George Holt, John Fillingem, Benjamin Hull, Matthias Hendrickson, Robert Scurrey, Jr., Robert Mansfield, Thomas Price (tanner), John Brice, Jr., Susanna Cox, Robert Walmsley, Thomas Marcer, Edward Veazey, Benjamin Pearce, Seth Ruley, Benjamin Price, John Winterbury, Thomas Beedle, Sarah Price, James Campbell, Andrew Price, Sr., Jacob Harper, Asel Gozdon, Alitear Terry (widow), John Wallace[?] [page torn], Otho Othoson, John Caulk, John Hall, Nicholas Farnley, Dr. Richard Smith, William Morgin, Henry Green, John Armstrong, Matthias Pippin [Rippin?], Thomas Etherington, Sr., Thomas Etherington, Jr., Barthow. Etherington, Jr., Thomas Davis, Sr., John Maulster, Perrigrine Frisbey, John Veazey, Sr., John Ward (surveyor), John Cann [Conn?], Nathaniel Ward, Hugh Boge, George Rice, Barthow. Etherington, Sr., Thomas Price, Sr., John Thomas, Robert Lusbey, Elexander Pratt, Ephraim Price, Samuel Penington, Hyland Beedle, Richard Wallace, Alexander Pratt, Robert Lusbey, Dorothea Roberts, Henry Hendrickson, Benjamin Etherington, John Goston, James Hayes, William Barnaby, John Money, Nicholas Money, Robert Scurry, Sr., John Lusbey, David Price, Henry Burnham, John Urin, Sarah Roberts, John Beedle, Jr., Thomas Beedle (son of William), William Beedle, Sr., John Beedle (son of William), William Ward, John Ward (son of Henry), Thomas Holland, William Cox, Richard Attwood, William Beedle, Jr., John Farley, Jehue Ryland, John Price (Lux Point), Henry Hayes, Ruth Hayes (widow of John), William Hayes, Charles Fourd, Frances Rennals, Robert Storey, Jon. Carnan, Jacob Jones, Jr., Thomas Ozle[?], Jon. Scott (millar), Jon. Stoops, William Smith, Andrew

Crocker, Jon. Cooper, Nicholas D---al [page torn], Charles Rumple, James Clark, William McBride, Jon. Welch, Nathan Newlin, James McCoy, Benjamin Benson, George Johnson, John Ward (Inspector), Henry Penington, John Latham, Anne Mauldin, Robert Marcer, Sr., Robert Marcer, Jr., James Coppin, and George Cuningham.

CONSTABLE NATHAN BAKER'S LIST OF PERSONS PAID FOR SQUIRREL SCALPS DESTROYED IN 1761: Nilkolus Carew, Col. James Baxter, Nathan Baker, Nicholus White, Thomas Hitchcock, William Forester, Joseph Hodghson, John Kirkpatrick, Joseph Richardson, John Anderson, Robert Hibets[?], Joseph Richardson, Jr., Joseph Corbett [Corlott?], John Judd, Jno. Weakfield, Alexander McFeegall, Andrew Ryon, Francis Lashley, Francis Handerson, James Meeks, Samiel Kirkpatrick, James Finley, Allen Steward, William Cruikshanks, Stephen Willcox, David Morrow, David Owens, William Adair, Benjamin Lawery[?], David Moor, David McCraking, William Camell, John Hedrick, Doctor Sliter Boshell, Roger Damengen[?], James Haphle[?], John Hale [Hall?], James Hewet, William Boyd, Mr. Francis Key, John Cisti, John Rudulph, Jacob Notteman, Benjamin Nelson, Charles Rumsey, Benjamin Rumsey, John Waller[?], Abraham Cazier, William Brown, Bryan McMuney, John Lewis, James Lawery[?], Henry Stidham, Andrew Gibson, Robert Smith, Joseph McNealy, Samuel[?] Miller, Thomas Miller, James Boughannon, John Brooking, Mathew Logan, Mathew Logan, Jr., Jno. Bing, Jno. Cheales[?], Jno. Nowland, Isaac Lythunam, Jno. Neale, Richard Hall, Thomas Whitacer, William Forster, Thomas Slycer, Thomas Cord, Charles Ragan, Christopher Jones, Samuel Patterson, James Freale[?], Samuel Karr, John McCoy, William Ewing, Sr., Samuel Gelospey, Robert Wuesry[?], Jon. Green, Jon. Green, Jr., James Garner, Augustune Passmor, William Howel, Benjamin Lee, Jno. Clarke, Jr., Phillup Nelson, Thomas Rage, Samuel Phillips, Jno. Stalkup, Francis Rack, Samuel Bard[?], Robert Lashly, John Stinson, Samuel Guilpin, Edward Oldham, Isaac Jenney, Jno. Thomas Hitchcock, Guning Justie [Justice?], Edward Wilson, George Black, John Henderson, Jonis Cooper, John Orsburn, John Miller, William Ford, Henry Miller, Thomas Newell, Patrick Shurkey, John Toulson, John Clarke, Samuel Clark, William Newell, James Ranolds, Simon Johnson, Henry Lenard, Richard Bradly, Jno. Short, Jno. Richardson, Jacob Johnson, Mathias Johnson, Joseph Hickman, Zebulon Oldham, David Brumfield, Morgan Swany, John Baker, James Glascow, William Marshall, Edward Daugherty, Thomas Ellut, Doctor James Spuwl[?], George Ankrum, Robert Alison, John Cuningham, Elexander Nuckel, Hugh Daugherty, Hance Hunderbirk[?], William Shearswood, Samuel Tagart, James Tagart, Thomas Tagart, Jno. McCullough, Joseph Orre, James Quaile, Robert Jones, Jno. Griffey, William Allison, Richard Simpus, John Simpus, Nathaniel Simpus, Jno. Rutter, Richard Claton, Jno. Camell, Robert Williams, Jno. McAwnekey[?], Jno. McCabe, Daniel Fragon [Dragon?], Edward Murphy, Steph Newel, Jno, Galaher, William Currer [Currerne?], Thomas Savin, Samuel McKeowne, James Wilson, Benjamin McVey, John Passmoor, Samuel Passmoor, Benjamin Dickson, Moses Rutter, Phillips Keatley, Thomas Murphy, Aron Grace, William Grace, Henry Sewell, Samuel Thomson, John Smith, John Reed, William Harvey, James Stephenson, Andrew Fraser, Robert Hill, Peter Justice, Richard Bennet, Andrew Coulter, Thomas

Palmer, James McCullugh, John Baily, Mathew Thompson, Edward Newell, Jr., Joseph Ellot, William Brunfield, Samuel Pritchet, Hance Rudulph, William Moffet, Robert Lutton, Mathew Hont [Hunt?], George Skipton, Hugh Browne, Adam Short, Hugh Nicholus, David Moor, Jr., John Walter, Robert Mills, William Ranalds, William Barnes, Joseph Wallace, John Scot, James Richey [Ruley?], Edward Tayler, William Hutchman[?], David Patterson, Jr., Robert Nelson, Joseph Rutherford, David Dickson, James Orr, John Griffey, Thomas Whiley [Whitey?], William McKeowne, Samuel McCullugh, Robert Nichals, John Nichals, Henry Miller (shoemaker), Ralph Whiteacer, Henry Baker, Thomas Forster, Archabald McCullugh, John Smith (farmer), David Henry, David Laramor, and George Ankarem.

CONSTABLE NICHOLAS GEORGE'S LIST OF DOG OWNERS IN NORTH ELK HUNDRED IN JUNE, 1766: Col. Nicholas Hyland, Thomas Crouch, Sr., Nicholas Hyland (miller), William Currer, Andrew Rion, Johanas Arants, Isaac Crouch, Jacob Rudulph, John Kankey, Mary Hyland, Mary Mauldin, Levina McDowell, Sampson Currer, Mary Lum, Joseph Thomas, Richard Simpers, John Rumsey, John Hitchcock, Ann Mauldin, Thomas Bedle, John Forster, Sr., William Veazey, Mary Veazey, Susanah McLaughlin, Jarvice[?] Orrick, Martha Hyland, Nicholas George, Lazaros Granger, and William Grace.

CONSTABLE PATRICK MCGARITY'S LIST OF DOG OWNERS IN NORTH SUSQUEHANNA HUNDRED IN AUGUST, 1766: Richard Downey, John G---- [worm hole in page], William Currier, James Corbit, John Kirkpatrick, William Glasgow, David Patterson, Jr., Andrew Barratt, George Johnson, Christopher Jones, Samuel Patterson, Andrew Touchstone, Joseph Rutherford, Robert Lyon, Charles Reagon, John Walker, William Rowland ("one dog his name Gunner, lately imported from Ireland"), David Patterson, Sr., William Callinder, Joseph Curlett, James Whitelock, William Hitchman, William Devaul, John Crockett, William Watts, John Stump, John Callinder, Richard Sedgwick, Thomas Bowen, Robert Finley, Robert Nelson, Richard Thomas, Mortey Mahon, John Miller (Phenice Chew, security), and Patrick McGarity.

CONSTABLE JAMES COPPIN'S LIST OF DOG OWNERS IN NORTH SASSAFRAS HUNDRED IN 1766: Samuel Taylor, Thomas Marra, John Marcer, Thomas Beard, Silvester Noland, William Bavington, Thomas Marcer, John Crouch, Richard Welch, Edward Furner, John Crosbe, James Oneal, Isaac Gibbs, Thomas Hynson, Benjamin Noland, Mary Ward (widow), Robart Lusby, William Rice, George Humberson, Jacob Jacobs, John Brockson, Nathnel Buckhannon, Daniel MacClan, William Jones, William Savin, William Savin, William Marcer, Stiphen Beedel, Beimine Marcer, Sarah Bordley, John Hood, Willim Ozer, Cornealus Vansant, and Daniel Charles Heath.

SUNDRY LIST OF DOG OWNERS IN MIDDLE NECK HUNDRED IN 1766: William Rumsey, William Chick, John Carnaan, James McCoy, William Smith, John Wiley, Charles Scott, John Feril, James Crowmell [Crom-

well?], Bryan O'Daniel, Mary Jacobs, James Rice, George Rice, Mary Nes-
bury[?], James Vance, John Scott, and John Scott (tavernkeeper).

LIST OF PERSONS WHO HELPED BUILD BOHEMIA PLANTATION
BETWEEN 1735 AND 1761. (Compiled from "The Bohemia Day Book" by
the Old Bohemia Historical Society's History Committee under the chair-
manship of Joseph C. Cann, 1976): Christopher Ailsbury, 1745; Bar-
tholemous Anderson, 1745, clothing; Henrietta Ailsbury, widow, 1742, dress
maker; Thomas Ashton, 1739-1751, factotum (manager); John Brown, 1753;
Peter Bayard, 1756, nails; Alexander Beard, 1745, quit rent; Dr. Douchet,
1759, customer; Robert Brent, 1748; Dan Brown, 1758, linens; Timothy Bran-
ham, 1742, tailor; Thomas Broderick, 1755, laborer; Humprey Best, 1735;
John Baine, 1750, shopkeeper; Benjamin Bradford, 1744; William Base, 1759;
Mary Betson, 1745 (Mr. Henry Neale, S.J., executor); Philemon Blake (no
date); Mat. Bartley, 1759, laborer; Col. John Baldwin, 1757-1761; Patrick
Brangham, 1760; Toby Bush, 1745; Bubenheims Store, 1739; Peggy Beatty,
1756, farming; John Bradly, 1740-1746; William Brooks, 1754, weaver; Suzan-
na Bradly, 1747-1753, shoes; John Burke, 1759, merchant; William Bradford,
1742; Charles Bradford, 1752; Thomas Bannister, 1750-1753; Susan Crosby,
1753-1755, spinner; Richard Cradick, 1735-1740, renter (20 lbs./year); James
Crosbey, 1753; John Crosbye, 1755-1756, factotum (manager); Col. Colvil,
1750; John Cazier, 1743-1748, shoemaker; Joseph Cockran, 1751, victualler;
John Cane, 1744-1751, planter (Kent County, Delaware); J. Crevet, 1755-
1756, oxen; Francois Chretien, 1745-1746; John Carnan, 1751, merchant;
Michael Cartwright, 1747; ---- Cully, 1751, house in Newtown (Chestertown);
Daniel Carrol, 1745-1748; John Cowgato [Cowgate?], 1758, merchant;
Nicholas Carnie, 1753, tanner and shoemaker in Warwick; Ann Chretian,
1756, farming; Timothy Carrol, 1746; Jane Carnie, 1753, knitting; Darby
Carty, 1753; Edward Costello, 1756; Thomas Cassons, 1759, smithy (black-
smith); ---- Cotringer, 1756, tailor; James Cockeran, 1759, customer; Miller
Campbell, 1759, millwright; Thomas Couch, 1751 (30 lbs. in part for ye mill);
William Cullen, 1758, customer; Archibold Cammel, 1746; Darby Dunleavy,
1736-1745, renter; Marcellous Douglas, 1742, tailor; ---- Dixon, 1750; William
Douglas, 1742; Patrick Doherty, 1758; Arch. Douglas, 1742; William Doland,
1745-1751, butcher (meat); Catherine Doland, 1754, spinner; John Dagnail,
1745; George Douglas, 1758; Timothy Dun, 1745; J. Driscoll, 1758, tailor;
Steven Driscoll, 1743, miller; Nathaniel Dawson, 1753, weaver; Valentine
Douglas, 1745; Margaret Dawson (Dorsy), 1748; Robert Eyler, 1745, carpenter; Evan Evans, 1750, lumber; Mary Eyler (no date); James Evans, 1756,
farming; Brian Farrell, 1745, well digger and tanner; Edward Foreigner,
1760; Thomas Fitzsimmons, 1756, merchant; William Farrell, 1748, well digger; Mrs. Farrell, 1751, tanning and currying leather; Peregrine Frisby, 1744,
tanner; --- Fayweather, 1751, merchant; James Frisby, 1744-1760, customer;
Terence Fitzpatrick, 1751, wigmaker; Archibold Fowler, 1753-1755, smithy;
Jacob Fowler, 1755, smith; Patrick Lawrence Fitch, 1750, wigmaker; Denis
Foley, 1759, merchant; Bryon Graham, 1744, smithy; Abraham Gooding,
1749-1750 ("borrowed 10 lbs."); John Galaher, 1745; Hugh Griffin, 1756-1759,
weaver; Neal G. Galaher, 1747-1760, tailor; Hugh Gallaher, 1742; Joshua
George, 1745, smith; Sidney George, 1760; Daniel Galaher, 1745-1755,
laborer; Joseph Gibbs, 1753, harness; Briant Garrety, 1745, laborer; Peggy

Galaher, 1756, shirtmaker; Bryan Grimes, 1753, victualler and smith; Charles Gordon, 1752; John Holland, 1751, druggist; James Paul Heath, 1744-1747, planter; Darby Hays, 1758, tallow and hides; William Havring, 1744; Mrs. Even Harper, 1756, weaver; William Hall, 1743-1755, merchant and customer; Cliff Hemings, 1755, renter; Owen Hagan, 1743; John Hanley, 1759, cobbler; James Hagan, 1745, butcher; Gavin Hutchenson, 1756, smith; Cliff Hammon, 1746, carpenter (rented "New Design"); Thomas Harper, 1757; John Honis, 1752; ---- Himmings, Jr., 1759, picture frames; Jonathan Hollins (no date); John Jackson, 1735-1740, doctor? ("1 years rent/20 lbs."); Jenny Jones, 1750; James Johnson, 1750-1753, lumber; Dave Jones, 1755 ("rec'd. on Mr. Beadnall order 16 lbs."); John Kaine, 1748; Mary Knarsborough, 1756, wax; Hugh Kelly, 1749-1750, merchant; ---- Kleinhoff, 1756, merchant; Anne Kelly, 1748; Robert Lloyd, 1755, servant; Christopher Long, 1750; John Loland, 1748; ---- Luna, 1751; Thomas Lavin [Savin?], 1756; Edward M. Loy, 1754, laborer; Joseph Lilly, Joseph, 1746-1752; Peter Lober, 1751, planter (Kent County, Delaware); Richard Lockwood, 1754, carpenter; ---- Lylly, 1750; Cornelius Mahoney, 1740-1754, customer; ---- More, 1751, millwright; William Murphy, 1745; Mrs. Meridith, 1751, left money on deposit; William Murdock, 1758, shoemaker; Patrick Murphy, 1759, laborer; Dr. Hugh J. Matthews, Sr., 1744-1753, borrowed 40 lbs.; Dr. Musgang, 1750, customer; Thomas Mills, 1755, axes; Thomas Murray, 1748, miller; Thomas Meighan, 1754, planter; Thomas Marr, 1752, smithy; Charles Maguire, 1756, merchant; Neddy Mainer, 1746; Francis McCabe, 1758, shoemaker; Edward McDermott, 1758; Dominic McDermott, 1760, tailor; Mary MacAdams, 1744, weaver; John McCombs, 1750, mason; John MacDermott, 1750-1753, borrowed 10 lbs. ("good customer"); ---- McDerry, 1751, veterinarian; Thomas McLaughlin, 1748, customer; ---- McCarty, 1753, cobbler; John MacNeal, 1752; James McDuel, 1753, customer; Widow McDermot, 1755, wool; Thomas McLean, 1758, customer; Peter Nugent, 1760; Richard Nicholas, 1751, millwright (16 lbs. for building mill house); Edward Neale, 1745; Andrew Nodine, 1750, tallow and hides; Matthias Noland, 1746-1751, carpenter, wheelwright; Mrs. Esther Noland, 1755; James Noland, 1744, plasterer; James Noland, 1751, draper (suit of clothes for Mr. Lewis, 3.10.0); Dennis Noland, 1742; Briant O'Daniel, 1755-1756, laborer; John O'Dell (no date); Denis O'Castle, 1751, thresher; James Porter, 1753; Nicholas Price, 1753, smith; James Patterson, 1753, smith; Dr. John Plunket, 1753, cared for Mr. Greaton, S.J.; Mrs. Mary Portlock, 1750; James Quin, 1753, painter; ---- Ringgold, 1754, newspaper; William Ryon, 1754, laborer; Samuel Roberts, 1756, cartwright; Elizabeth Richardson, 1759, stocking maker; Brian Reyley, 1749; Braint Reyleigh, 1751, customer; Nicholas Reynolds, 1735, planter; ---- Rumsey, 1751, contractor; Thomas Rutter, 1744; James Reed, 1751, merchant; Sam Stampson, 1735-1740; Daniel Swan, 1751, horse trader; William Sergeant, 1737; Charles Scotty, 1752, cobbler; Cornelius Smith, 1735; William Savin, 1756, quit rents; Dan Sorrell, 1751-1754, Culley's House, Newtowne (Chestertown), paid rent; Captain Spence, 1739; Harry Scots, 1750, negro; Prince Snow, 1744-1751; Charles Shaddock, 1753, laborer; James Stanley, 1744; Mrs. Sheppard, 1758, knitting and spinning; Anthony Shoemaker, 1747; Martha Shea, 1749-1755, customer; Thomas Smith, 1745, smithy; Alexander Stell, 1746, mowers; James Schloss, 1756, dry goods; Felix Summers, 1745; William Tweedy, 1754, cobbler; Ann Taylor, 1744; John Toland, 1752, weaver; George Vicars, 1754; Edward Veasey, 1750, auctioneer; Cornelius

VanSant, 1753, smith; B. VanHorn, 1755; Andrew Wyatt, 145-1759, School Master at the Bohemia Academy; William Williams, 1758, Frederick [Town], nails and planks; David Watherspoon, 1749-1753, planter; Joseph Wallace, 1751, ax layer; Thomas Watts, 1738-1740; Mrs. Henrietta Ward, 1739-1756, midwife; Nichols Woods, 1743-1748; Henry Woods, 1751, stocking maker; John Waters, 1745, mason and bricklayer; James White, 1753, merchant; and, Charles Wilson, 1753.

TAXABLES IN MIDDLE NECK HUNDRED IN 1759: Sidney George and John Carty, plus 8 negroes; John Carnan and 3 negroes; John Ozier and 3 negroes; John Simson; Henry Penington, Stephen Penington and Isaac Penington; Charles Rumsey, William Cox, Joseph Hattry, and 1 negro; Walter Scott, Walter Scott, and 4 negroes; William Price; Jonathan Hollings and John Hollings; "To" Mary O'Hagan and 1 negro; Walter Burk, Richard Chandler and 1 negro; John Driscool; Brian Garitty; Thomas Reynolds; Edward Rumsey, Sr.; Edwatd Rumsey; Patrick Harris and Nicholas Harris; John Rian; Robert Story; Thomas Yorkson; James Clark and William Tench; Elias Eliason, Elias Eliason and 2 negroes; Alexander McFarlen; Samuel Steuart; Nicholas Seeds; William Lollar; Thomas Aken and William Kar; John Cazier, George Carpenter and 3 negroes; John Arel; William McElhany; William Smith; Alexander Steuart and 2 negroes; Thomas Steuart (farmer) and 2 negroes; Patrick Newgent; Barnet Vanhorn and David Gray; Hugh McDonel and 4 negroes; Benjamin Elsbery; James Manycousins; Philip McLoughlen; Michael Manycousins and 1 negro; Evart Evarson and 3 negroes; Benjamin Hull, security for John Akes; "To" Mary Knaresbrough, Michael Knaresbrough, Robert Love, and 1 negro; Richard Flenton; James Reynolds and Jeremiah Reynolds; James Harper, security for Edward Bushnal; John Scott; James Vance, James Steel and Isaac Vandike; Moses Stewart; William Clark, Jr., security for Richard Jones, and Thomas Shears; John Eliason; Cornelius Eliason; Veazey Husband; Richard Reynolds; James McCoy and 2 negroes; William Paul; Robert Faris; Edward Price Willmoor, John Farrel, James Farrel, and 4 negroes; Walter Diven and 1 negro; Denish Kelley; Michael McGowen; John Harper (farmer) and 1 negro; James Cochran and William Cochran; William Weathers, security for James Rody; Zebulon Weathers; John McCoy; Ephraim McCoy and 1 negro; John Cochran; William Reed; John Fillinggam and John Fillinggam; Bartholomew Jacobs, William Cazier and 3 negroes; John Bohannan; Jacob Evarson and 4 negroes; Charles Gorden and 5 negroes; John Houston; Charles Scott, Will Scott and 3 negroes; John Dowbin and 4 negroes; John Elsberry and 2 negroes; Peter Cowarding and 4 negroes; William Rumsey and 4 negroes; George Berwick; David Herring; Jacob Harper and John Hogans; John Carnan; Evart Evarson; William Rumsey. Jacob Harper, Constable.

TAXABLES IN SOUTH SUSQUEHANNA HUNDRED IN 1759: Archibald Ankrim; Arthur Allexander; John Allexander; James Ankrim; Richard Bennet; Mr. Nathan Baker, Thomas Baker and 4 negroes; Robert Boyd; Mr. Henry Baker, Jethro Baker, Isaac Jonson, Robert French, 5 negroes and one chair, 2 wheels; James Baxter, 10 negroes and 1 chair, 2 wheels; Daniel Brumfill; John Baker; John Cuningham; William Caruthers and William Lessle [Lesslie]; James Cuningham; John Cannon; William

Cathur; John Cathur; William Cambell; Peter Cazier; Richard Cazier and William Jones; John Clarck; Samuel Clarck; William Cruickshanks; Hugh Dougherty; Thomas Dugan; Phillip Dougherty; Archibald Eakin and Michael Galloher; William Foster; Thomas Foster; William Ford; James Freeland; John Guffe; John Glasgow; Robert Givens, William Givens and Cornelius McCulgan; Andrew Gibson and James Allen; John Green, Jr.; James Glasgow and William Glasgow; John Green, Sr.; George Hadrick; Robert Hill; Joseph Hodgson and 1 negro; Francis Henderson; John Hall and James Hall; Thomas Hartshorn and Arthur Marshall; Peter Justis, Peter Justis, Jr. and Edward Justis; Isaac Jeaney and Thomas Woodard; Thomas Jeaney; David Keloch; William Kelly, Anthony Kelly, John Kelly and Andrew Davis; Nicholas Kelly; Mr. Francis Keys, James Neilson, and 2 negroes; Samuel Kirkpatrick; Matthew Logan and Matthew Logan, Jr.; Robert Leslie and Hugh Nikel; Francis Leslie; John Moor; David McCrackin; John Mc-Crackin; Oliver Miller; Cornelius McCray and Lackland Duffe; Thomas Mahaffey; Archibald McColloch; Henry Miller and John Bogs; William Mc-Colloch; James McMullen; Joseph McNealy; John McClure; Ellexander Moor; Thomas Murfy; William McKeown and William McKeown, Jr.; William Marshall; Samuel McKeown and William McKeown; Benjamin Mc-Veay; James McClure; Francis Maybury; Robert Nikel and John Nikel; John Neal; Robert Neilson, William Tomson and Thomas Beckett; Stephen Newill and Joshua Newill; Zebulon Oldam; James Ore; Samuel Pritchard; Richard Patten; Walter Rogers; Joseph Richerson; Joseph Richerson, Jr.; William Sheerswood; Morgan Sweny; Thomas Sliser and James Burfrit; James Smith; James Stephenson; William Stephenson; Mr. William Thornton; Robert Thackery; Thomas Underhill; Robert Williams, Robert Knox and Daniel Fagan; William Weltch and Charles Busy; John Willson; James Willson; William Willson; Stephen Willcox; Thomas Willey; Samuel Yeamans; Ellexander Ewing; George Hadrick, security for Matthew Reily; Robert Hill, security for David Hill; James Glasgow, security for John Smith; John McVeay; Hugh Christy. "Insolvents refusing to give in their names and keeping out of ye Constable's way: James Hunter, John Rardon, and Andrew Freeland." Thomas Hartshorn, Constable.

LIST OF TAXABLES IN 1759 (Badly torn, soiled and in pieces): William A---[?], security for William Ebbey[?]; John Anderson; George Taylor, security for Thomas ---on[?]; ---- Williss[?]; ---- Kirk; ---- Kenney; ---ert Love and 1 negro; ---- Lynch[?]; ----m Love; ---as Love and 2 others; Richard George[?], John N---[?] and 2 others; Stephen Gelespie, Stephen Markwright and 1 slave; Joseph Patterson; James Porter and sons Andrew[?] and James, and John Campble and Agness [sic]; John Poake; Stephen Porter; Andrew Porterfield; Doctor Andrew Porter and 2 others; James Thomson[?]; A---[?] Sloan[?]; and others names torn off.

LIST OF TAXABLES BELONGING TO ELK FORGE IN 1762: David Thomas, Caleb Thomas, Patrick Holland, Jesse Graves, Amos Standup, James Henry, Thomas Hayse, Thomas Mills, Robert Mills, James McGuire, John Carey Sr. and John Carey Jr., Isaac Young, Jesse Hollingsworth, Negro Scipio, James Daugherty, and John Caroll. "The within to be each levy free. Filed August 11, 1762."

LIST OF INSOLVENTS IN ST. MARY ANN'S PARISH IN 1764 RETURNED TO THE WORSHIPFULL JUSTICES IN 1765 BY RICHARD THOMAS, SHERIFF OF CECIL COUNTY. North Susquehanna Hundred: William Anderson - in Pensa [Pensilvania]; Patrick Bannan - run; William Carson - run; James Davis - poor; Edward Harding - run; John Henderson - run; William Hanneman - run; John Jackson - dead, no effects; John Marquis - gone to Carolina; John McCue - in Baltimore; Walter McKinny - run; John McDeed - run; James Neilson - dead, no effects; Terrence Neal - in Baltimore; William Porter - run; Francis Potter - run; James Patton - run; Abraham Sewall - run; Andrew Smith - son; James Taggart - in Baltimore; and, Thomas West - run. South Susquahanna Hundred: Alexander Akin - run; William Boyd - run; William Carruthers - in Pensilvania; Robert Clandinnan - twice chgd.; John Damason - run; James Gardner - poor; David Larrimore - run; James McMullin - run; Thomas Mahaffey - run; James McCulloch - in Baltimore; Thomas Murphy - run; James McCartney - run; James McDonald - run; Richard Nowland - run; Joseph Penington - run; Matthew Simpson - run; William Sturgan - run; and, Benjamin Stevenson - run. North Milford Hundred: Daniel Alexander - not in the county; John Brown - run; John Beatty - run; William Chambers - run; Robert Chaffin - run; John Forker - run; William Gillespie - run; William Hall - run; Nicholas How - in Baltimore; James King - run; John McCloud - run; James Rea - run; Samuel Stevenson - run; William Spear - run; James Sands - run; and, Joseph Wilkison - run. South Milford Hundred: Hugh Baird - dead, no effects; John Carroll - run; Jacob Morton - run; William Moor - run; and, John Patton - run. Elk Hundred: Alexander Hannah - run; and, John Walmsley - run. Octarara Hundred: Joshua Brown - run; Mordecai Cloud - run; John Haughew - not known; John Laughlan - not known; John Magonagal - in Pensa [Pensilvania]; Kenneth McKinzie - in Pensa [Pensilvania]; James McNaught - in Pensa [Pensilvania]; and, Nicholas Troy - in Pensa [Pensilvania]. North Susquehanna Hundred: Robert Cursal - not known, additional tax; James McGaw - run, additional tax; William Kelly - in Baltimore, additional tax; William Dickson - run, additional tax; and, John Spear - not in county, additional tax. South Susquehanna Hundred: Samuel McChesney - in Baltimore, additional tax. South Milford Hundred: John Gray - in Pensa [Pensilvania], additional tax. Charles Town: Richard Barns - in Baltimore; William Brown - in Baltimore; Robert Edgar - run; James Ingram - run; Joseph Maybury - run; William Powers - run; Thomas Pritchard - run; Samuel Pritchard - run; and, Martin Wilcox - run. "St. Mary Ann's Parish, Charles Town Included - 94 taxes."

LIST OF INSOLVENTS IN ST. STEPHEN'S PARISH IN 1764 RETURNED TO THE WORSHIPFULL JUSTICES IN 1765 BY RICHARD THOMAS, SHERIFF OF CECIL COUNTY. North Sassafras Hundred: Alexander Doyle - run; and, John Lashley - in Kent. West Sassafras Hundred: James Horney - not in county; John Loftus - run; Andrew Munro - in Pensa [Pensilvania]; John Nicholas - run; and, Jacob Pennington - run. Bohemia Hundred: James Kemp - run; Andrew Clements - not known; Hans York Power - old and poor; and, Mary Severson - not known.

LIST OF INSOLVENTS IN AUGUSTINE PARISH IN 1764 RETURNED TO THE WORSHIPFULL JUSTICES IN 1765 BY RICHARD THOMAS, SHERIFF OF CECIL COUNTY. Manor Hundred: Henry Cooper - run; James Erwin - charged twice; John Gruffey - not in county; William Lancaster - in custody; William Plunket - in Baltimore; John Scanlan - in goal [jail]; and, Cornelius Scanlan - dead, no effects. Middle Neck Hundred: George Campbell - not in county; Joseph Carroll - dead, no effects; Rees Howell - not known; Richard Jones - charged in this and Manor Hundred; Richard Meekins - in Pensilvania; Michael McGowan - run; John McClure - not known; Edward McDonald - not known; Alexander Purse - not known; John Paul - not in county; Silvester Reyling - twice charged and taken in West Sassafras; James Stewart - not known; John Scott, Jr. - not known; Thomas Teague - dead, no effects; and, Edward Price Wilmer - in Kent County. Back Creek Hundred: John Barbert - not known; David Cader - not known; William Crath - not in county; Nicholas Knight - run; Andrew Price, Sr. - dead, no effects; William Paget - in Pensilvania; and, James White - not in county. Augustine and St. Stephen's Parishes - 55 taxes.

LIST OF TAXABLES IN NORTH ELK HUNDRED IN 1766: Col. Nicholas Hyland, Isaac Hyland, Jacob Manley, and 6 negroes; Thomas Crouch, Sr. and Stephen Crouch; Nicholas Hyland (miller), Edward Garish, Thomas Crouch, Jr., and 1 negro; Thomas Hart; George Knight; William Lassells; William Grace and Thomas Keitley; John Waram; William Newell and Abraham Waram; John Wakefield, John Barr and Archabel Barr; Peter Bayer, James Price and 2 negroes; Francis Rock and Hugh Jones; William Currer and 5 negroes; Nathanel Simpers, William Hart, James Brooks and 1 negro; Thomas Brooks; Andrew Rion; Alexander Dogan; John McDowell and William Fan; James Roach; Joseph Richardson and Benjamin Richardson; John Stalcop and Willson Buckmaster; William Cox; William Neavel and John Neavel; William Bristow and 4 negroes; Robart Hart and 4 negroes; James Hart and 3 negroes; John Kankey, John Byard and 3 negroes; Jacob Ashbaugh; Edward Oney; Johanas Arrants, Harman Arrants and Nathan Arrants; Jacob Rudulph; Stephen Hyland, William Beeks [Becks?], and 1 negro; William Veazey, Levi Veazey and Robart Steel; Mary Veazey, Elisha Veazey and 1 negro; William Rutter; John Lewis; William Haslett; Harman Kankey, Michel Smith, and 2 negroes; Susannah McLaughlin, Charles Malattre[?], and George Robinson; Mary Hyland, Richard Fedrey, and 2 negroes; Mary Mauldin and 4 negroes; Francis Mauldin; Benjaman Mauldin, John Orton, and 2 negroes; Levina McDowell, Hyland Money, James Waram, and 2 negroes; Sampson Currer and 1 negro; John Keitley; William Forster; Mary Lum, Jacob Lum, and 2 negroes; Joseph Thomas; Jacob Dawson; Thomas Sumers; John Moody; Alaxandar Moody and John Gillis; Richard Simpers; William Rynalds; John Rumsey and 5 negroes; John Hitchcock and Thomas Hitchcock; Benjaman Avron "to one tax son Thomas Avron;" Henry Avron; William McHue[?]; James Fleming; James Moody, William Starkey, and John McKnob; Thomas Murphey; George Ball; John Little; Ann Mauldin and 3 negroes; James Redman; Moses Jones and Aron Jones; Thomas Bedle and 1 negro; John Forster, Sr., John Forster, Jr., Nathan Forster, and Patrick Campbal; Samuel Phillips, Joseph Phillips and Zeblon Phillips; Mathew Cleghorne and John Cleghorne; John Rutter and William Rutter; Moses Rutter and 1 negro; Thomas Savin and 3 negroes;

John Morrow; James Lowrey; Samuel McKenney and John McKenney; William Ranken and William Curfhaver[?]; Nicholas George, William Jones and 2 negroes; Alaxander Grey; James Orrick and 19 negroes; Martha Hyland, Nicholas Hyland, Jr., John Hyland, and 6 negroes; Daniel Orton; and, Col. Nicholas Hyland, security for Lazarus Granger. Taken June 10, 1766.

LIST OF TAXABLES IN SOUTH MILFORD HUNDRED IN 1766:
Thomas Armstrong; John Anderson; Thomas Allison, James Allison and William Allison; Ezekiel Andrews, William Shierwood and Elisha Millier; Samuel Anderson and John Bristo; Hugh Brown, James Brown and Joseph Barnett; Hugh Beard; Samuel Bond and 1 slave; Richard Bond and 1 slave; John Bing and George Bing; John Baily and James Matthews; Widdow Black and James McGill; William Black and 6 slaves; James Bethorn; Robert Boulton; John Campbell and Patrick Campbell; Richard Clayton and Obediah King; James Campbell; Robert Creswell; Allexander Crowlee; James Coffy and Robert Coffy; James Campbell; William Cloward; Robert Coughran; Richard Coulter; John Coughran; Adam Dobson, Richard Dobson, Evan Jones and William Mauldin; James Dugan; James Elliot; James Frazer; Samuel Farier; William Forsythe; William Finley and Allexander Finley; Henry Graham; John Glass; George Glen and James Young; Samuel Gilpin, Sr., Samuel Gilpin, Jr., Thomas Booth, Ephraim Byard, and 1 slave; George Hall and George Cully; John Hunter; Richard Hall and James Pinkerton; Thomas Huston and Robert Hamelton; Matthew Hodson and Jonathan Hodson; John Huston; William Hull; Joseph Hickman; William Hilles; Robert Jones, John Jones and Samuel Jones; Simon Johnston; Jacob Johnston, Henry Keitley, and William Hitchcock; Mathias Johnston; Robert Lutton, Sr. and Robert Lutton, Jr.; Thomas Maffitt, Samuel Maffitt, Adam Kennedy, and 1 slave; Henry Miller, Michael Hagerty and Daniel Robb; James Mackey, John Mackey and 1 slave; Robert Mackey, John Mackey, William Mackey and 2 slaves; Thomas McCrery, Sr., Thomas McCrery, Jr., and Samuel McCrery; Barnibas Murry; William McKinney; John McDowell and Robert Smith; Thomas Miller; Hugh McBride; John Mullinax; William Murfy; Barnabas McCauley and John McCauley; James Morrow; James Morgan; John Nowland; Thomas Nash; Joshua Newell; Igs. Read, security for James Newell; Hugh Nickles; Hugh Oskeli; Richard Oldham, Nathan Oldham and 1 slave; Augustine Passmore; William Passmore and 1 slave; John Read, Andrew Read, Hugh McDonnald, and 2 slaves; John Read; Thomas Rodgers and David Dougherty; John Richardson; Allen Stuart; Robert Smith; Adam Short; John Simpas and 1 slave; John Short; Thomas Short; William Todd; John Todd and James Todd; Matthew Thompson; Samuel Thompson, John Shanahan and Robert Oar; John Taylor; Matthew Taylor, Sr., Henry Taylor and Matthew Taylor, Jr.; Joseph Thompson; Edward Wilson; Thomas Whiticar and Ralph Whiticar; Michael Wallace, Thomas Wallace, Robert Wallace, and 4 slaves; John Wilson and James Wilson; Robert Young and Thomas Gilliland.

LIST OF TAXABLES IN NORTH MILFORD HUNDRED IN 1766:
George Catto, George Starlin, 6 slaves and 3 dogs; Samuel Sheppard, Thoms Hollandsworth, Andrew Beetle, and 1 "fiste" dog; Thomas Simpers, Richard Lewis, 4 slaves and 1 dog; James Elliot, John Gillis and George McColagh;

John Brown; James Hoxley; Caleb Rickets, Nim Roth, John Broadly, William Allen and Jacob Richardson; John Richardson; Henry Hollandsworth, Jacob Hollandsworth and 4 slaves; John Wilson and John Gillaspie; Jonathan Booth and William Gillis; James Reed; John Tuse; John Smith; George Ash; Petter Baldwin; Robert Barr and Robert Barr, Jr.; John Barnes; Zeblon Hollandsworth, John Shohansie, Thomas Killie and Abraham Mitchel; Joseph Gilpin, Benjamin McGavardy, William Stanup and Joseph Morrison; Herman Gevil; Widow Brown "to one slave Rachel;" Daniel Baily and John Bayly; Robert Fleemin; Robert Evens, Phillipe McMacan, 6 slaves and 1 dog; Edward Talor and William Wallace; Abraham Holms, John Holms, Abraham Holms, and 1 dog; John Langley; William Fleman; William Gray; Joseph Parkes, Thomas Noble, and 2 dogs; Robert Corey and 1 slave; William Langwill, Benjaben Mason, and 1 dog; Thomas Beety; Hughe Langwell; Hezekiah South; Joseph Hear; Edam Willson; John Allexander, 1 slave and 1 dog; Robert Willson and James Reed; Amos Alexandra, John Mechlin, Robert Hoot [Scoot?], and 1 slave; James Alexandra and 4 slaves; Theophlous Alexandra and 1 slave; Samuel Hill and 2 dogs; Frances McClintock and 1 dog; Pattrick Colberson; Joseph Herise; Thomas Coock; Able Hodgson; John Makey, James Makey and William Cofey; Samuel Gay, Hugh Gay, and Samuel Gay; Samuel Beety; Marthew McCracken, John McCracken, and Thomas McCracken; William Gibson; Daniel Torner, Thomas Torner, and John Torner; James Wilken; Robert Roland, 3 slaves and 1 dog; John Strawbridge and 1 dog; George Lawson, John Lawson, 1 slave and 1 dog; Samuel Campell [sic]; John Larrimor; Charles Williams; Samuel Poak; John McElwee; John Duglas; William Davison, John Davison and 1 dog; James McCleland; William Armstrong and John Armstrong; Ritchard Brodley, Gorge Brodley and Neale Brodley; Silvaster Nugin; James Hamphill and William King; William Hervey and Simon Gillespy; Andrew Hervey; William Hervey; Andrew Freser; Thomas Chesnut; Archebald Armstrong, William Armstrong, Peter Daley, and 1 slave; Mr. James Finley, 2 slaves and 1 dog; John McCaye, James McCaye, Beety McCaye, and 1 slave; Edward Weave and Thomas Weave; Joseph Wallace, William Riley, Robert Wallace, Francis Davison, and 2 slaves; Thomas Killgor and William Killgor; William Smith; David Read; Robert Townsley; Daniel Cain; James Brafort; John Hilles and Mathew Hilles; John Gilliland; Andrew Barnet; Jes Holingsworth and 3 dogs; John Rikits and 1 slave; Tobias Rudulph, John Rudulph, and 3 slaves; Thomas Ricketts, Benjaben Ricketts, James Oglvie, Hendrey Hopeff[?], John Crow, 1 slave and 1 dog; Christifor Thomas, Hendrey Thomas, and William Thomas; John Pritchard; William Thompson and 1 dog; Edward Crow; John Freeman; John Medowl [McDowell]; Robert Latta; John Corethers; William Finly and Samuel Finly; Francis Corrithers; and Robert Corrithers; William Willson; David John; William Whan and Samuel Whan; Forgus Smith and William Murvan[?]; Moses Andrew, John Singer, and 1 slave; Doletree[?] Cohran, Andrew Cohran, James Cohran, William Cohran, and 2 dogs; Samuel Hall, Robert Hall, and 1 dog; James Chambers and William Thomson; Andrew Means, Andrew Dugan, and Benjaben Means; David Hallem[?]; Andrew Beer; Robert Fleman, Robert Evens "beal"; Joseph Keeler, William Davison "beal"; John Lowrey, John Burns "beal"; James Kerell, Jorge Lawson "beal"; John Murgan, Jorge Lawson "beal"; William Dulap, Edward Weave "beal"; John Gray and William Gray, Robert Roland "beal."

LIST OF TAXABLES IN CHARLES TOWN HUNDRED IN 1766: Edward Mitchell, Phillip Creamer, John Winchester, and 6 slaves; Jeames Cooper, Henery Jakson, William Jakson, and Edward Jakson; Thomas Bruce; Thomas Ellot and 1 negro; Robert Edger; John Lekey; Gorge Gwine[?]; Ratchford Dupretor[?]; Joseph Ellot, Thomas Price, and Robert McCannehan; William Barns; John Houell; Bengemin Moor; Jacob Poatherman[?]; Thomas Weest [West], Mickell Boullan; Daniell Care, Thomas Pallmer "his belr"[?]; Thomas Pallmer; William Walker; Samuell Kilpatrick; Revd. John Hamltown [sic], James Byerds, and 1 negro; David Morrie [Murrie?]; John Forest; Robert Good; Isack Benbever [VanBeber?]; David Clayton; James Mitchrt [sic], John Phillips, Mathew Kenney, and Henery Toutchstoon; Samuell Crockett and Petter Condin; Andrew Coalter and John Coalter; Robert Allison; John Hudbark[?]; Samuell Devis [Davis?]; Edward Docherty; Isack Jonson; Francis Bromphield; James Cunnigam; Allaxander Mor; William Winchester; Edward Besely and Suttin Smith; James Quaill and Jacob Nell; Charles Rumsey and 1 negro; John Sisly and 1 mulata; Mr. Francis Keys, Henery Allan, William Wattson, and 4 negroes; John Kirkpatrick and 1 negro; Andrew Groob[?]; Mr. Bengmin Rumsey and 2 negroes; John Rigbee and 1 molato.

LIST OF TAXABLES IN NORTH SAFFRAX (SASSAFRAS) HUNDRED IN 1766: Mathias Olaners[?] and 14 negroes; John Marcer and 3 negroes; Cornelus Ticen; William Gudeon; William Carnan; Prince Snow, Guy Snow, and 1 negro; William Jones; Stephen Ryland; Isaac Gibbs, James Makaniy [sic], and 1 negro; Benimine Bodys and 1 negro; Thomas Marcer; Daniel MacClan; James Oneal; Samuel Taylor; Charles Heath, Thomas Patterson and Willim Darnell; John Ward; Richard Lee; Richard Welch; Thomas Hynson, John Hynson, Nathnel Hynson, and 1 negro; Morries Kilingim; Olever Caulk and 4 negroes; Richard Caulk; William Savin, Sr., and 4 negroes; Thomas Beard, Sr., Thomas Beard, John Walker, and 4 negroes; Lewis Beard; Beniman Noland, Daniel Noland, and 2 negroes; Alisha Weeb; Larance Branfeald; Nathan Newland and William Shafley; Nathan Canbuy; Sarah Penington (widow), Araham Penington, and 1 negro; Otho Penington; Ephram Noland; William Marcer, Stepen Marcer, and 1 negro; Silvester Noland and 3 negroes; Mary Ward, Perigren Ward, and 7 negroes; John Ward and 5 negroes; Stephen Beedle, Augasteen Beedle, and 2 negroes; Frances Long; Richard Crouch; Owen Kelly; Thomas Carson, Archabel Grahm, and 1 negro; Nicklos Vanhorn and 1 negro; Hugh Matteus [?], Patt Carney, and 12 negroes; William Bavington, Dennis Noland, and 5 negroes; Beniaman Marcer; John Williams; Elizebeth Paterson and James Paterson; Daniel Gears; Nathniel Buckhanan; Robart Lusby and 2 negroes; Thomas Marra; William Rice and John Sillcox; Sarah Bordley and 4 negroes; John Crouch; George Humberston, Johnothon Humberston, and Jacob Humberston; Gabrel Sillcox; Patrick Dagnel; Enock Gibbs, George Taylor, and Joseph Chambers; John Arterge; John Hood, James Forrell [Ferrell?], and 2 negroes; Jacob Jacobs and 1 negro; William Ozer; Thomas Savin and 2 negroes; John Guy; James Hessey; Benimine Cleave; Thomas Chapman; William Warner; Edward Furner, James Power, and 1 negro; Cornelus Vansant; Daniel Welch; John Brockson and Thomas Brockson; John Batman; John Crosbie; Joseph Smith; Daniel Charles Heath, Philip Pratt, John Brown,

Abraham Poor, and 4 negroes; Nathniel Hynson and 4 negroes; John Simson; James Beard; Joseph Carmon; Neal Golloherr; James Coppin, Andrew Monrow, and 7 negroes. James Coppin, Constable. Additional list: Benjamin Johns and Patrick Brogan.

LIST OF TAXABLES IN BACK CREEK HUNDRED IN 1766 (Original list badly eaten with worm holes): Sammil Adear, Abrm. Adear, and Benjman Cochran; John Allexander, James Allexander, Aron Allexander, and 2 slaves; David Allexander; Elli Allexander and 1 slave; James A----oe[?]; John Armstrong; Thomas Bedle, Sr., and 2 slaves; Even Bell; Thomas Bravard and Thomas Patton; John Bevington and 1 slave; James Boulding, Elidgah Boulding, Elisah Boulding, James Boulding, and 1 slave; Nathan Boulding and 1 slave; Jessey Boulding and Joseph Chick; Thomas Bedle, Jr. and 2 slaves; Benjman Bravard and Charles McNealus[?]; William Bohanan and Robert Bohanan; William Bedle; John Beard and 1 dog; John Bohanan (Cripple) "to 2 taxes to wit Caleb Allexander, Danal McWillimson" and 1 dog; Noble Bedle and 1 slave; William Barns and Thomas Barns; Elidgah Barns, Sr. and Elidgah Barns, Jr.; John Barbert; Thomas Burnom; Hyland Bedle and 1 slave; Henery Bedle and 1 dog; Richard Bedle, Dominick Bedle, Benjman Bedle, and 3 slaves and 1 dog; Thomas Boulding, John Cowan, James Cowan, 1 slave and 2 dogs; William Clark, William Steward[?], Hugh McGinis, and 6 slaves and 2 dogs; David Clark, Robert Whiteside, and 2 slaves; Nathanal Chick and 1 slave and 1 dog; Cornelus Conaly; David Cader; Michal Canshale[?]; Taxables for George Catto's Quarters - Moses Jones and 7 slaves; Nathanal Dawson; Joseph Dawson; John Elwood, Andrew Hughs, and 1 dog; Richard Ellise and 1 slave; Philip Elwood; John Foard and Richard Foard; George Foard, Sammil Hughs, and 1 slave; David Ferice; Robert Ferice; Allexander Hudgeson and 2 slaves; Rodger Hammil; David Henery; Richard Hukle, Jeramiah Hukle, and 1 dog; Manasah Harley, William Harley, John Harley, and 1 dog; John Hall, Sr. and John Hall, Jr.; Thomas Hollings, George Lankester, Danal Murphey, and 1 slave and 1 dog; Andrew Jones and John Jones; Mary Lowrey "to one tax to wit" Robert Lowrey; Robert McCulley; Robert Mire and John Brown; Andrew McKiney; Abraham Miller, Benjman Miller, and 1 slave and 1 dog; William Miller and 2 dogs; Andrew Miller, George Moor, and 1 slave; Thomas Moody; John McCartney; John Morefield; John Nash, John Redin[?], and 1 dog; Sammil Nash and 1 dog; Elias Oyns [Ossus?]; Thomas Ogle and 1 dog; Jaramiah Poulson; Isaac Parker and 1 dog; William Price and 1 slave; Thomas Price, Veazey Price, and 4 slaves and 1 dog; Abrm. Penington and Hyland Penington; James Phillips; David Phillips; Joseph Pue; Charles Quigley and 1 dog; Thomas Richason and 6 slaves and 1 dog; John Snowhill and 1 dog; Allexander Scott, Charles Derumple, and 1 dog; Michael Sticke and "Sumbody Else" [Somebody Else?]; Sammil Sharp; Hester Snell, security for Allexander Snell, and 1 dog; Moses Scott, Andrew Zillafroe, and 1 dog; Thomas Steward[?]; Benjman Thomas, Isaac Thomas, and 1 slave; Richard Thompson, Sr. and 4 slaves; Richard Thompson, Jr., Abrm. Thompson, Richard Thompson "miner" and Ephram Thompson, and 1 slave and 5 dogs; Ephram Thompson, Isaac Hamm, Jonathan Malone, 1 slave and 1 dog; Jaramiah Taylor; Griffith Williams, Richard Bever, and 1 dog; James Wallace, Adam Wallace, Sammil McDowal, and 1 slave; Benjman Whittom and Hanse Athabaugh; James Williams; John Williams; John Williams (carpenter); Andrew Wallace; Edward Armstrong, Wm. Trotters, and 1 dog. Edward Armstrong, Constable. Additional list: Hugh Kilpatrick, Abraham Miller, security; Samuel Marshal[?].

LIST OF TAXABLES IN MIDDLE NECK HUNDRED IN 1766. (Original list badly eaten with worm holes): William Rumsey and 3 negroes; Sidney George, John Penington, 8 negroes, James Hukell, 6 negroes, Cornelius Hukill, 5 negroes, Benjamin Elsbury, 7 negroes, Richard Smith, 5 negroes; Thomas Morgen; Martha Harper's taxables, 2 negroes; Thomas Vandike, Jr. and Thomas Vandike, Sr.; Joseph Hattery; Patrick Laden; John Ryan; John Vail; Edward Rumsey and 1 negro; Edward Rumsey, Jr.; Isaac Pennington; John Bell; James Morrison; William Lawler[?]; William White and son Charles; John Jones; William Chick, William Chich, Jr., and Nathaniel Chick; John Scott (tavernkeeper) and Cornelius Calvin; William Clark (cooper) and 2 negroes; Cornelius Eleson and his sons John and Cornelius, and 1 negro; Elias Elieson and 2 negroes; Elias Elieson, Jr. and his brother Abraham; Richard Reynolds and Isaac Chick; William Weathers, John Diven, James Sea, John Parkerson, and 1 negro; James Warten, Wm. Weathers, security; Ephraim McCoy, John Daniel, and 1 negro; Thomas Cornwell; John Davidge and 1 negro; John Chick, John Joyce, and James Megillin; John Canaan and 4 negroes; James McCoy and 2 negroes; Samuel Stuart and 1 negro; William Smith, John Idhares[?], and 1 negro; John Wiley and his sons Garret and John, and 2 negroes; Barnet Vanhorn and his sons Jacob and Nicholas; Charles Scott, William Scott, and 4 negroes; John Ferel and William Smith; George Wilkin; Jacob Harper; William Bavington's taxes in Middle Neck Hundred - 4 negroes; Alexander Stuart, Samuel Michal, and 3 negroes; Richard Jones; George Sewel Douglas; Jonas Jones; James Crowmell [Cromwell?]; Augustine Saven; John Elsbury and 2 negroes; James Quigley; Jonathan Hollands; Bryan Odaniel; Charles Gorden, Benjamin Sheperd, and 7 negroes; James Runnels; John Bradley; Jacob Evertson, James Anderson, and 2 negroes; Richard Flintham; James Bartley; James Roberts; Bryan Garrety; John Simpson; John Hanna; John Ozier and 2 negroes; Mary Jacobs taxables - Nathaniel Sapenton and 2 negroes; Hiland Benson and Benjamin Benson; Daniel Linch; Michael Manycousins and his son Michel, and 2 negroes; James Rice, John Murphy, and 2 negroes; Timothy Brannen and Solloman Thomas; Justis Gonce, Rudolph Gonce, Abraham Gonce, and George English; George Rice; Patrick Mudgen[?]; Jeremiah Runnels; Mary Neesbury's taxables - Michael Neesbury and 2 negroes; Robert Story and John Bryans; James Vance, Neel McInintire, Andrew Burns, William Ha---, Thomas ----ns, and 1 negro; John Scott and James Scott; John Cazier and his son John, and 4 negroes. [Note: Incomplete due to poor condition of original list].

LIST OF TAXABLES IN NORTH SUSQUEHANNA HUNDRED IN 1766: Antoney Alecock; Samuel Allison; Solomon Allen; John Anderson; Edward Arnit and William Laughlin; John Ash and 1 negro; William Adair; Samuel Arnit; Samuel Anderson; Elisabeth Anderson and Robert Anderson; John Anderson; Arthur Alexander; Benjamin Blades; James Buchanan, John Buchanan, and Michael Connel; John Bleak; Lazarus Barckley; James Brisbin; Robert Bell and Henry McKeever; Andrew Barrat and 6 negroes;

Thomas Bowen, William Bowen, and Jonathan Bowen; William Borris;
James Bankhead and John Bankhead; James Cowan and James Cowan, Jr.;
William Callinder; John Crockett and 6 negroes; Benjamin Chew and 4
negroes; John Callinder, Jr.; Alexander Coughron and William Coughron;
Joseph Corlett; Robert Creswell; William Currier and James Currier; James
Corbit, William Corbit, and James Corbit, Jr.; George Caruthers; Nicholas
Carter; Phenice Chew, Abraham Pearpoint, John Miller, and 4 negroes; Sar-
rah Chew and 6 negroes; John Carson; John Camble, James Camble, and
John Killbreath; John Cartmill, Charles Gorden, with Jean Whitelock,
security; Simon Coser [Cozer?]; Aron Dun; James Devis [Davis?]; Richard
Downey; John Death; John Donoway; William Dickson; John Ewing and
John Freeborn; Moses Ewing; James Evans and 2 negroes; Samuel Ewing
and Amos Ewing; Amos Evans, John Evans, and 1 negro; Robert Finley and
1 negro; James Graham; James Gantley; Richard Griffee and John Conner;
William Glasgow; Robert Glasgow, John Glasgow, and James Bailey; John
Good, Henry Good, and Robert Good; Marius Glanvil; William Griffee and
Daniel Lesly; Jonath Hartshorn, William Maxwell, and 1 negro; James
Hunter; Thomas Hopkins; William Hitchman, Charles McMeans, and 1
negro; John Hunsdon; Thomas Hughes and 10 negroes; George Johnson,
David Hampton, and 6 negroes; Jackson, Edward; Christopher J--kes and 1
negro; James Kidd; Samuel Kerr; John Kirkpatrick, Abraham Kirkpatrick,
Benjamin Coats, and William Barnet[?]; Thomas Kelly[?]; John Kelly[?];
Andrew Kidd and Thomas Taylor; John Kidd and John Kidd, Jr.; Robert
Lyon and David Cleek; John Lyon, Robert Lyon, and Hugh Lyon; Tobias
Long and Israel Long; Robert Little and William Porter; Alexander Long
and Patrick Finigan; Lee Lues; Cornelius Lesly and Jacob Johnson; Joseph
McNeely; John McCoy, Thomas Mollon, and 3 negroes; Roelef Morgan;
John Morgan, John Herring, and 1 negro; Mortey[?] Mahon, Isaac Johnson,
William Mahon, and 2 negroes; Thomas Miller and 2 negroes; Samuel Miller
and 2 negroes; William McClure, James McClure, and Patrick Shields; Walter McChesney; John Murphy; Robert Miller; Adam Meek and 1 negro;
Robert Marquis and George Marquis; Patrick McGarity, James McGarity,
and James Gibson; Theophilus Morrias; Samuel McMullen and Robert Mc-
Mullen; Robert Nelson[?] and Ferch ----[?]; Charles O'Nail, John Callinder
(bail); Thomas O'Nail; Joseph O---; Israel P---; Joseph P---; Samuel Patterson and 2 negroes; Andrew Porterfield; Charles Porter; Robert Porter; Wil-
liam Patton; David Patterson; Armstrong Porter; David Patterson, John
Patterson, Michael Mearn, and 2 negroes; William Rowland, John
Armstrong, George Martin, and 2 negroes; Charles Reagon and Jacob
Death; Joseph Rutherford and William Lilly; John Riddle and Samuel Rid-
dle; William Randles; Lowdewick Rudolf; Benjamin Stevens; John Slone and
Patrick Sloan; John Stump and 2 negroes; James Smyth; James Skillron; John
Smyth, David Henry, and 3 negroes; Andrew Scott; Andrew Smyth; James
Spear; Richard Sidgwick, John Dun, and 2 negroes; Samuel Thomas and 18
negroes; Thomas Tagart; Samuel Tagart, Alexander Tagart, and Matthew
White; Cardiff Tagart; John Taylor and Thomas Taylor; Richard Thomas,
Charles Coats, and 9 negroes; Andrew Touchstone and Soloman Long; John
Touchstone; Henry Touchstone; John Walker; James Whitlock and Daniel
Money; John Wood and Benjamin Pinel[?]; William Willson; John Welch,
Andrew Welch, and John Welch, Jr.; William Wattson, Joseph Powers,

Abraham Wattson, and 2 negroes; Decon Issac Wattson; Daniel Wade; and William Wright. Patrick McGarity, Constable.

MISCELLANEOUS LISTS OF TAXABLES IN 1766: William Hunter, Thomas Tagert, security; Alexander McCulley, John Anderson (farmer), security; William Boner, Samuel Miller, security; John Chambers, John Good, security; James Brumfield; William Gallaugher; Joseph Commins; Andrew Carson; George Key; Thomas Baird; John Othoson and John Henderson; Perigrin Kees, Henry Bun---m, security; Jeremiah Crummey, John Ward, security; Otho Othoson, Constable, Boheamy (Bohemia) Hundred; Richard Thomas, Sheriff, Cecil County. [Note: Francis Key's account was completely eaten up with worm holes and was totally impossible to handle, let alone read].

LIST OF TAXABLES IN OCTORARA HUNDRED IN 1766: George Anderson; Simond Allit; Andrew Baxter; John Braley; Ezekiel Berry; Jeams Cleark; John McCreary; Daniel Chalihon, George Tailor (Beal); Thomas Mc-Dowel; Patt Doyle; Henry Dougherty and Arsbald Dougherty; James Downey; Samuel Ewing, Natt Ewing, and 2 negroes; Patt Ewing and 1 negro; William Ewing, Jr.; William Ewing, Sr. and 3 negroes; Robert Ewing; Jeams Elder; Hugh Emison; Frances Fulton and Daniel McDaniel; Samuel Fulton and William Snodgrass; Dinnis McFading; Robert Forcher [Fercher?]; Samuel Gillespie, Robert Gillespie, Steaphen Gillespie, and 3 negroes; William Gillespie; Samuel Gillespie, Jr. and 1 negro; Richard Gay; John Mc-Gonigal; Natt Gillespie; William Husband and 7 negroes; Joseph Husband and Whitten Rutter; James Hunt, Elihu Hall, Joseph Hall, and 9 negroes; James Hagon; Elihu Hall, Sr. and 10 negroes; John Thieff [Thiess?], William Ewing (Beal); Thomas Love, Robert Love, and 1 negro; Robert McMaster; Robert Maxfield, Richard Gay (Beal); William Means, Robert McMaster (Beal); James McLeer and Thomas Porter; Andrew McKinney and John Sidwill; William Mitchel; James Porter, George Porter, John Tagert, and 3 negroes; Robert Porter; Andrew Porter, Sr., Andrew Porter, Jr., John Porter, James Carnihon, and 2 slaves; William Porter, George Ewing, and Daniel Rider; William Porter, Sr.; George Dalton and John Hamelton; Luke Peacock, William Gash, and 2 slaves; Andrew Rogan; John Sloan; Robert Willson; John Widdowfield; Andrew Weer; Robert Walker; George Tailor and Hans Becker[?]; James Tomson and John Anderson; Thomas Moor, Robert Porter (Beal); Daniel McCay [McCoy?]; John Craig and Andrey [sic] Craig; Hezekiah Balch, Mr. James Hunt (Beal). Samuel Ewing, Constable, August 5, 1766.

LIST OF TAXABLES IN BOHEMIA HUNDRED IN 1766: John Armstrong and Joseph Severson; Revd. William Barroll, Richard Barclay, and 3 negroes and 1 dog; John Beedle, Perrigrine Beedle, and 4 negroes and 1 dog; Samuel Beedle, Bennidick Beedle, Raimon Beedle, and 1 dog; John Beedle, Jr. and 2 negroes; Francis Boys and Francis Boys; Henry Burnham, Raimon Burnham, and 2 negroes; John Barnaby; William Barnaby; John Bellarmin[?]; James Beard; William Bateman, Andrew Bateman, and 1 dog; John Bateman; John Bulley and Edward Lusbey; Thomas Bibbin and Benjamin Burchaner[?]; Thomas Beedle, son of John; William Beedle, William

Owenns, and 1 dog; John Cox, Edward Parish, and 4 negroes and 1 dog; Rebekah Cox, Benjamin Walmsley, and 4 negroes; Nathaniel Childs and Thomas Grimes[?]; William Cox and 1 negro; Benjamin Chrisfield; Mary Cann and Robert Can; John Caulk, James Dorrall, and 3 negroes; Hezekiah Co---[?]; Thomas Davis and 1 negro; William Davis, John Davis, and 4 negroes; Thomas Etherington, Jr. and 1 dog; Barthow. Etherington, Jr. and 2 dogs; Bengam. Etherington, Thomas Wilkins, John Marcer, and 1 dog; Barthow. Etherington, John Childs, 3 negroes and 1 dog; Thomas Etherington and 1 negro; Perrigrine Frisbey, William Martin, William Hodges, 15 negroes and 3 dogs; Samuel[?] Glenn and 3 negroes; Alfanco Gosdon, James Eades, and 1 negro; Samuel Hutchison; James Hayes; George Holt; Jessey Holton and Spencer Pryce; Henry Hayes and John Hayes; John Hall, John Gofton, and 4 negroes; Leaticia Howell and 2 negroes; Henry Hendrickson, Augusten Hendrickson, John Hendrickson, William Gilligan, and 2 negroes; Isaac Holt; Anraham Hollings; Francis Hill; Charles James and James James; Zachariah Kirk and 1 dog; George Kilgore; James King and John Cannon; William Lynch, 1 negro and 1 dog; Mary Louttit, John Spargoe[?], William Boyls, and 10 negroes and 2 dogs; Robert Moody; Thomas Marsh, John Morgan, and 5 negroes and 2 dogs; Robert Marcer, Jr., John Gooding, and 1 negro; William Morgan; John Money, John Money [sic], Thomas Bankett, 6 negroes and 2 dogs; Robert Marcer, John Knowland, 6 negroes and 1 dog; Robert Marcer (son of William); Rebekah Money and 1 negro; William Marin (a millar); Hugh Manley, Ephraim Pryce, security; Charles Murphy; Otho Othoson; John Olover, Thomas Etherington, security; Ephraim Pryce, 2 negroes and 1 dog; Samuel Penington, 5 negroes and 1 dog; William Pryce; Rebekah Penington, 1 negro and 1 dog; Benjamin Pearce and 1 negro; David Pryce and 2 negroes; Hyland Pryce; William Pryce, Jr., William Pryce, Lewis Pryce, and 1 dog; Pantom[?] John Pryce and Perrygn. Pryce; Thomas Pryce (tanner) and 2 negroes and 1 dog; Hugh Pouge; Barthow. Parsley, Thomas Parsley, and Samuel Hamm; Alexander Pratt; York Hance Powel; William Bayer Penington; Robert Penington and Urias Penington; William Pearce and 2 negroes and 2 dogs; Benjamin Pryce and 3 negroes; John Pryce and John Penney; John Pryce, son of John; Joseph Phelps; John Wd. Penington; Andrew Pryce; Henry Wd. Pearce, Joseph Hauge, 10 negroes and 4 dogs; John Roberts and 1 negro; Dorothy Roberts, Roberts Roberts, Thomas Roberts, and 1 dog; Morgan John Roberts; Anthony Ruley and Benjamin Batt; John Ryland; Fredas Ryland and John Milvin; Jehue Ryland and Daniel Bridges; Thomas Severson, Henry Pryce, and 1 dog; Ezekiall Severson and 1 negro; John Sullivin; Richard Smith, Robert Soper, 10 negroes and 2 dogs; Robert Scurry; Robert Scurry, Jr.; Charles Smith, Thomas Pryce, security; William Seden[?] and 1 dog; Joseph Sturgis; John Stogton, Joseph Stockton, Benjamin Stockton, 4 negroes and 1 dog; William Savin, Daniel Sartin[?], and 3 negroes; John Sutton and 1 dog; Jeremiah Sutton; John[?] Thomas; John Urin; Edward Veazey, Anthony Henderson, Richard Wallace, 10 negroes and 1 dog; Benjamin Vickers, Ephraim Lee, and Nicholas Pryce; Daniel Veazey, Henry Hendrickson, security; John Veazey, William Veazey, and 5 negroes and 1 dog; James Wroth and 3 negroes; William Walmsley, Jr., John Dyer, and 1 dog; William Walmsley, John Walmsley, 2 negroes and 1 dog; Richard Welch, James Morgan, and 1 negro; Robert Walmsley, Nicholas Walmsley, Joseph Pryce, 2 negroes and 1 dog; Nathaniel Ward and 2 negroes; William Ward, Robert Penington, and 5 negroes; John Ward (son of Henry), William Hawkins, and 5 negroes; John Winterburey; John Ward (Surveyor), Richard Brown, William Calloishon [Callocohon?], and 6 negroes; John Ward (Inspector), Alexander McClouds, 4 negroes and 2 dogs; James White, Henry Hayes, security; John Veazey Ward, 6 negroes and 2 dogs.

LIST OF INSOLVENTS IN ST. MARY ANN'S PARISH IN 1768: Octorara Hundred: George Anderson - not in county; Cottril Baily - not in county; Patrick Doyle - run; Jonathan Guy - run; Andrew McKinney - run; John Mc-Gonagal - run; Daniel McCoy - run; James Russell - run; James Clark - not in county. North Susquehanna Hundred: Edmund Briggs - run; Lazarus Bartley - run; John Death - not in county; John Davis - run; Joseph Hill - not in county; Arthur Maxwell - not in county; Andrew Smith - not in county; James Welsh - run. South Susquehanna Hundred: William Boyd - run; Thomas Bradley - run; John Constable - run; William Clark - run; Charles Carty - dead, no effects; Nicholas Farnley - dead, no effects; James Gardner - old and very poor; Aaron Grig - not in county; William Johnson - run; Edward Johnson - run. North Milford Hundred: Abraham Arnitt - not in county; Andrew Bears - run; Andrew Barnett - run; James Elliott - run; Widow Broom - denies; John Gray - denies; James Hucksley - dead, no effects; William Hillas - run; John Larrimore - run; Robert Latta - run. North Milford Hundred: John McFee - run; John Richards - gone to Philadelphia; John Snowhill - dead, no effects; William Smith - gone to Carolina; Adam Wilson - run; Samuel Wiggans - run. South Milford Hundred: William Cloward - run; James Elliott - run; Thomas Gilliland - in Pennsylvania; William Jamison - run; James Morgan - run; Hugh Nicols - run. Elk Hundred: William Cox - run; Henry Brooks Calver [Culver?] - run; Joseph Hill - dead, no effects; William Nevil - run; Andrew Ryan - run; Benjamin Richeson - run; William Hasslett - not in county; John Morrow - not in county. Charles Town Hundred: Alexander Andrews - in Baltimore; William Barnes - in Baltimore. INSOLVENT TAXES NOT ALLOWED LAST YEAR: William Boyd - run; James Gardner - old and very poor; William Gibson - in Pennsylvania; John Larrimore - run; James Dugan - run; Jacob Dawson - dead, no effects; John Morrow - not in county; William Nevill - run; and, William Murphy - run.

LIST OF INSOLVENTS IN ST. STEPHEN'S PARISH IN 1768: North Sassafras Hundred: John Crouch - in Kent; Nathan Canby - in Kent; Maurice Celligan [Culligan?] - in Kent; Patrick Dagney - run; Henry Gillispie - in back woods; John Jackson - dead, no effects; William Jones - not in county; Thomas Nicholson - in Pennsylvania; Joseph Smith - not in county; John Wilson - in Pennsylvania. West Sassafras Hundred: James Englis - in Pennsylvania; John Jones - in Kent; George Loyd - pensioner; Thalwell Loftus - dead, no effects; John Martin - in Queen Anns; Robert Porter, Jr. - released by Assembly; William Welsh - not in county; Benjamin Warner - in Kent; James Warner - in Kent. Bohemia Hundred: Thomas Davis - released by Assembly; Nathaniel Glen - in Pennsylvania; John Martin - in Kent; John Parsons - not in county. INSOLVENT TAXS NOT ALLOWED LAST YEAR: Neil Gollaher - very poor; William Warner - very poor; Daniel Jackson - in goal (jail); Richard Blackburn Jackson - released by Assembly; Thomas Ryland, Jr. - released by Assembly; Hans York Powell - very poor.

LIST OF INSOLVENTS IN ST. AUGUSTINE PARISH IN 1768: Manor Hundred: Benjamin Devin - not in county; John Johnson - run; John Mc-Carty - not in county; James Sea - not in county. Middle Neck Hundred: Benjamin Armstrong - not in county; James Aul - not in county; James Crutchley - not in county; William Campbell - not in county; Henry Downey - not in county; George Sewell Douglass - denies; Joseph Hook - not in county; Richard Jones - not in county; John Ryan - died in goal (jail); Thomas Vandyke - not in county; James Pearcey - not in county. Back Creek Hundred: Thomas Burnham - denies; John Carson - not in county; James Erwin - not in county; Thomas Hollings - dead, no effects; Thomas Richardson - denies; Richard Thompson - denies; Griffith Williams - released by Assembly; Benjamin Whittom - denies. INSOLVENT TAXES NOT ALLOWED LAST YEAR: John Barbett - not in county; Robert McCulley - run; Griffith Williams - released by Assembly; John Williams - not in county.

CECIL COUNTY OVERSEERS OF ROADS, 1760-1773: OVERSEERS IN 1760 - North and West Sassafras: Philip Stoops, Prince Snow, William Savin, Sr., Isaac Gibbs. Bohemia: Thomas Etherington, Capt. John Brown, William Price (wicked or wicker?), Thomas Severson. Middle Neck: John McCoy, Sidney George; Back Creek: Robert Thompson, William Boulding, Abraham Miller. Bohemia Manor: Joseph Neide, Thomas Wallace, Charles Ford. North Susquehannah and Octorara: William Husband, Robert Finley, John Ewing, William Rowland, John McCullough. South Susquehannah: William McKeown, Andrew Touchstone, John Glasgow, Murthy Mahon, George Hedrick, James Buchannan, Joseph McNeely, Robert Lesslie, Samuel Gilpin, Samuel Bond, Robert Thackrey. North and South Millford: John Alexander, John Passmore, Robert Rowland, Thomas Ricketts, Samuel Shepherd, Joseph Gilpin, Charles Quigley, John Alexander; Elk: William Manley, Harman Kankey, Robert Hart, William Bristow, Hanse Rudulph. OVERSEERS IN 1761 - Joseph Neide, William Morgan, John Smith (at the Head of Elk), Thomas Wallace, Robert Rowland, Jno. McCullough, Joseph Gilpin, James Veazey, George Vansant, William Manley, John Holland, Jr., Richard Bond, Moses Cochran, Samuel Adair, John Passmore, Jacob Everdson, John Fillingham, James Smith, Joseph Rutherford, James Spear, John Baird, Joseph Thomas, John McVey, Samuel McKeown, James Orr, Archibald McCullough. OVERSEERS IN 1762 - Samuel Gilpin, James Reynolds, William Savin, Sr., Daniel Jackson, John Roberts, Jr., Moses Cochran, Peter Sluyter, Richard Foard, George Ancram, Samuel McCulloch, James Stinson, Phineas Hodgson, Jacob Johnson, Robert Smith, James Orrick, William Grace. OVERSEERS IN 1765 - Henry Pennington, Richard Flintham, Sylvester Nowland, Edward Furroner, Thomas Etherington, James Hughes, Jr., William Walmsley, Thomas Price (tanner), John Davidge, Sidney George, James Smith, James Wallace, Abraham Miller, William Craig, Robert Mansfield, Richard Ford, William Husband, Richard Griffee, Andrew Porter, William Rowland, George Ankrim, Samuel McCulloh, James Whitelock, James Stinson, Richard Thomas, Esq., William Welsh, Matthew Logan, Joseph McNealy, William Baxter, Esq., Richard

Bond, John Alexander, William Pasmore, Samuel Hill, John McDowell, Jona. Booth, Robert Smith, Benjamin Thomas, John Rumsey, John Wakefield, Robert Hart, Joseph Thomas. OVERSEERS IN 1766 - John Cooper, John Ozier, Benjamin Nowland, Robert Thompson, Ephraim McCoy, William Clark, Frederick Elsberry, Solomon Hearsey, George Hedrock, Samuel Miller, Thomas Slicer, Augustine Passmore, Daniel Bailey, Michael Wallace, Archibald Armstrong, Matt. Johnson, Peter Bouyer, James Roach, Andrew Ryan, David Ricketts, Robert Thackery. OVERSEERS IN 1767 - James Coppen, Charles Heath, William Mercer, Edward Furroner, Henry Hayes, John Dockery Thompson, William Savin, Thomas Price (tanner), Charles Scott, Alexander Smith, James Wallace, Abraham Miller, James McCoy, Solomon Hearsey, Joshua Donoho, William Husband, Richard Griffee, Andrew Porter, William Rowland, George Ankrim, Thomas Kenney, James Whitelock, James Stinson, Phineas Chew, Robert Thackery, Charles Brookins, Thomas Slicer, William Baxter, Augustine Passmore, Daniel Bailey, Michael Wallace, Robert Rowland, Archibald Armstrong, Andrew Frazier, Robert Smith, Jacob Rudulph, James Roach, William Currier, Robert Hart, David Ricketts, Peter Bouyer, Francis Fulton. OVERSEERS IN 1768 - James Beard, John Roberts, Benjamin Price, Michael Kneasberry, George Ford, Thomas Ogle, Jr., Joseph Cochran, Jonathan Hutchison, James Porter, Samuel Paterson, Francis Carrithers, Harman Kinkey [Kankey?], David Price, Jesse Hollingsworth. OVERSEERS IN 1770 - Alexander Williamson, Charles Heath, Lewis Beard, Daniel Charles Heath, William Walmsley, Hartley Sappington, John Roberts, Benjamin Price, John Ward (Warwick), Nathaniel Chick, James Wallace, Abraham Miller, William Withers, Andrew Gordon, George Beaston, George Ewing, Samuel Patterson, Samuel Ewing, William Rowland, Joseph Rutherford, Thomas Jenney, Robert Lytle, James Stinson, Phineas Chew, Robert Thackery, Charles Brookins, Nicholas Kelly, William Baxter, Ralph Whitacre, Jacob Rudulph, Michael Wallace, Francis Caruthers, Andrew Harvey, Jonathan Booth, Robert Smith, Benjamin Thomas, Benjamin Mauldin, Thomas Savin, Robert Hart, David Ricketts, William Phillips, David Price, Thomas May, Thomas Smith. OVERSEERS IN 1771 - John Cooper, John Hood, William Pearce, John Elsbury, George Ford, Alexander Scott, Andrew Lawrenson, Thomas McDowell, William Glascow, William Edmundson, William Foster, Thomas Maffitt, Robert Evans, Richard Dobson, John Kankey, Nicholas Hyland, Jr., Benjamin Vickers. OVERSEERS IN 1773 - John Crosby, Benjamin Vickers.

CECIL COUNTY CONSTABLES APPOINTED IN EACH HUNDRED, 1760-1771: In 1760 - Thomas Savin, Jr., North Sassafras (Hartly Sappington in 1762, James Coppin in 1765, John Hood in 1766, Thomas Marr in 1767, John Mercer in 1768, Benjamin Nowland in 1770, Augustine Beedle in 1771); Elisha Terry, West Sassafras (Jacob Jones, Jr., in 1761, Ebenezer Pennington in 1762, Henry Pennington in 1765, James Chetham Wood in 1766, Nicholas Dorrell in 1767, William Pearce in 1768, William Crocker in 1770, John Cox [Jr.?] in 1771); Otho Othoson, Bohemia (John Lusby in 1761, Otho Othoson in 1765-1766, Thomas Parsley in 1767, Augustine Hendrickson in 1768-1771); John Cazier, Middle Neck (John McCoy in 1761, John Ozier in 1762, John Cazier in 1765, William Chick in 1766, John Chick in 1767, Ephriam McCoy in 1768, James Scott in 1770, James McCoy in 1771); William Kleinhoff, Bohemia Manor (Peregrine Vandergriff in 1765, Peter Sluyter in 1766, Andrew Lawrenson in 1767, James Boyle in 1768, Richard Hukill in 1770-1771); Thomas Bouldin, Back Creek (Edward Armstrong in 1761-1767, Alexander Scott in 1768, Elie Alexander in 1770, Alexander Smith in 1771); Thomas Mason, North Milford (James Holms in 1761, Moses Latham in 1762, Fergus Smith in 1765, Francis Carrithers in 1766, Andrew Cochran in 1767, Samuel Hall in 1768, Abel Hodgson in 1770, Patrick Culbertson in 1771); Matthew Taylor, South Milford (Richard Bond in 1761, Thomas McCleary in 1762, Samuel Maffitt in 1765, John Anderson in 1766, Jacob Johnson in 1767, Lawson Beard in 1768, Robert Sutton in 1770, Andrew Read in 1771); James Corbit, North Susquehannah (Andrew Barratt in 1761, William Glasgow in 1762, Patrick McGavity in 1765, William McClure in 1766, John Lyon in 1767, Arthur Alexander in 1768, John Good in 1770, John Patterson in 1771); Zebulon Oldham, South Susquehannah (Samuel Clark in 1761, William Cather in 1762, Robert Lasley in 1765, Samuel McKeown, Sr. in 1766, John Glasgow (tanner) in 1767, Benjamin McVey in 1768, Thomas Williams in 1770, John Crookshanks in 1771); Henry Stidham, Elk (John Hyland in 1761, James Roach in 1762, Nicholas George in 1765, Francis Mauldin in 1766, Sampson Currier in 1767, William Ruttur [Rutter] in 1768, Alexander Gray in 1770, Jacob Mainley in 1771); John Hedrick, Charles Town (Jacob Northerman in 1762, Samuel Killpatrick in 1765, Jonas Cooper in 1766, Edward Beazley in 1767, Francis Brumfield in 1768, Christian Guither in 1770, Jacob Neal in 1771); William Gillespie (tanner), Octorara (William Graham in 1761, William Gillespie, Sr. in 1762, Samuel Ewing in 1765, Richard Gay in 1766, John McCrery in 1767, James Gallaspie in 1768, John Craig in 1770, Samuel Fulton in 1771). Sheriffs: James Baxter (1761-1762) and Edward Mitchell (1767-1768).

CECIL COUNTY PRESS MASTERS APPOINTED, 1760-1771: North Side of the Elk River - John Read (1760), Jesse Hollingsworth (1761), Henry Hollingsworth (1762-1771); South Side of the Elk River - Jacob Hamm (1760), John McDuff (1761-1770), James Hughes (1771).

NAMES GLEANED FROM THE ACCOUNTS OF MR. THOMAS RUSSELL AT NORTH EAST FORGE, 1764-1774. [Note: Actual ledger covers the period from October, 1764 to October, 1782. Ref: Maryland Historical Society, Manuscripts Division, MS.1117, Box 1]. In 1765 - Benjamin Chandley, Edward Mitchell. In 1766 - Grace Smith, David Rhea, John Hylton. In 1767 - Dr. Morrow, Grace Smith, George Russell, Stephen Furnea Hoomes, Edward Mitchell. In 1768 - Grace Smith, Andrew Coulter, Dr. Lloyd, Thomas Archer, George Russell, David Rhea, Mr. Philips, Thomas Smith, John Rhea, John McCalla. In 1769 - Grace Smith, George Russell, William Baxter, Jonathan Smith, Mr. Rhea, Mr. Elliott, Richard Thomas, Richard Ireland, Mr. Randall. In 1771 - Tom Giles, Jacque the Barber. In 1772 - Gibson Granbury, "Smith son of Russell," Thomas Charleton, Samuel Pleasants, Philip Thomas, Samuel & Jonathan Smith, William Russell, Edward Mitchell, George Russell "brother of Thomas Russell," Alexander Davey, John Southall. In 1773 - schooling John Smith's children, Thomas Charlton, Mrs. Maybury, Christie & Boyd, Mr. Peale, Tobias Rudulph, Mr.

Roberts, William Russell, Mr. George Roberts, Messrs. Cox & Furman, William Baxter (deceased), Mr. Thomas, Mr. David Rhea, John Hamilton, Esq. (Sheriff), Philip Thomas, Mr. Bird, Baruch Williams, Tobias Rudulph, John Campbell, Thomas Huggins, Peter Turner, Smith son of Russell, Mr. George Roberts, Thomas Russell "brother of William Russell," John Willson, Joseph Baxter, Thomas Jones, Philip Creamer, William Young, Reese Meredith, Joseph Trimble, Timothy Kirk, Rowland Rogers, John Sinclair, Edward Parker, Samuel Pleasants, Richard Dobson, George Rock. In 1774 - Thomas Huggins, Mr. Bird, Mr. Millick, Robert Hill (labourer), Tobias Rudulph, Mrs. Smith, Thomas Russell "his brother William Russell in favor of Smith son of Russell," Francis Maybury, Jonas Cooper, Thomas Charlton, Mr. Brumfield, John Willson (Rock Run), John Barnaby, Ann Glenn, Tom Giles, Mrs. Rathell, Parson Read, George Rock, Negro Manty, Thomas Ricketts, J. Giles, Edmond Warriner, William Durbin, Thomas Giles, Philip Creamer, Abram & Tom ---[?], John Hamilton, Michael Simpson, James Haggarty, William Johnson, William Smith, William Simpson, John Hull, Andrew Robinson (Schoolmaster), Thomas Manuel, Robert Whitley, David Frew, Negro Bess, Michael Gallispie, John Wakefield, James Pritchard, Meredith & Clymer, Samuel Maffitt, Mr. Currer & Mr. Thomas, Col. John Lyme, Thomas Thomas.

A LIST OF TENEMENTS ON BOHEMIA MANOR IN 1768. (Ref: Maryland Historical Society, Manuscript Division, Augustine Herman Papers, MS.1556): Capt. John Veazey (3), Jacob Ozier (3), Richard Ford (1), Nicholas Wood (1), Moses Cockron (1), Alexander Clark (1), Richard Reynolds (2), Alexander Stuart (1), John Carnan (1), Jacob Harper (2), Martha Harper (1), Joseph Ensor "Bought in" (5), Thomas Ogle (2), Thomas Moore (1), John Kirk (1), James Smith (1), John Holland (4), William Harling (1), John Carty (1), Andrew Lawrenson (2), Elizabeth Marr (1), Ephraim and George Beastin (1), Hyland Price (1), Peter Lawson (3), Richard Hukill (1), Anthony Lynch, Jr. (1), Anthony Lynch, Sr. (1), Joshua Donoho (3), William Taylor (2), Mary Harr [Hann?] "now Donoho" (1), Jonathan Hodgson (2), John Mullin (1), Joseph Neidie (1), Frederick Elsberry (2), William Weathers (1), William Clark (1), John Wyley (2), William Cox (1), Elias Aliason (2), Cornelious Aliason (1), Rebeckah McCoy (1), Robert Veazey (1), Joseph Taylor (1), John Garty [Gaily?] (1), Richard Wallace (1), Philip Noble (1), Manasah Loage (1), Peter Rider (1), William Craige (1), James Boyle (4), Mart Canter (1), and Joseph Rider (1). Total: 78.

CECIL COUNTY REPRESENTATIVES IN THE LOWER HOUSE OF THE MARYLAND GENERAL ASSEMBLY (Gleaned from *A Biographical Dictionary of the Maryland Legislature, 1635-1789*, by Dr. Edward C. Papenfuse, et al., Maryland State Archives, 1979): 1674/1675 - Henry Ward, Abraham Wilde, John Vanhack, Thomas Salmon; 1676 to 1682 - James Frisby, Jonathan Sybray, William Pearce, Nathaniel Garrett; 1682 to 1684 - James Frisby, William Pearce; 1686 to 1688 - William Dare, Edward Jones; 1689 to 1692 - Charles James, Edward Jones, William Dare, James Frisby; 1692 to 1693 - William Dare, St. Ledger Codd, Edward Jones, George Warner, James Wroth, Thomas Theakston, Robert Crooke; 1694 to 1697 - St. Leger Codd, John Thompson, William Pearce, Casparus Augustine Herman;

1697/98 to 1700 - William Harris, Hans Hanson, John Thompson, John Carvile, William Pearce; 1701 to 1704 - William Harris, St. Leger Codd, John Thompson, Matthias Vanderheyden, Thomas Frisby; 1704 to 1707 - William Pearce, Edward Blay, Thomas Frisby, William Dare; 1708 to 1711 - Thomas Frisby, Matthias Vanderheyden, John Ward, Edward Larramore, Henry Ward; 1712 to 1714 - James Frisby, Matthias Vanderheyden, William Dare, Peregrine Frisby; 1715 - John Ward, Matthias Vanderheyden, Ephraim Augustus Herman, Francis Mauldin; 1716 to 1718 - Matthias Vanderheyden, Ephraim Augustus Herman, John Ward, James Frisby; 1719 to 1721/22 - William Dare, Ephraim Augustus Herman, James Frisby, Roger Larramore; 1722 to 1724 - John Ward, Josiah Sutton, Francis Mauldin, William Freeman; 1725 to 1727 - John Ward, Ephraim Augustus Herman, Francis Mauldin, Thomas Johnson; 1728 to 1731 - Thomas Johnson, Jr., Ephraim Augustus Herman, Stephen Knight, Joshua George; 1732 to 1734 - Joshua George, Ephraim Augustus Herman, John Ward, Joseph Wood; 1734/35 to 1737 - Joshua George, Ephraim Augustus Herman, John Ward, Joseph Wood, Thomas Johnson, Jr.; 1738 - Joshua George, Thomas Colvill, William Rumsey, Alphonso Cosden; 1739 to 1741 - Joshua George, Thomas Colvill, William Rumsey, Thomas Johnson, Benjamin Pearce; 1742 to 1745 - Joshua George, Thomas Colvill, Benjamin Pearce, Nicholas Hyland; 1745/46 to 1748 - Nicholas Hyland, Joshua George, Benjamin Pearce, Peter Bayard; 1749 to 1751 - Benjamin Pearce, Peter Bayard, John Baldwin, Richard Thompson, Thomas Colvill, Nicholas Hyland, Henry Baker, James Baxter; 1751 to 1754 - Michael Earle, Benjamin Pearce, Sidney George, Nicholas Hyland; 1754 to 1758 - Nicholas Hyland, Michael Earle, Henry Ward, Henry Baker; 1758 to 1761 - Michael Earle, Henry Baker, Henry Ward, Francis Mauldin, John Veazey; 1762 to 1763 - Michael Earle, Henry Baker, Francis Mauldin, William Ward, Nathan Baker; 1765 to 1766 - Michael Earle, Henry Baker, Nicholas Hyland, William Ward; 1768 to 1770 - John Veazey, William Ward, William Baxter, Henry Baker, Joseph Gilpin; 1771 - John Veazey, Benjamin Rumsey, William Baxter, William Ward; 1773 to 1774 - John Veazey, Jr., William Ward, Joseph Gilpin, Stephen Hyland.

CECIL COUNTY DEBT BOOKS, 1734-1766: NAMES, TRACTS, YEARS.
(Reference: Maryland State Archives, Index Card File 58).

Abbot, William - Freemans Park, Daniels Den - 1739-1766.

Adair, Samuel - Sligoe, Alexandria - 1749-1766.

Addison, Rev. Henry - Clifton, Manevaren [Manwaren?] Hill, Heaths Third Parcell, Dividend, Maniwarring Hall - 1754-1766.

Alexander, Andrew - Hispaniola, Bullens Range, Newcastle Back Landing, Blankensteins Park Resurveyed - 1739-1758.

Alexander, Arthur - New Munster - 1734-1761.

Alexander, David - New Munster, Sligo, Bullens Range, Hispaniola - 1734-1766.

Alexander, Elias - New Munster, State Hill - 1734, 1760.

Alexander, Ephraim - No tract listed - 1734.

Alexander, Francis - Sligoe, Alexandria - 1734-1761.

Alexander, Isaac - Blankensteen Park Resurveyed - 1754-1761.

Alexander, James - New Munster - 1734-1766.
Alexander, James (farmer) - New Munster - 1739.
Alexander, James, Jr. - New Munster - 1739, 1766.
Alexander, John - New Munster - 1739-1766.
Alexander, Joshua - No tract listed - 1734.
Alexander, Joseph - New Munster - 1734, 1760.
Alexander, Martin - Sligoe - 1734-1761.
Alexander, Mary - Sligoe - 1734, 1760.
Alexander, Moses - Sligoe - 1734-1766.
Alexander, Samuel - Sligoe - 1734, 1760.
Alexander, William - No tract listed - 1734, 1739, 1760.
Allason, Thomas - Smiths Discovery - 1734, 1760.
Allison, James - Society - 1749-1757.
Allen (Allin), Daniel - Monns - 1734, 1760.
Allene (Allyne), Samuel - No tract listed - 1758.
Altam, Widow - Triangle - 1739.
Altham (Alton), John - Triangle - 1734, 1760.
Anderson, James - Welsh Point - 1734.
Anderson, Widow - Success - 1739, 1749, 1754.
Andrews, Moses - Lessaroon - 1749-1766.
Andrews alias Johnson, Simon - Success - 1734.
Arbuckle, James - Teagues Endeavour - 1749-1766.
Armstrong, Archibald - Arianna, Addition, Clements Venture - 1739-1766.
Armstrong, Edward - Boldings Rest, Armstrongs Venture, Jones Green Spring - 1755-1766.
Armstrong, Francis - Representation - 1758-1766.
Armstrong, James - Clements Adventure, Addition - 1739-1757.
Armstrong, John - Clemerson - 1766.
Arrants, Johannes - St. Johns Manor, Lums Venture, Stoney Ridge - 1749-1766.
Arther, Matthew - New Munster - 1739-1761.
Aston, James - New Turkey Point - 1734, 1760.
Atkey, Ann - Pains Lot - 1739.
Atkey, John - Pains Lot, Kings Payne - 1734, 1749, 1760.
Attwood, Peter - Askmore - 1734, 1760.
Atwood, Richard - Cockatrice - 1758, 1761, 1766.
Avalon, Sarah - No tract listed - 1734, 1760.
Bailey, John - Providence - 1755-1766.
Bailes, Daniel - New Munster - 1766.
Baird, Thomas - Norland, Martins Nest - 1749-1766.
Baird, Hugh - Drumgena - 1766.

Baker, Henry - Colleton, Contention, Landoar, Raccoon Range, Antcastle, Gorrey, Philips Neglect, Smiths Addition, Vulcans Rest, Venter, Vanbebbers Forest - 1749-1761.

Baker, Nathan - Buck Hill - 1749.

Baldwin, John - Macgregorys Delight, Baldwins Dispatch, Corborough, Baldwins Enlargement, Mapleton, Conelias Town, Mathiason, Mattinson Range, Stoney Chace, Rumnys Retreat - 1734-1760.

Barbott, James - Savons Lott - 1734, 1760.

Barker, Henry Sr. - No tract listed - 1734.

Barney, William - Dares Desire - 1734, 1760.

Barns, William - No tract listed - 1734.

Barr, Robert - Mount Joy - 1766.

Barren, Dorothy - Perry Point - 1760.

Barrett, Philip - Cox's Purchase - 1739.

Barry, Andrew - Confusion, Successor - 1734-1760.

Bateman, William, Jr. - Batemans Trial, Kings Aim - 1756-1766.

Bateman, William, Sr. - Batemans Trial, Kings Aim - 1734-1766.

Bavington, John - Addition - 1734, 1760.

Baxter, Andrew - Sargents Neck - 1749-1766.

Baxter, James - Hearts Delight, Gotham Bush, Anna Catherina, Part of Carpenters Point - 1754-1761.

Baxter, John - Sargents Neck - 1739.

Bayard, James - Georges Friendship, Rollings Rest, Bristol, Uppermost - 1734-1766.

Bayard, Peter - Bohemia Manor, Morris Neck, Bouldings Rest, Bristol, Uppermost - 1734, 1758-1761.

Beadle (Beedle), John, Sr. - Abrahams Promise, True Game - 1749, 1766.

Beard, Thomas - Martins Rest, Norland - 1734-1761.

Beck, Edward - Barton, Reserve - 1734, 1760.

Beck, Jonathan - Cockatrice, Rattlesnake Nest, Kings Delight, None So Good, Benjamins Level and Marys Enlargement, Middle Grounds - 1734, 1760.

Beedle (Beetle), John, Jr. - Abrahams Manor, St. Johns Manor, Beedles Promise, True Game - 1734-1761.

Beedle (Beadle, Beetle), John, Sr. - Jones Adventure - 1734, 1760, 1761.

Beedle, Richard - Bohemia Sisters - 1766.

Beedle (Beetle), Samuel - Jones Adventure, Essex Lodge - 1749-1766.

Beedle (Beetle), Thomas, Sr. - Boldings Rest, Bristol, Uppermost - 1734-1766.

Beedle (Beetle), William - Colleton, Prices Neglect, Fryars Hill - 1749-1766.

Beesly, Jeffery - St. Johns Mannor - 1739.

Beesting, William - Swan Harbour - 1734.

Beeston, William - Swan Harbour - 1739, 1760.

Bellah, Moses - Creswell, Steels - 1755, 1761, 1766.

Bennett, Richard - Yorkshire, Stockton Addition, Convenient Rest, Tryall, Palmers Island, Emorys Satisfaction, Greenbury, Turkey Point, Marksfield, Coxes Purchase, Bennington Resurveyed, Sargents Neck, Stockton, Skelton - 1734-1760.

Benson, Benjamin - Daniels Den, Jones Venture, Money Worth - 1754-1766.

Benson, Mary - Kings Ayme (Aim) - 1734, 1760.

Bing, John - Beckers Addition - 1749-1766.

Blackiston, Ebenezer - No Name - 1734, 1760.

Bladen, John - No tract listed - 1734.

Blake, John - Harts Delight, Gotham Bush - 1734, 1739, 1760.

Blankesteen, William (Heirs - Baltimore County) - Requittal - 1760, 1734 [sic].

Blunt, Robert (Kent Island) - Wheelers Delight - 1734, 1760.

Bodle, John - Colleston - 1734, 1739, 1760.

Boggs, William - Providence - 1749, 1754.

Bolden, Thomas - Bristoll - 1755.

Bond, Samuel - Batchelors Funn, Rumseys Rambles - 1749-1766.

Bonner, Francis (Heirs) - Clemerson, Seversons Delight - 1739-1766.

Booker, Richard (Virginia) - Uppermost - 1734, 1760.

Boom, Rachel - No tract listed - 1758.

Booth, Jonathan - Successor - 1766.

Booth, Thomas - Succession - 1749-1761.

Bordley, Beal - Blenham - 1754, 1755.

Bordley, Thomas - Bordleys Beginning - 1734, 1760.

Bordley, William - Bordleys Beginning, Painters Rest - 1739-1766.

Borne, John - Borns Forrest - 1734, 1760.

Born (Bourne), William - Hack Town - 1734, 1760.

Bouchell, Peter - Bohemia Manor - 1734, 1755-1761.

Bouchell, Susannah - No Name - 1734, 1760.

Boulding, Richard - Richards Chance, Belleaugh - 1734-1760.

Boulding, Thomas - Bristoll - 1758, 1761.

Boulding, Thomas, Jr. - Uppermost, Bristol, Boldings Rest - 1739, 1755-1766.

Boulden, Thomas - Bristol - 1756, 1757, 1766.

Boulding, William - Knowlwood - 1739-1766.

Bowlding, William - Bowldings Neglect, Bristow, Uppermost - 1734.

Bowlin, Wiliam - No tract listed - 1734.

Boyer (Bowyer), John - Johns Mannor [sic] - 1734, 1760.

Boyer, Peter - Lums Venture, St. Johns Manor, Stoney Range - 1739-1766.

Boys, Nathaniel - Martins Delight, Martins Enlargement - 1739.

Bradford, Elizabeth - Hearts Delight, Gotham Bush - 1749.

Bravard, John, Sr. - Charles Camp, Sligo - 1749, 1754.

Brent, Hugh - No tract listed - 1734, 1760.

Bravard, Benjamin - Suttons Forrest and Range, James Venture - 1758, 1761, 1766.

Brevard (Breward), John, Jr. - Charles Camp, Sligo - 1734-1766.

Bravaird, Thomas - Hispaniola, Glasgow - 1766.

Brice, John - Frisbys Prime Choice, Frisbys Forrest, Addition to Forrest, Harris Venture, Brices Discovery, Brices Triangle, Long Neglected - 1749-1766.

Brimingham, Richard - No tract listed - 1734, 1760.

Bristol (Bristow), John - Bristows Conveniency - 1734, 1760.

Bristowe, William - Thompsons Town, Hopewell, St. Johns Manor, Society, Confusion - 1734-1766.

Broome, Robert - Batchelors Hope, Batchelors Chance, Sorances Chance - 1758, 1761, 1766.

Browne, Daniel - Chairing Chance - 1734, 1760.

Brown, Capt. John - Dunton, Thompsons Inspection, Long Lane, Coroborough, Addition, Augustinia Defence - 1754-1761.

Brown, Thomas - Martins Delight, Martins Enlargement - 1749-1766.

Browning, Thomas - Essex Lodge, Cedar Branch Neck - 1734, 1760.

Broxam, John (Heirs) - Strawberry Bank - 1734, 1760.

Broxen, William - Mulberry Dock, Strawberry Bank - 1734, 1760.

Buchanan, John - Buchannans Endeavour, Newcastle Back Landing, Catharines Lott - 1734-1766.

Buchanan, Robert - Tryangle - 1734, 1760.

Buchanan, William - No tract listed - 1734.

Buck (Bucke), John - Spencers Harbour - 1755-1766.

Bull, James - Collets Town - 1734, 1739.

Bull, Thomas - Colletts Town - 1734, 1760.

Bully, Mathew - Henricks Choice - 1739, 1749, 1754.

Buntington, John - No tract listed - 1756, 1757.

Burgess, Charles - Bullens Range - 1734, 1760.

Bush, Mathew - No tract listed - 1758.

Bushell, Dr. Peter - No tract listed - 1754.

Buttler, Cacelius (St. Marys) - Roystones Purchase - 1734, 1760.

Buttler, James - Navington Green - 1734, 1760.

Caldwell, James - State [Slate?] Hill - 1755-1766.

Caldwell, Samuel - Three Partners Part - 1749-1766.

Calvert, Philip (Heirs) - Squall, Morton - 1734, 1760.

Cammell, John - Deviding, Thompsons Town, Prices Adventure - 1734.

Campbell, Elinor - Thompsons Town, Two Sisters - 1749, 1754, 1766.

Campbell, James - Connaught, Campbells Dividend - 1734, 1749-1761.

Campbell, John (Heirs) - Prices Venture, Thompsons Town - 1734, 1739, 1755-1761.

Campbell, Rebeccah (Heirs) - New Garden - 1734, 1760.

Cankers, Thomas (Heirs) - Cankers Neck - 1734, 1760.

Carmack, Peter - St. Johns Mannor - 1734, 1739, 1760.

Carr, Richard - No tract listed - 1734.

Carr, Thomas - Williams Chase - 1734, 1760.

Carr, Walter - Society - 1749-1766.

Carroll, Charles - Society, Addition, Smiths Addition - 1734-1760.

Carroll, Dominack (Heirs) - Addition - 1734-1749, 1760.

Carruthers, Francis - New Munster - 1749-1766.

Cartmill, Martin - Good Will - 1734, 1739, 1760.

Carter, James - Holt (lies in Kent County) - 1739-1766.

Carter, Joseph - Kingsby - 1734, 1760.

Cartis, John - Mulberry Point - 1760.

Carvill, Daniel - No tract listed - 1760.

Carvill, Deborah - No tract listed - 1760.

Cato, Capt. George - Thompsons Town, Friendship, Cattos Range - 1754-1766.

Cattlin, Robert, Jr. - Long Acre - 1734, 1760.

Cattline, Robert, Sr. - Long Hope - 1734, 1760.

Caulk, Isaac - Worlds End, Larramores Neck Enlarged, Larramores Addition, Wheelers Point - 1734-1761.

Caulk, John - Larramores Neck Enlarged, Larrimores Addition, Wheelers Point - 1766.

Caulk, Oliver - Worlds End, Caulks Addition - 1739-1766.

Cazier (Crazier), Philip - Smiths Addition, Vulcans Rest, Coxes Forrest - 1734, 1739, 1760.

Cecil Town Proprietors - Mulberry Dock, Mulberry Mould - 1739-1755.

Chambers, Jonas - Chambers Venture, Chambers 4th Vacancy, Golden Ball - 1766.

Chambers, Rowland - Mount Joy - 1734, 1760.

Cheston, Daniel - Frisbys Farm, Frisbys Prime Choice - 1749-1758.

Chetwind, William and Co. - Gotham Bush, Gefaruson, Partnership, Addition to Forge Mills - 1739-1766.

Chew, Benjamin - Perry Neck - 1739-1766.

Chew, Bennett - Convenient, Turkey Point, Palmers Island - 1755-1766.

Chew, Samuel - Frisbys Meadows, Pains Lott - 1766.

Childs, Benjamin - Shrewsbury - 1739.

Child, George - Shrewsbury - 1734, 1760.

Childs, Nathaniel - Daniels Den, Sisters Dowry - 1734, 1760.

Christian, Thomas - Colletton, Roundstone, Norland - 1734, 1760.

Clark, David - Francina - 1756-1766.

Clark, William - Francina - 1758-1766.

Clauson, Peter - St. Johns Manor - 1734, 1760.

Clauson, William - Waram - 1734, 1760.

Clayton, Richard - Batchelors Fun - 1734-1766.

Clemence, Margaret - No tract listed - 1734.
Clemens, Isaac - Homely, Smoaking Point - 1739.
Clements, Cornelius - No tract listed - 1734.
Clements, Gabey - No tract listed - 1734.
Clements, Gabriel - Deery Hill - 1734, 1760.
Clements (Clemens), Michael - Clemens Venture - 1734, 1760.
Clemerson, Abraham - Clemerson - 1734, 1760.
Clemerson, Ann - No tract listed - 1734.
Clemerson, Cornelius - Homely, Smoaking Point - 1734, 1760.
Clifton, Thomas - No tract listed - 1734.
Cloud, Mordecai - No tract listed - 1758.
Cochrane, John - Fair Hill - 1755-1761.
Cochran, Joseph - Addition, Goodwill, Lydias Joynture, Fair Hill - 1749-1766.
Cochran, William - New Munster - 1749-1766.
Cocks, John (Heirs) - Good Luck - 1734.
Colwell, James - State Hill - 1754.
Coldwell, Samuel - Three Partners - 1739.
Collett, Abraham - Perry Point, Mount Pisgah - 1734.
Collett, John (Heirs - England) - Broad Neck - 1734, 1760.
Collins, George - Maidenhead - 1734, 1760.
Collins, James (Talbot) - Mount Pleasant - 1734.
Colson, Thomas - Glass House - 1739, 1749, 1754.
Colvill, John - Knowlwood - 1734, 1739, 1760.
Colvill, Thomas (Virginia) - Horn Point, Knowlwood - 1734-1766.
Comegies, Cornelius - Glass House - 1734.
Cook, Thomas - More Lowe, Buntington - 1734, 1760.
Cooper, John - Middle Neck, Happy Harbour - 1739-1755.
Coppen, James - James Lott - 1754, 1756, 1757.
Coppen, John - Middle Neck, Happy Harbour - 1756-1766.
Coppin, Angelico - Buntington, Coppins Chance, Silvanias Folly - 1749-1758.
Coppin, James - James Lott, Coppins Chance - 1755-1766.
Coppin, John - Buntington, Silvanias Folly - 1734, 1760-1766.
Coppen, Widow - Coppens Chance, Silvanias Folly - 1739.
Copson, John (Heirs) - Copsons Forrest, Copsons Intent, Coxex Park, Mistake - 1734-1761.
Cosden, Alphonso (Heirs) - Addition alias Hacks Addition - 1734-1766.
Coursey, Col. William - Ladys Delight, Timber Ridge - 1734.
Courtier, William - Chives Chace, Hopewell - 1734.
Covill, John - No tract listed - 1734.
Covell, Thomas - Knowlwood, Horn Point, Bohemia Sisters - 1754.
Cox, Benjamin - Civility - 1766.
Cox, John - Barbadoes, Corneliouson, Jamaica, Mattsons Town - 1734-1766.
Cox, Thomas - Cockatrice - 1734, 1760.

Cox, William - Levell - 1734, 1749-1766.

Cozine, John - St. Johns Mannor, Booker - 1734, 1760.

Cazier (Crazier), Philip - Coxs Forrest - 1734, 1739, 1760.

Cresswell (Creeswell), James - Steels - 1755, 1761, 1766.

Crocker, Capt. - None So Good - 1739.

Crocker, Thomas - Knavery Outdone - 1766.

Crouch (Croutch), Thomas - None So Good, Triumph - 1734-1758.

Crozier (Crosier), John - Hispaniola, Glasgow, No Name - 1755-1761.

Culmery, William - Maidenhead, Parkers Parcels - 1761.

Cummings, Robert - Netherland, Arundel - 1754-1766.

Cuniliffe, Foster - Prices Venture - 1734, 1739, 1755-1761.

Cunningham, George - Buntington - 1766.

Currier, John - Chivy Chace - 1739, 1749, 1754.

Currier, Sampson - Hopewell, Small Hopes - 1754-1766.

Currier, William - Hopewell, Copsons Intent, Deer Harbour, Curriers Lott, Curriers Addition - 1734-1766.

Curry, Robert - Snow Hill Addition - 1734, 1760.

Curson, Henry - New Connaught - 1734, 1760.

Curtis, John - Mulberry Point - 1734.

Dare, William - Lower Triumph, Travelers Refreshment, Two Neck - 1734, 1760.

Darnal, Henry - No tract listed - 1755.

Davage, John - Wormust, Addition, Hacks Addition - 1754-1761.

David, Fouch (Heirs) - Middle Ground, Benjamins Level - 1734, 1739.

Davis, Thomas - Marys Jointure, Cockatrice, Frisbys Farm, Frisbys Prime Choice, Kings Delight, Rattlesnake Neck, Tullys Lot - 1739-1766.

Davis, William - Levell - 1734, 1760.

Davis, William, Jr. - Addition - 1734, 1760.

Davidson, Samuel - Davidsons Fancy, Emorys Endeavour, High Park - 1749-1766.

Dawson, Joseph - Wallaces Scrawl - 1749-1766.

Death (Dearth), Randall - Glass House - 1734-1761.

Demondadesy, Katherine Massey - Katharines Lott - 1734, 1760.

Dempster, John - Bouldings Rest, Bristoll, Uppermost - 1749-1757.

Dennis, Richard - Brereton - 1734, 1760.

Denton, Henry - Ashmore - 1734.

Denton, Vachel - Ashmore - 1734.

Deoran, James - Mount Quigley - 1734, 1760.

Diggs, Edward - Coasters Refreshment - 1760.

Dillon, James - Harts Delight - 1734.

Dobson, Adam - Hollowing Point, Succession, Good or Bad, Veazys Lot - 1749-1766.

Dobson, Richard - No tract listed - 1734.

Donelson, Major - Londonderry - 1760.

Donnel (Donalds), William - Hail Hill, Snow Hill, Snow Hill Addition - 1739-1761.

Dorrell, Nicholas - Rook and Pill - 1734-1766.

Dorsey, John Hammond - Success, Biters Bit - 1755-1766.

Dougherty, Nathaniel - Daughertys Desire, Daughertys Endeavour - 1734, 1760.

Douglas, Archibald - Vulcans Rest - 1749-1758.

Douglas, George - No tract listed - 1734.

Douglas, Joseph - No tract listed - 1734.

Douglas, Susannah - Dividends - 1734, 1760.

Douglas, William - Smiths Addition - 1734, 1739, 1760.

Dowdle, Capt. John - None So Good, James Forrest, Trevalin, Sheffield - 1734, 1760.

Dowdall, Richard - No tract listed - 1734.

Drake, William (Heirs) - Civility - 1734, 1760.

Drummond, John - Larramores Neck, Larramores Addition, Hazle Branch - 1749-1766.

Dumagin (Duming), Roger - Sinequa Point - 1754-1766.

Duvall, Samuel - Larkins Desire - 1739.

Earle, James (Heirs) - Anna Catharina - 1739, 1749.

Earle, Michael - Addition, Resurvey of Swan Harbour, Stockton - 1734, 1754-1766.

Edmonds, Evan - Dollvaine - 1734, 1755-1760.

Edmond, Thomas (Heirs) - Buckler Hill, Thomas Lot - 1734, 1760.

Edmundson, John - Providence - 1739, 1749, 1754.

Edmunson, William - Providence - 1739.

Edrington, Thomas - Neighbours Neglect, Hendricksons Oversight, Edringtons Hope - 1749, 1754.

Edward, John - No tract listed - 1758.

Edwards, Philip - Dayleys Desire - 1734, 1760.

Elder, David - Society - 1754-1761.

Elliott, Benjamin - Pleasant Mount - 1766.

Elliott, Francis - Pleasant Mount - 1749-1761.

Elliott, James - Killavilla - 1749, 1754.

Ellis, William - No tract listed - 1758.

Elstone, Ralph, Sr. - Elstone - 1734, 1760.

Elstone, Ralph, Jr. - Love - 1734, 1760.

Elswick, John - Raccoon Point - 1739.

Emory, George - High Park, Emorys Endeavour - 1734, 1760.

Emory, Lydia - High Park - 1734, 1760.

English, John - No Name - 1760.

Erwing, Alexander - Levell - 1754.

Erwin, William - Providence - 1749, 1754.

Etherington, Bartholomew - Jamaica, Shrewsbury - 1739-1766.

Etherington, Benjamin - No tract listed - 1755.

Etherington, Thomas, Sr. - Etheringtons Hope, Hendricksons Oversight, Neighbours Neglect, Ethringtons Chance, Ethringtons Tryal - 1739, 1755-1766.

Evans, Elias - Bohemia Sisters - 1739.

Evans, James - Holland, Heaths Adventure - 1755-1766.

Evans, John - Bohemia Sisters, New Munster - 1734, 1739, 1760.

Evans, Robert - New Munster, Successor, Duck Neck, Addition, St. Johns Town, Prices Venture - 1749-1766.

Everard, John - Everards Fortune - 1734, 1760.

Everard, Thomas - Norwick - 1734, 1760.

Everson, Elias - Successor - 1734.

Everson (Evertson), Evert - Middle Parcel, Second and Fourth Heaths Parcel - 1739, 1754-1761.

Everson (Evertson), Jacob - Sarahs Jointure, Sedgefield, Heaths Range, Middle Parcel, Stocktons Addition - 1739-1766.

Ewing, Alexander - Levell - 1734-1761.

Ewing, James - Holland, Heaths Adventure - 1754.

Ewing, John - Holland - 1756, 1757, 1766.

Ewing, Joshua - Bourns Forrest and Addition, Deviding - 1734-1761.

Ewing, Nathaniel - Bourns Forrest and Addition, Deviding - 1734-1761.

Ewing, Patrick - Bourns Forrest - 1766.

Ewing, Samuel - Deviding - 1766.

Ewing, William, Jr. - Levill - 1766.

Ewing, William, Sr. - Deviding, Long Lane - 1755-1766.

Faris, John - Jones Green Spring - 1755-1766.

Faires, Moses - New Munster - 1749-1761.

Fedderay, Richard - Fedderays Meadow - 1758, 1761, 1766.

Finlow, James - Castle Fine, Garners Gift - 1755-1766.

Finlowe, John - Fair Hill - 1734-1760.

Fisher, William (Heirs) - Albans - 1734, 1760.

Fogg, Amos - Clay Fall - 1749-1757.

Forbes, George - Simms Forrest - 1739, 1749, 1754.

Ford, Charles - Bohemia Sisters - 1766.

Ford, George - Richards Chance, Bristoll - 1749-1766.

Foster, James - Joans Green Spring - 1739.

Forster, John - Brereton - 1749.

Forster, Richard - Brereton - 1739.

Forster, William - Joans Green Spring - 1739.

Foster, Benjamin (Heirs) - Prices Venture - 1734, 1755-1760.

Foster, James (Heirs) - Joans Green Spring - 1749-1766.

Foster, John - Brereton, Johnsons Addition, Jones Green Spring - 1754-1766.

Foster, Richard - Brereton - 1734, 1749-1766.

Foster, Thomas - Clay Fall - 1749-1757.

Foster, William - No tract listed - 1734.

Fotterell, Edward - No tract listed - 1734.

Franks, David - No tract Listed - 1758.

Frazier, Alexander - No tract listed - 1734, 1760.

Frazer, Andrew - Batchelors Content - 1766.

Frazier, James - Buckhead Hill - 1755-1766.

Frazier, Joseph - Teagues Forrest - 1739, 1749-1766.

Frazier, Philip - No tract listed - 1734.

Free School Visitors of - Banks - 1734, 1739, 1749, 1754.

Freeman, Timothy - Freemans Joy - 1734, 1760.

Freeman, Anne - Kings Aim - 1755, 1756, 1757.

Freeman, William - Wheelers Point, Daniels Den - 1734-1760.

French, Robert - Londonderry, Duffield - 1734, 1760.

Frisbye, Mrs. Ariana - Frisbys Venture - 1734, 1760.

Frisby, James - Frisbys Meadows, Rounds - 1749-1766.

Frisby, Perregrine - Burleys Journey, Frisbys Addition, Frisbys Wild Chace, Baltimore Fields Resurveyed, Paines Lott, Frisbys Point, Frisbys Meadows - 1734-1766.

Frisby, Thomas - Frisbys Farm, Frisbys Forrest, Frisbys Prime Choice, Frisbys Meadows, Frisbys Point, Hargraves Choice - 1734, 1760.

Frisby, William - Frisbys Purchase - 1734, 1760.

Fryer, James - New Munster - 1755-1761.

Fulton, Alexander - Resurvey of Emorys Satisfaction, Teagues Chance, Doughertys Desire - 1761, 1766.

Fulton, John - Doughertys Endeavour - 1755-1766.

Gale, George - Tuscarora Plains - 1734, 1760.

Gale, John - Stillington - 1734, 1760.

Gale, Levin - Hackley - 1766.

Gallaspye (Gillaspie), John - New Munster - 1734, 1760.

Gallaway, James - No tract listed - 1734, 1760.

Garrett, Amos (Anne Arundel) - Middle Neck - 1734, 1760.

Gears, Daniel - Micum, Rook and Pill - 1734, 1739, 1760.

Gears, John - Happy Harbour, Carrington - 1749-1766.

Geist, C. - Gratitude - 1734.

George, Joshua, Jr. - Little Bohemia, Dividend, Sarahs Jointure, Salem, Murphys Forrest, Warren, 1/2 lot in Frederick Town - 1734-1761.

George, Nicholas - Highlands, Triumph - 1734-1766.

George, Richard - No tract listed - 1734.

George, Sampson (Heirs) - Turkey Harbour - 1734, 1760, 1766.

George, Sidney - Little Bohemia, Clifton, Strange Upon Resurvey, Salem - 1754-1766.

Gilder, Hickle [Hukill] - Wasp Nest, New Spain - 1754.

Gilder, John - New Corborough, Friendship - 1734, 1760.

Gilder, William - Gilders Forrest - 1734, 1760.

Gillaspie (Gallaspye), George (Heirs) - Bourns Forrest and Addition, Level - 1749-1766.

Gillespie (Gilaspie), George - Bourns Forrest and Addition, Greenberry - 1754-1761.

Gillespie, William - Mount Gillespie - 1766.

Gillis, Thomas - Tuscarora Plains - 1734, 1760.

Gilpin, Joseph - Heddrys Meadow, Beaver Dam - 1766.

Gilpin, Samuel - Coxs Park, Rumseys Rambles, Stoney Chace - 1734-1766.

Givens, Robert - New Munster - 1749, 1754.

Glassford (Glashford), Henry - Philips Bottom - 1755-1761.

Glinn, Robert - No tract listed - 1734, 1760.

Goldsmith, George (Heirs - Baltimore County) - Bohemia - 1734, 1760.

Goodman, Edward (Heirs - Virginia) - Norfolk - 1734, 1760.

Gording, James - Deviding - 1734.

Gordon, Charles - Dividend, Sarahs Jointure, 1/2 lot in Frederick Town - 1754-1766.

Gray, John - Matthias Hills - 1755-1761.

Gray (Grey), Miles - Grays Lot - 1734, 1760.

Graham, John (Heirs) - Pembroke, Teagues Delight - 1739-1766.

Graham, Robert - Hopewell, Teagues Endeavour, Resurvey on Teagues Delight - 1766.

Graham (Grayham), William - Pembroke - 1755-1766.

Green, Thomas - Coxs Prevention - 1734, 1760.

Grimes, John (Heirs) - Matthias Hills - 1755-1766.

Grimes, Samuel - New Munster - 1749-1766.

Grimes, William - Holland, Heaths Adventure - 1754.

Griffee, Richard - Glass House - 1755-1766.

Griffin, Charles - Brownings Neglect - 1734, 1760.

Griffin, Thomas (Heirs - England) - Welch Point - 1734, 1760.

Griffith, Edward - No tract listed - 1734.

Griffith, Nicholas - Compound - 1734, 1760.

Grubb, Emanuell - Cornwell, Cornwell Addition - 1734-1760.

Grubb, Thomas - Cornwall, Cornwall Addition - 1749-1766.

Grundy, Andrew - Andrews Delight - 1734, 1760.

Grundy, Robert - Anchor and Hope - 1734, 1760.

Guilder, Hukil - Wasps Nest, New Spain - 1739.

Gunnery, Sprye (Baltimore County) - New Hall - 1734, 1760.

Guy, Richard - Level - 1766.

Hack, George - Hackly - 1734, 1756-1760.

Hack, Peter - Hackly - 1734-1761.

Hall, Andrew - Hollingsworths Second Parcel - 1739, 1749, 1754.

Hall, Elihu - Halls Lot, Halls Choice, Hope, Halls Fishery, Baldwins Dispatch - 1739-1766.

Hall, Francis - Hackly, Sprys Hills - 1739-1766.

Hall, George - Coxes Purchase - 1739.

Hall, James - Snow Hill - 1734.

Hall, John - Knowlwood, Coxes Purchase, Marksfield - 1734-1766.

Hall, Richard - Hollingsworths Second Parcel, Halls Discovery - 1734, 1755-1766.

Hall, Samuel - Black Marsh - 1766.

Hamilton, Rev. John - Mount Joy, Society - 1766.

Hammond, John (Heirs) - Borns Forrest - 1734-1760.

Hammond, Thomas - Land of Delight, Success - 1734, 1760.

Hampton, David - Succession - 1749, 1754.

Hargrave, Isaac - Withers - 1734, 1760.

Harper, Nicholas - No tract listed - 1734.

Harman, Col. Ephraim Augustine - Bohemia Manor, Misfortune, Small Hopes, Copings Chance - 1734.

Harris, Ariana Margaretta - Hargroves Choice, Frisbys Prime Choice - 1754-1766.

Harris, James - Neglect, Adventure, Joans Green Spring - 1734, 1760.

Harris, Matthias - Coasters Harbour, Wormust, Pasture Point, Wheelers Warren, Bromley, Rounds, Locust Neck, High Park - 1749-1766.

Harris, Thomas - Resurvey of Welch Point - 1758, 1761, 1766.

Harris, William (Heirs) - Jones Green Spring - 1734-1760.

Harrison, Richard - Halls Lott, Hope - 1734, 1760.

Hart, James - Triumph alias Wadmores Neck - 1766.

Hart, Robert - Triumph, Highlands - 1749-1766.

Hartshorn, Jonathan - Holland - 1766.

Hawkins, John - No tract listed - 1734.

Hays, John - Essex Lodge, Abrahams Promise - 1749-1766.

Haynes, Thomas - No tract listed - 1734, 1760.

Heath, Charles - Heaths Level Parcels, Heaths Range - 1734-1766.

Heath, James - Addition, Heaths Range, Heaths Level Parcels, Norland, Sedgefield, Scraps - 1734, 1760, 1766.

Heath, James Paul (Heirs) - Addition, Addition to Heaths 3rd Parcels, Chance, Forlorn Hope, Gee [Goe] Look, Heaths Range, Heaths Level Parcel, Hog Pen Neck, Heaths Outlet, Mount Harman, Mesopotamia, Norland, Sheffield, Mannering Hall, Sarahs Jointure, Sedgefield, Killington, Toas Purchase, Scraps, Holt, Worsall Manor, Larramores Neck Enlarged - 1739-1757.

Heathod, Thomas - Plain Dealing - 1734, 1760.

Hedges, William - Heaths Range 1st Part, Heaths Outlet, Toes Purchase, Holt, Worsall Manor - 1754-1766.

Hendrickson, Barth - No tract listed - 1734.

Hendrickson, Chris - Hendricks Addition - 1734.

Hendrickson, Henry (Heirs) - Cockatrice Addition, Crouches Oversight, Indian Range, Cockatrice, Hendricksons Addition, Marys Park, Henry and Ward, Levell, Jamaica - 1634-1766.

Hendrickson, Matthias - Marys Park - 1754-1766.

Henrick, Bartho - No tract listed - 1760.

Henry, William - Black Marsh, Cafiruro - 1749-1766.

Herman, Ephraim Augustine - Bohemia Manor, Copings Chance, Misfortune, Small Hopes - 1734, 1760.

Herman, Col. (Heirs) - Bohemia Manor - 1739.

Herrickson [Henrickson], Christopher - Henricksons Addition - 1734, 1760.

Heyland, Nicholas - Chesnutt Level, Poplar Valley, Johns Mannor, Johnsons Adventure, Hylands, John and Marys Highlands, Triumph, Surplus of Triumph, Hylands Forrest, Hyland, New Kent - 1734.

Highland, John - Highlands, St. Johns Manor - 1756-1758.

Highland, Nicholas - Hylands, Hylands Forrest, Johnsons Adventure, St. Johns Manor - 1739-1758.

Hill, John (Heirs) - Sedgefield - 1739.

Hill, Dr. Richard - Maidenhead, Middle Neck - 1734, 1760.

Hill, Capt. Richard - No tract listed - 1734.

Hill, Samuel - New Munster - 1734, 1749-1766.

Hill, William - Sarahs Jointure - 1739.

Hillin, Nathan (Heirs) - Hillins Grove - 1734, 1760.

Hinton, Reece - Hintons Conveniency, Inspection - 1734, 1760.

Hinton, Thomas (Heirs - England) - Hintons Adventure - 1734, 1760.

Hitchcock, Thomas - St. Johns Mannor - 1734, 1739, 1760.

Hoar, John - Town Point - 1734, 1760.

Hoax, John - Town Point - 1734.

Hodgson, Phineas - Pleasant Garden - 1749-1766.

Hodgson, Robert - Hodgsons Choice, Pleasant Garden - 1734, 1760.

Hodson, Joseph - Pleasant Garden - 1739.

Hogshead, John - Loveroon - 1734, 1739, 1760.

Holland, Col. William - Mount Arrarat - 1734, 1760.

Hollinsworth, Abra - Picture Parcels, Hollingsworths Parcels, Inlargement - 1734, 1760.

Hollinsworth, Catherine - Mount Hope - 1734, 1760.

Hollingsworth, Henry - New Munster, Successor, Gabriel Old Field, Friendship - 1734, 1755-1760.

Hollinsworth, John - Fair Hill - 1734.

Hollinsworth, Lydia - Hollowing Point - 1734, 1760.

Hollinsworth, Mary - Mount Hope - 1734, 1760.

Hollingsworth, Stephen - Successor, Three Tracts, Mount Pleasant - 1734, 1755-1760.

Hollinsworth, Thomas - Jacobs Adventure - 1734, 1760.

Hollinsworth, Zebula - Hollingsworth Inspection, Swamp - 1734-1766.

Hollowell, Richard - Londonderry - 1734, 1760.

Holms, Abraham - New Munster - 1755-1766.

Holt, Obediah - Bohemia Manor - 1734, 1760.

Holtham (Haltham), John -- Spencer [sic] - Luck - 1754-1766.

Holey, Ann - Society - 1758, 1761.

Holy, Robert (Heirs) - Confusion, Holys Expedition, Mount Joy, Society, Holys Contrivance, Hopewell - 1734-1761.

Hood, John - Hog Pen Neck - 1749-1761.

Hooper, Henry - No tract listed - 1734.

Hopkins, Joseph - Mount Hope - 1734, 1760.

Hopkins, Thomas - Cedar Branch Neck - 1734, 1760.

Houston, Richard - Pennyworth- 1755, 1758.

Houston, Samuel - Philips Bottom - 1749, 1754.

Howe (How), Richard - Knowlwood - 1734, 1760.

Howard, Gorden - Wallaces Scraule [Scrawl] - 1734, 1760.

Howton, Richard - Pennyworth - 1739.

Huberson, John - St. John's Mannor - 1760.

Hughes, James - Happy Harbour, Lot 20 in Frederick Town, Buntington - 1749-1766.

Hughes, John - Happy Harbour - 1758, 1761.

Hughs, Joseph - No tract listed - 1755.

Humberson, John - St. Johns Manor - 1734.

Humberton, John - No tract listed - 1734.

Humberstone (Umberstone), George - Heaths Outlet - 1749-1766.

Humphrys, Thomas - Geist, Gratitude - 1734, 1760.

Hunt, Rice - Grange - 1734, 1760.

Husbands, Herman - Hermans Rambles - 1755, 1757.

Husbands, James (Heirs) - Hog Pen Neck - 1739.

Husbands, William - Level, Mount Pisgah, North Addition to Level, Walnut Thicket, Mount Pleasant - 1734-1766.

Hutcheson, Alexander - Griffin - 1734-1766.

Hutcheson, Gavan - New Intersection - 1734, 1760, 1766.

Hutchison, Phinias - Pleasant Garden - 1755.

Hutchman, William - Holland, Widows Lot - 1754-1766.

Hutton, David - Killa Villa, Huttons Grudge - 1755-1766.

Hyatt, John - Dares Desire - 1734, 1760.

Hyde, Capt. John (England) - Widows Lot - 1734, 1754-1761.

Hyde, Samuel (Heirs - London) - Smiths Fort - 1754-1761.

Hyland, John, Jr. - St. Johns Manor, New Amster - 1766.

Hyland, John - Highlands, St. Johns Manor, White Marsh, Kenneys Desire, Johnsons Adventure, Hylands Forrest - 1739-1766.

Hyland, Nicholas - Highlands Part, St. Johns Manor, Highlands, Highlands Forest, Johnsons Adventure, Highlands Chance - 1739-1766.

Hynson, Charles - Salem - 1739, 1749, 1754.

Hynson, John - Worlds End, Thomsons Town - 1734, 1760.

Hynson, Nathaniel - Worlds End, Urinson, Martins Nest - 1734-1766.

Hynson, Thomas - Worlds End - 1734, 1756-1766.

Inglish, John (Heirs) - No tract listed - 1734.

Inveir, Francis - No tract listed - 1734.

Irwin (Irvin), John - Skelton - 1758, 1761, 1766.

Irvin, William - Providence - 1755-1761.

Isaac, James - Elk Plains - 1734, 1760.

Ivan, James - Griffin - 1734, 1760.

Ivory, Theopha - St. Johns Manor - 1734, 1760.

Jackson, Edward - Gotham Bush, Hearts Delight - 1734, 1739, 1760.

Jackson, Dr. John - Daniels Den, Hills Adventure - 1749-1766.

Jacobs, Bartholomew, Sr. - Stockton - 1749, 1754.

Jacobs, Bartholomew - Skelton, Stockton - 1739-1766.

Jacobs, Jacob - Skelton - 1749-1761.

Jacobs, Joseph - Three Partners - 1755-1766.

Jacobs, Thomas (Heirs) - Dares Desire, Friendship, Gift, Chance, Jacobs Bottom, Newcastle Back Landing, Three Partners, Jacobs Chance - 1734-1766.

Jacobson, Bartholomew - No tract listed - 1734.

Jawart, John - Town Point - 1734, 1760.

Jenings, Edmund - Frisbys Farm, Frisbys Prime Choice, Hargraves Choice, Frisbys Venture, Frisbys Forrest - 1739.

Jenkins, Francis - Pashoare - 1734, 1760.

Jobson, John - Civility, Happy Harbour - 1734, 1760.

John, Aaron - No tract listed - 1734, 1760.

John, David - Hill Foot, Rumseys Success - 1749-1766.

Johns, Thomas - St. Johns Manor - 1749-1766.

Johnson, Bartholomew - Newcastle Back Landing - 1734-1760.

Johnson, Edward - Purchase, New Amster, Johnsons Addition, St. Johns Manor - 1734-1766.

Johnson, Hannah alias Watson - Kirkminster - 1754-1766.

Johnson, Henry - Feddard - 1734, 1754, 1760.

Johnson, Jacob - Chesnut Ridge - 1766.

Johnson, John - Perry Neck - 1734, 1760.

Johnson, Matthias - Batchelors Content - 1749-1761.

Johnson, Samuel - Gardners Advice - 1734, 1760.

Johnson, Simon alias Andrews - Successor - 1734, 1739.

Johnson, Simon - Friendship, Successor - 1749, 1754, 1760.

Johnson, Simon, Jr. - Succession - 1749, 1754.

Johnson, Thomas - New Amster, Triumph - 1734, 1739, 1754, 1760.

Johnson, Wooly - Feddart - 1739.

Johnson, William (Elk River) - Oldfields Lot - 1734, 1760.
Johnson, William (Heirs - England) - Bryans Lot - 1734, 1760.
Jones, Charles (Baltimore County) - Charles Camp - 1734, 1760.
Jones, Elizabeth - Happy Harbour, Jones Addition - 1755-1761.
Jones, Hugh - Clifton - 1758, 1761.
Jones, Jacob, Jr. - None So Good in Finland - 1766.
Jones, Jacob - Happy Harbour, Jones Addition - 1766.
Jones, John - Hills Adventure, St. Johns Manor, Dolevain - 1734, 1760.
Jones, John (cooper) - Buckhead Hill - 1739, 1749, 1754.
Jones, Lewis - Bella Connell - 1734, 1760.
Jones, Moses - White Marsh, Dorsons Point - 1754-1761.
Jones, Peter (Heirs) - Happy Harbour - 1758-1766.
Jones, Reese - New Munster, Sarenam - 1734, 1760.
Jones, Thomas - Happy Harbour - 1734-1760.
Jones, William, of Thomas - Happy Harbour, Jones Addition - 1754.
Jones, Willim - Happy Harbour - 1754-1758.
Judd, Michael (Baltimore County) - Tuttle Fields - 1734, 1760.
Kankey, Harman - St. Johns Mannor, Harmans Addition - 1766.
Kankey (Kinkey), John - St. Johns Mannor - 1734-1749, 1766.
Kear (Kerr), Samuel - Steels - 1755, 1761, 1766.
Kelham, William - New Munster - 1749, 1754.
Kelton, Major Thomas - Jamaica - 1734, 1760.
Kember, Thomas - Hendricksons Choice - 1734, 1760.
Kempstone, Richard - High Offley - 1734, 1760.
Kennedy, Daniel - Buck Range - 1734, 1755-1760.
Kennedy, Hugh - Kennedys Adventure - 1734, 1760.
Kersey, Thomas - Perry Neck - 1734, 1760.
Key, Francis - Anna Catherine, Carpenters Point - 1766.
Key, John - Pennyworth - 1734.
Killgore (Kilgow), Thomas - Wallaces Scrawl - 1749-1766.
Kimball, Rowland (Baltimore County) - Contrivance, Kimballs Addition - 1734.
Kimbol (Kimbar), John - Rattlesnake Neck, Cockatrice, Kings Delight, None So Good - 1739, 1749.
Kimboll, Richard - Partners Choice - 1734, 1760.
Kimboll, Rowland - Kimbolls Addition, Contrivance - 1760.
Kingsbury, James - Hope - 1734, 1760.
Kingsbury, John - Hope - 1734, 1760.
Kinkay, Harman - St. Johns Mannor - 1734, 1760.
Kinkey (Kankay), John - No tract listed - 1734-1749, 1760.
Knaesbrough, Mary - Addition to Heaths Parcel, Mannering Hall - 1758, 1761, 1766.

Knight, Rachel - Clifton, Mannering Hall, Heaths Third Parcel, Addition to Heaths Third Parcel, Dividend - 1749.

Knight, Stephen - Clifton - 1734, 1739, 1760.

Knox, James - Coxes Prevention - 1749-1766.

Land, Francis - Batchelors Hope, Chance, Beaver Dam, Bella Connell, Bedfords Chance - 1734-1760.

Langent, John - No tract listed - 1734, 1760.

Larimore, Augustine - Larramores Neck, Hazle Branch, Chance, Larramores Addition - 1739.

Larramore, Ed - No tract listed - 1734.

Larramore, Roger - Larramores Neck, Larramores Neck Enlarged, Two Branches, Hazell Branch, Larramores Addition, Chance - 1734, 1739, 1760.

Lashley, Robert - No tract listed - 1758.

Lashley, William - Wallaces Scraul, Leith - 1734, 1760.

Lathan, Aaron - Welch Point - 1734, 1749, 1754.

Latham, John - Welch Point - 1755-1766.

Latham, Moses - Mount Hope - 1749-1766.

Lawrence, David - Providence - 1734.

Lawrence, Samuel - Coxes Prevention - 1749-1758.

Lawson, David - Providence - 1734, 1760.

Lawson, George - Addition, New Munster, Providence alias Goodwill, Society, Whites Folly, Fair Hill, Holys Contrivance - 1749-1766.

Lawson, Hugh - Colerain - 1734, 1739, 1760.

Lawson, John - Bohemia Manor - 1754-1761.

Lawson, Mary - Bohemia Manor - 1766.

Lawson, Roger - Society - 1734, 1739, 1760.

Leak, Richard - Addition, Fork - 1734, 1760.

Lee, Francis - Smiths Addition - 1749.

Leeds, John - Mount Hope - 1734, 1760.

Lesly, William - Wallaces Scraul - 1739.

Levin, Aaron - Town Point, Welch Point - 1734.

Levy, Isaac - No tract listed - 1758.

Lewellin, Richard - Picadelli - 1734, 1760.

Lewin, Aaron - Town Point, Welch Point - 1739, 1760.

Lewis, John - St. Johns Manor - 1739, 1754-1766.

Lewis, Richard - St. Johns Manor - 1734, 1749-1760.

Lewis, Robert - No tract listed - 1758, 1766.

Lillingstone, John - Anna Catherina - 1734, 1760.

Linsey, Thomas - Doughertys Endeavour - 1739, 1749, 1754.

Lloyd, Edward - Emorys Satisfaction, Greenbury - 1755-1761.

Lloyd, Phill - St. Augustine Manor, Rich Neck, Bohemia Manor - 1734, 1760.

Loftain, Thomas - Mount Pisgah - 1734.

Loftus, John - Lots 37 and 53 in Frederick Town - 1748, 1754.

Logan, Alexander - Snow Hill, Snow Hill Addition, Guile Glass - 1739-1766.

Longwell, Hugh - New Munster - 1766.

Longwell, William - New Munster - 1755-1766.

Losstain [Lofftain?], Thomas - Mount Pisgah - 1739, 1760.

Louttit, James - Chance, Skillington, Hog Pen neck, Sheffield, Go Look, Forlorn Hope, Harmans Mount, Mount Marman, Mesopotamia, Larrimores Neck Enlarged - 1766.

Love, Thomas - Loves Arrowhead, Hopewell, Level Addition - 1756-1766.

Lowe, Nicholas - Mount Harman, Sprys Hills - 1734, 1760.

Lowe, Col. Vincent - Lows Lott, Timber Ridge, Ladys Delight - 1734, 1760.

Lowman, Joseph - Kirkminster - 1749.

Lowman, Samuel (Heirs) - Brereton - 1734, 1739, 1760.

Lowry, James - Feddart - 1749-1766.

Lum [Lunn?], Michael - St. Johns Manor, Lums Venture, Stoney Range - 1749-1766.

Lusby, John - Larramores Neck Enlarged, Hazle Branch, Chance - 1749-1761.

Lucky, Robert - Emorys Endeavour - 1739.

Lunch, Anthony - Locust Thicket, Dividings - 1754-1766.

Lynes, Phil (Heirs - Charles County) - Friendship, Bella Connell - 1734, 1755-1760.

Lyon, John - Widows Lott - 1766.

McClintock, Francis - Hail Hill, Snow Hill, Snow Hill Addition - 1766.

McClure, James - New Munster - 1739.

McCoy, John (Susquehanna) - Glass House - 1761, 1766.

McCoy, John - New Munster - 1749-1766.

McCrackin, James - Mount Hope - 1749-1766.

McCreerie, John - Three Partners - 1766.

McCulloch, John - Addition, Providence - 1749, 1754.

McCutcheon, Samuel - Fair Hill - 1756-1761.

Mutchion [McCutchion?], Samuel - No tract listed - 1755.

McDaniell, John - Buck Hill - 1734, 1760.

McDonnel, John - Buck Hill - 1739.

McDowell, Alexander - Berrys Chance, Confusion, Chance, Society - 1754-1761.

McDowell, Jacob - Larramores Neck Enlarged, Larramores Addition - 1754-1761.

McDowell, Samuel - Newcastle Back Landing - 1749-1766.

McDowell, Thomas - Martins Delight - 1766.

McDowel, William - Martins Delight - 1739-1761.

McFarlin, Joseph - Rumseys Rambles, Society - 1739.

McHaffey (Machffey), Hugh - New Munster - 1749-1766.

McHeate, John - Hispaniola - 1760.

McKenny (Mackenny), Alexander - Feddard - 1734, 1760.

McKenny (McKinney), Garret - Feddart - 1739, 1749, 1754.

McKenny, Thomas - Strugle - 1734, 1760.

McKey (Mackey, Maccay), James - Hopewell, Mount Pleasant - 1734-1766.

McKey, John - Pleasant Garden - 1754-1766.

McKey, Robert - Hopewell, Bristows Convenience, Providence and Enlargement - 1749, 1754.

McKinley, John - Drum Greena - 1754.

McKnitt, Elizabeth - Glasgow, Hispaniola - 1749-1757.

McKoy, John - New Munster - 1754.

McManus, John - None So Good - 1734, 1739.

McNetts [McNitts?] Heirs - Glasgow, Hispaniola - 1739.

Maccay (McKey, Mackey), James - Hopewell, Mount Pleasant - 1734, 1749-1766.

Maccay (McKey), Robert - Bristolls Conveniency, Hopewell, Providence, Confusion, Barrys Chance, Society - 1734, 1749-1766.

Maccubbin, Zachariah - Wallnutt Thickett - 1734, 1760.

Mackenny (McKenny), Alexander - Feddard - 1734, 1760.

Mackey, Mrs. Araminta - Grange, Friendship, Bella Connell, Inspection, Elk Plains, Hintons Conveniency, Thompsons Town - 1749.

Mackey (McKey, Maccay), James - Hopewell, Mount Pleasant - 1734, 1749-1766.

Mackey, John - Pleasant Garden - 1749.

Macklehany, Thomas - No tract listed - 1734.

Macknett, John - Glasgow, Hispaniola - 1734, 1760.

MacNeale, John - Hispaniola - 1734.

Maffett, James (Heirs) - Maidenhead, Hollinsworth, Partners Parcels - 1734-1761.

Maffett, William (Heirs) - Bell Tarr, Gorrey, Tilly Broom, Vanbebbers Forrest - 1756-1766.

Mainly, John (Heirs) - Colletstown - 1734-1761.

Manado, Peter - St. Johns Mannor - 1734, 1760.

Mansell, Thomas - St. Xabarias, Woodbridge, Worsall Mannor, Ignatious - 1734, 1760.

Manycozens, Michael - 2nd and 4th of Heaths Parcels, Middle Parcels, Stocktons Addition, Scraps - 1734-1766.

Marsh, Thomas - Middle Plantation - 1739-1766.

Marshall, Mary - No tract listed - 1734.

Marshall, Thomas - No tract listed - 1734, 1760.

Matthews, Hugh (Papist) - Vulcans Rest, Coxes Forrest - 1758, 1760, 1761.

Mathews, Dr. Hugh, Jr. - Vulcans Rest, Coxes Forrest - 1734-1766.

Matthiason, Hugh - Mattson Town - 1749, 1754.

Mathison, Mathias - Cornelienson, Successor, Sweedland - 1734, 1760.

Mathiason, Mathew (Heirs) - Mathiasons, Matsons Range - 1734, 1760.

Matthewsson, Widow - Successor, Sweedland - 1734, 1760.

Matthiason, Mary - Matthiason - 1739.

Mattinson, James (Heirs) - Mattinson - 1734, 1760.

Mauldin, Benjamin (Heirs) - Two Necks, Colletstown - 1749-1766.

Maulding, Francis - Collets Town, Two Necks, Mount Colleston - 1734, 1749-1766.

Mauldin, Widow - Collets Town, Two Necks - 1739.

Meekins, Peter - Meekins Adventure - 1755, 1758.

Mercer (Marcer), Robert - Barbadoes, Indian Range, Mountsfield, Addition to Mount Herman, Hermans Mount, Mountsfield Addition, Larramores Neck - 1734-1766.

Mercer, Thomas - Indian Range, Hermans Range - 1734, 1739, 1760.

Mercer, William - Dayleys Desire - 1734-1766.

Middleton, Lutener - Clayton - 1734, 1760.

Miller, Abraham - Simms Forrest - 1755-1766.

Miller, Andrew - Knowlwood - 1766.

Miller, David - No tract listed - 1758.

Millar, Jane - Whites Folly - 1739.

Millar (Miller), Thomas - Collets Town, Steelmans Delight - 1739-1766.

Milligan, George - Baldwins Enlargement, Corborough, McGregorys Delight, Savins Rest, Skelton - 1754-1766.

Mills, Thomas - Jones Green Spring - 1749, 1754.

Millson, Saunders - Ransom Cell - 1734, 1760.

Miner, Thomas (for Adam Wallace's Heirs) - Kirkminster, Blankensteins Park - 1739.

Mirick, David - Griffin - 1739.

Mitchell, Edward - Siniqua Point - 1758, 1761, 1766.

Mitchell (Mitcell), Robert - New Munster - 1749-1761.

Mitchell, William - Coxes Fancy - 1734, 1754-1766.

Mollyneux, Richard - Woodbridge, Askmore, St. Ignatius, St. Xavarius, Worsell Mannor - 1749.

Money, John - Larramores Neck, Larramores Neck Enlarged, Mesopotamia, Fryers Neglect, Augustines Defiance, Head of the Ponds, Homely, Hendricks Choice - 1749-1766.

Money, Robert, Sr. - Larramores Neck Enlarged - 1734-1760.

Moore, Mordecai (Anne Arundel) - Timber Ridge - 1734, 1760.

Moore, Nathaniel - Addition, St. Johns Town - 1755-1757.

Moore, Thomas - St. Johns Town, Addition - 1739, 1749, 1754.

Morgan, Ann - Fryers Hills - 1766.

Morgan, Edward - Shrewsbury, Jamaica - 1749.

Morgan, Hugh - Zebulans Fancy - 1734-1760.

Morgan, James - Shrewsbury, Fryers Hills - 1734-1760.

Morgan, John - Friars Hills - 1739.

Morgan, Robert - Mount Johnson - 1755-1766.

Morgan, William (Heirs) - Larrimores Neck Enlarged - 1734, 1754-1766.

Morris, John (Heirs) - Batchelors Folly - 1734, 1760.

Morris, Robert (Heirs) - Lovell [Levell?] - 1734, 1760.

Mounts, Christopher - Soleson, Mounts Field - 1734, 1760.

Mount [Mounts], Martha - Hollowing Point - 1734, 1755, 1758.

Mullineaux, Richard - Woodbridge, Askmore, St. Ignatius, St. Exavarius, Worshall Manor - 1739.

Nash, Richard (Heirs) - High Park - 1734, 1760, 1761.

Nash, John - Nashes Adventure - 1754.

Nash, Thomas - Nashes Adventure - 1755-1766.

Nicholls, Griffin (Griffith) - Land Oare, Contention, Dolvain - 1734, 1755-1760.

Nowland, Daniel - Green Spring - 1734, 1739, 1749-1766.

Nowland, Darby (Heirs) - Brandon Bridge - 1734, 1760.

Nowland, Dennis - Brandon Bridge, Coxes Forrest, Worsal Manor, Wood Bridge - 1734-1761.

Nowland (Noland), James - Brandon Bridge, Coxs Forrest, Worsall Manor, Wood Bridge, Vulcans Rest - 1758, 1761, 1766.

Nowland, Mary - Hopewell - 1734-1761.

Noland, Silvester - Dayleys Desire - 1758, 1761, 1766.

Nowland, William - Glass House - 1755-1761.

Noxon, Peter - Heaths Level Parcel - 1749-1761.

Numbers, Isaac - Salem - 1734, 1760.

Numbers, John - St. Johns Manor - 1734, 1760.

Numbers, Peter (Heirs) - Clemerson, Clemerson Addition - 1734, 1739, 1760.

Nutt, John - Black Marsh - 1749-1761.

Ofley, Michael (Heirs) - High Offley - 1734, 1760.

Ogle, Thomas - Knowlwood, Bohemia Sisters, Francina - 1755-1766.

Oldfield, George - Georges Friendship, Bristow Moyety, Gloster Moyety - 1734, 1760.

Oldham, Edward - Oldhams Venture, Kennedys Adventure - 1749-1766.

Oldham, Zebulon (Heirs) - Siniqua Point - 1766.

Onion, Stephen - Stoney Island, Nostradamus, Rupel Onion - 1739-1761.

Onion, Stephen and Co. (Iron Works) - Gefarruson, Partnership, Gotham Bush, Perke Island - 1734, 1760.

Osman, Catherine - Perry Point - 1734.

Othoson, Robert - Clemerson, Homely - 1739.

Otterson, Garrett - Homely, Clemerson - 1734, 1760.

Otterson (Othoson), Otho - Head of the Ponds, Homely, Heaths Range, Norland - 1734-1761.

Owens, Stephen (Heirs) - No tract listed - 1755 [1758?].

Ozier, John - Swan Harbour - 1739, 1749.

Paine, John - St. Johns Town - 1734, 1760.

Painter, Nicholas (Heirs) - Gloster Moyety, Bristow Moyety - 1734, 1760.

Palmer, William - Dover - 1734, 1760.

Parish, Edward - Hay Down - 1734.

Parsons, William - Town Point - 1734, 1760.

Passmore, Augustine - Bear Point, Doe Hill - 1749-1766.

Pasmore, John - Content, Jacobs Adventure, Partners Parcel, Frisbys Venture, New Munster - 1739-1766.

Pate, Richard - Boerne - 1734, 1760.

Patten (Patton), Robert (Heirs) - Hispaniola, Bullens Range, Uppermost - 1739-1766.

Patterson, David - Widows Lott - 1766.

Patterson (Pattison), Robert - Larkins Desire, Teagues Chance, Doughertys Desire - 1749-1761.

Patterson, Samuel - Larkins Desire, Holland - 1766.

Paulson, Paul - Glass House - 1734, 1739, 1756-1760.

Peace (Pearce), Henry Ward - Bohemia Sisters, Haydown, New Intersection, Poplar Neck, Pearces Lane, Pearces Beginning - 1761, 1766.

Pearce, Andrew - Addition to the Rounds, Andrews Square, Carborough, Rounds, Pearces Lott, Pearces Meadow - 1758, 1761, 1766.

Pearce (Pierce), Benjamin - Rounds, Addition to Rounds, Corbrough, Andrews Square, Sheer Mould and Colter, Larimores Conveniency, Money Worth, Poplar Neck, Haydown, New Intersection, Bohemia Sisters - 1749-1760.

Pearce, Col. Benjamin (Heirs) - Addition to Rounds, Andrews Square, Corborough, Rounds - 1734-1761.

Pearce (Peirce), Daniel - Worlds End, New Munster - 1734, 1760.

Pearce (Peirce), Henry - No tract listed - 1734.

Pearce, Henry Ward - See "Henry Ward Peace," q.v.

Pearce (Peirce), Thomas - Gibbons Green, Vacancy to Gibbons Green - 1734-1766.

Peirce, Col. William - Addition to Rounds, Andrews Square, Corborough, Rounds - 1734, 1758.

Pennington, Abraham - No tract listed - 1734, 1760.

Pennington, Benjamin - Two Branches - 1766.

Pennington, Ebenezer - Buntingtons Addition, Civility - 1766.

Pennington, Henry, Sr. - Buntingtons Addition, Civility - 1749-1761.

Pennington, Henry, Jr. - Buntington - 1754-1766.

Pennington, Henry (Heirs) - Buntington - 1734-1758.

Pennington, John, Sr. - Two Branches - 1739.

Pennington, John - Two Branches - 1734, 1749-1761.

Penington, John (N. E. River) - Arundel, Two Necks - 1734, 1760.

Pennington (Penington), Otho - Heaths Range - 1749-1766.

Pennington, Rebecca - Gibsons Green - 1739-1766.

Pennington, Richard - Pains Lott - 1754.

Pennington, Robert - Mulberry Mould - 1734, 1755-1766.

Pennington, Robert, Sr. - Mulberry Dock - 1739, 1749, 1754.

Pennington, Robert, Jr. (Heirs) - Happy Harbour, Buntington - 1739.

Pennington, Samuel - Two Branches, Rich Lott - 1766.

Pennington, William - Norland - 1739, 1749.

Pennington, William Boyer - Hazle Branch - 1766.

Perkins, Isaac - Hopewell, Lydias Joynture - 1734.

Perks, Edmond - Honey Island - 1734, 1760.

Perry, George - Perry Point - 1734, 1760.

Perry, John - Perry Point - 1734, 1760.

Peters, Anthony - Outer Light - 1734, 1760.

Peters, Christian - Vanbebbers Forrest - 1739-1761.

Peters, Christopher - Vanbebbers Forrest - 1734, 1760.

Peterson, Adam - Fatigue - 1749-1761.

Phillips, Nathaniel - St. Johns Mannor - 1734, 1739, 1749, 1760.

Phillips, Samuel - St. Johns Mannor - 1739, 1749.

Phillips, Thomas - Raccoons Range, Philips Bottom - 1734, 1739, 1760.

Phips, Isaiah - No tract listed - 1734.

Picoe, Peter - St. Johns Manor - 1734, 1739, 1760.

Pilgrim, Thomas (Barbadoes) - New Munster - 1734, 1760.

Pinkerton, Alexander - Fox Harbour - 1755-1761.

Pollard, Edward (Heirs - England) - Anchor and Hope - 1734, 1760.

Pollock, William - New Munster - 1734, 1739, 1760.

Polyoung, John - Coxs Forrest - 1739.

Poor, Walter - Perry Point - 1734.

Popish Clergy - Askmore, St. Ignatius, St. Xaverius, Worsall Manor, Woodbridge - 1754-1766.

Porter, Andrew - Smiths Fort - 1766.

Porter, George - Banks - 1766.

Porter, James (Octarora-Susquehanna) - Hopewell, Poplar Valley, Slate Hill, Strugle, Steels, Good Luck - 1755-1766.

Porter, James (Sassafras) - Benjamins Level, Middle Grounds - 1734, 1749-1766.

Porter, Robert - Hazle Branch - 1749-1766.

Poulson, Paul - Glass House - 1754, 1755.

Poulson (Poalson), Peter - Feddard - 1749-1766.

Prentice, William - Prentices Second Choice - 1734, 1760.

Presbury, George - No tract listed - 1734.

Price, Andrew - Dividings - 1749-1758.

Price, Benjamin - Locust Thicket, Maidenhead - 1758-1766.

Price, Ephraim - Clemerson, Clemersons Addition - 1749-1766.

Price, Henry - No tract listed - 1734.

Price, James - Indian Range - 1760.

Price, John - Indian Range, Mesopotamia - 1734, 1739, 1760.

Price, Joseph - Coxes Purchase - 1739, 1749.

Price, Joshua - Coxes Purchase - 1754.

Price, Nathaniel - No tract listed - 1755.

Price, Nicholas - Henricksons Choice - 1756-1761.

Price, Thomas - Horns, Meekings Adventure, Spernons Delight, Wales - 1734-1766.

Price, Thomas, Jr. - Uppermost - 1739, 1755.

Price, William - Maidenhead, Locust Thicket - 1734, 1739, 1760.

Price, William, Jr. - Dividings - 1734-1766.

Price, William, Sr. - Abrahams Promise, Locust Thicket, Maidenhead, Dividings - 1734, 1749-1766.

Pronce, Charles - Pronceys Discovery - 1734, 1760.

Proprietors of Cecil Town - Mulberry Mould, Mulberry Dock - 1739-1766.

Quigly [Quigley], Charles - Quigley's Lodge - 1734-1766.

Ranbrey, John - Plump Point Fork - 1754.

Rankey, John - Plumb Point Fork - 1755, 1758, 1761.

Rankin (Rinkin), Adam - New Munster - 1739.

Rawson, Laurence - Steels Head - 1734, 1760.

Read, John (Pennsylvania) - Kingsley, Reads Addition - 1766.

Read, John - Kingsley, New Munster, Reads Addition - 1734, 1749-1766.

Redgrave, Abraham - Batchellors Folly - 1734, 1760.

Redgrave, Joseph - None So Good in Finland - 1749-1761.

Redman, William Fitts - No tract listed - 1734.

Reese, William - Bohemia Sisters - 1734, 1760.

Regan, Charles - Glass House - 1766.

Revell, Randell - New Arte [Ark?] - 1734, 1760.

Reyley, Bryan - Vulcans Rest - 1749.

Reynolds, Edward - Sarahs Joynture - 1734, 1739, 1760.

Reynolds, Henry - Marsh - 1734, 1760.

Reynolds, Hugh - Essex Lodge, Mill Pond - 1766.

Reynolds, James - Sarahs Jointure - 1749-1766.

Reynolds, John - Swan Harbour, Sarahs Joynture, Foxes Palace - 1734, 1760.

Reynolds, Nicholas - Sarahs Joynture - 1734, 1760.

Reynolds, Richard - Knowlwood - 1734-1760.

Reynolds, Thomas - Reynolds Fortune - 1734, 1760.

Reynolds, William - Sarahs Joynture - 1734, 1739, 1760.

Richardson, John - Willer Brook, Northampton - 1734, 1760.

Richardson, Richard - No tract listed - 1734.

Richardson, Thomas - Hispaniola - 1766.

Richardson, Widow - Chance - 1739.

Richardson, William - Hispaniola - 1734, 1754-1761.

Richey, James - Sligoe - 1749-1761.

Richey, John - Sligo, Monin - 1734, 1739, 1760.

Richey, Robert - Sligo, Monin - 1734, 1739, 1760.

Richard, William - Hispaniola - 1760.

Rickets, Caleb - Bottle, Resurvey of Smiths Discovery - 1766.

Rickets, David - Kings Aim - 1749-1761.

Rickets, John - Smiths Discovery, Bottle, Rickets Triangle - 1749-1766.

Rickets, Mary - Kings Aim - 1766.

Rickets, Thomas - Flint Hill - 1755, 1760, 1761.

Ricketts, Thomas (Heirs) - Dole Dife, Killa Villa, Laranim, Worth Little, Flint Hill - 1734-1766.

Ridgley, Nicholas - Greenfield, Quigleys Grove - 1734, 1760.

Rigbie, John - Stoney Chace - 1766.

Rigbie, Sabina - Antigua, Antcastle, Little Chance, Money Worth, Prevention, Pig Point, Rumseys Discovery, Rumseys Double Parcel, Virginity - 1766.

Rippin, Capt. Henry - Essex Lodge - 1734, 1739, 1760.

Roberts, Dorothy - Fryers Hills, Horns - 1766.

Roberts, James (Heirs) - Two Necks - 1739-1766.

Roberts, John, Sr. - Horns, Mesopotamia - 1734-1766.

Roberts, John, Jr. - Fryars Hills - 1749-1761.

Robertson (Robinson, Robison), George - Consent - 1734-1766.

Robertson (Robinson), Valentine - Brereton - 1749-1766.

Robinett, Samuel - Providence - 1734, 1739, 1760.

Robison, Valentine - Brereton - 1749-1766.

Rock, George - Arundel - 1749, 1754.

Rodes, Nicholas - Larkins Desire - 1734, 1760.

Rogers, Matthew - Prevention - 1734, 1760.

Rogers, Parnall - Wheelers Point, Chance, Goe Look, Forelorne Hope, Addition - 1734, 1760.

Rogers, Thomas - Clemerson - 1734, 1760.

Rogers, William - Providence - 1758, 1761, 1766.

Ross, Hugh - New Munster - 1739.

Ross, John (for Vansant) - New Munster - 1749, 1754.

Ross, Widow - Griffin - 1739.

Rowland, Robert - Society, Confusion, Rowlands Chance, Rowlands Venture - 1754-1766.

Rudolph, Hanse - St. Johns Manor - 1754-1761.

Ruley, Anthony - Maidenhead - 1766.

Ruly, Michael - Maidenhead - 1739-1761.

Ruley, Sarah - Addition to Campbells Dividend - 1749-1757.

Rumsey, Benjamin - Bailey, Round Stone, Withers, Necessity - 1766.

Rumsey, Charles - Newhall, Addition to Newhall, Concord, Swan Harbour - 1734, 1760, 1766.

Rumsey, Edward - Rumseys Rambles, Wrights Lott - 1734, 1760.

Rumsey, Sabina - Manwarring Hall, Stocktons Addition, Money Worth, Dividend, 2nd and 4th Heaths Parcels, Triumph, Small Hopes, Davids Sheep

Fold, Baily, Round Stones, Shear Mould and Coulter, Middle Parcel, Wademores Neck, New Hall, Virginity - 1749, 1754.

Rumsey, William - Baldwins Lott, Dividend, Davids Sheepfold, 2nd and 4th Heaths Parcels, Little Addition, Manwering Hall, Middle Parcel, Rumseys Range, Stockton Addition, Shear Mould and Coulter, Sarahs Jointure, Small Hopes, Third of Heaths Parcels, Adjunction, Happy Harbour, Rumseys Negligence, Variation - 1754-1761.

Russell, James - Beaver Dam - 1754-1761.

Russell, William - Carloe - 1734, 1760.

Rutherford, Joseph - Widows Lott - 1766.

Rutter, Moses - Claybank - 1755-1766.

Rutter, Ralph - Claybank - 1734, 1760.

Rutter, Richard - Claybank - 1739, 1749, 1754.

Ryland, John - Seedfield alias Sedgefield - 1734-1761.

Ryland, John, Jr. - Mulberry Mould, Mulberry Dock - 1734-1761.

Ryland, Rebecca - Mulberry Mould - 1749-1757.

Ryland, Silvester - Mulberry Mould - 1758, 1761, 1766.

Ryland, Thomas - Mulberry Mould, Mulberry Dock - 1766.

Ryley, Micholas - Greenfield - 1734.

Ryley, Patrick - Rumford - 1734, 1760.

Ryley, William - Greenfield - 1734, 1760.

Sappington, Hercules - Dayleys Desire - 1766.

Sappington, Mathew - Dayleys Desire - 1734, 1760.

Sappington, Nathaniel - Dealeys Desire - 1739-1761.

Savin, John - Green Spring - 1749-1761.

Savin, Thomas, Sr. - Indian Range - 1739-1766.

Savin, William, Sr. - Dayleys Desire, Green Spring, Eyla - 1734-1761.

Savin, WIlliam, Jr. - Green Spring, Prosperity - 1756-1766.

Schee, Harman - Sedgefield, Heaths Range - 1734, 1760.

Schee, James - No tract listed - 1739, 1758, 1761.

Scott, Charles - Askmore - 1739-1766.

Scott, James - New Munster - 1749, 1754.

Scott, John - Francina - 1755-1757.

Scott, Walter - Askmore, Clifton - 1734, 1749-1766.

Scott, Walter, Sr. - Clifton - 1739.

Scott, Walter, Jr. - Askmore - 1739.

Sealy, George - Sealys Delight - 1734, 1760.

Seegar, John - Society - 1734.

Seferson, John - Sefersons Delight, Helmby [Holmley] - 1734.

Sequence, John - Arundel being part of Netherlands - 1734, 1760.

Sereney, Samuel - Bella Connell - 1734.

Severson, Ezekiel - Homely, Smoking Point alias Seversons Delight - 1766.

Severson, John - Sefersons Delight, Homely - 1739, 1760.

Severson (Sefferson), Thomas - Sefersons Point, Plantation, Prices Intelligence, Larrimores Neck - 1734-1766.

Sewell, Henry (Heirs) - Dividend - 1734, 1760.

Sewell, N. - No tract listed - 1734.

Sexton, George - Cornax Town - 1734, 1760.

Sharpe, Samuel - Blankesteens Forrest, Larrimores Neck - 1766.

Sharpe, Thomas - Confusion, Society - 1734-1766.

Sheppard, Thomas - Anchor and Hope, Larkins Desire, Rycrofts Choice - 1739, 1749-1766.

Sherwell, Adam - Three Partners - 1734, 1760.

Sherwell, William, Jr. - Three Partners - 1734, 1755-1761.

Simco, George - Anna Catharina - 1734-1766.

Simpers (Simpus), John - Simpus Meadows, Simpus Chance, Wasps Nest, New Spain - 1754-1766.

Simpers (Simpus), Thomas - Successor, Simpus Forrest, Concord, Tryal - 1734, 1755-1766.

Slayter, Petrus alias Vorsman - Bohemia Manor - 1734, 1760.

Smallwood, Holy - Mount Joy, Society - 1766.

Smith, Anthony (Anne Arundel) - Heaths Adventure, Holland - 1734, 1760.

Smith, Bartholomew - Dailys Desire - 1739.

Smith, Casper - Swan Harbour - 1734, 1760.

Smith, Fergus - Springs Head - 1739, 1749, 1754-1766.

Smith, Francis - Knowlwood, Locust Point - 1734, 1760.

Smith, Henry - Kirkminster - 1734, 1760.

Smith, James - Coxes Park, Rumseys Rambles - 1749, 1754.

Smith, John - New Munster, Bella Connell, Friendship, Wormust, Hacks Addition, Bewdly - 1734, 1755-1766.

Smith, Capt. Richard (Calvert County) - Smiths Fork - 1734.

Smith, Richard (Attorney) - Bennetts Grove - 1734, 1760, 1766.

Smith, Richard (Prince Georges) - Bennets Grove, Dailys Desire - 1739, 1755-1761.

Smith, Robert - Gorrey - 1766.

Smith, Samuel - Hollan, Heaths Adventure - 1749.

Smith, Thomas - Bryleys Desire - 1734, 1760.

Smith, William, Jr. - Thompsons Town, Duck Neck - 1734, 1760.

Smithson, Thomas - Pains Lott - 1760.

Snell, James' widow - Triangle - 1755-1761.

Snell, Jane - Triangle - 1766.

Snicker, Henry - Slate Hill, Mount Johnson - 1734, 1739, 1760.

Spencer, George (Heirs) - Danby - 1734, 1760.

Sprott, John - Clements Venture - 1739.

Spurne, Nicholas (Calvert County) - No tract listed - 1734.

Starett, John - New Munster - 1734, 1739, 1760.

Starkey, William - Worth Little - 1756-1766.

Stedman, Capt. John Hance - Successor, Long Point, Steelmans Point - 1734, 1760.

Stedham, Lulaff - Feddard - 1734.

Stedham, Rocloff - Feddart - 1739.

Steel, Archibald - New Munster - 1756, 1757.

Steel, Elizabeth - Steels - 1755-1766.

Steele, James - Gardners Forrest - 1734, 1739, 1760.

Steel, John - Parks Island (Perks Island), Bourns Forrest and Addition - 1749-1766.

Steele, Joseph - Society - 1734, 1739, 1760.

Steele, Walter - Success - 1755, 1758, 1761.

Stevens, George (Heirs) - Carroborough - 1734, 1760.

Stevens, John - London and Content - 1734, 1760.

Steward, William - Francina - 1755-1757.

Stidham, Lulaff - Feddard - 1760.

Still, Exell (Heirs) - No Name - 1734, 1760.

Stockton, John - New Garden, Abrahams Promse, Eyla - 1749-1766.

Stoops, John - Pains Lot - 1734, 1758-1766.

Stoops, Philip - Becks Meadows, Rook and Pill, Buntington, Frisbys Neglect, Hendricksons Oversight, Kings Aim, Mickum, Mapleton, Pains Lot, Pennworth, Philips Addition, Stoops Folly - 1739, 1749-1766.

Storey, Enoch - Storeys Meadows, Partnership - 1755-1766.

Storey, Robert - Netherland - 1734, 1739, 1760.

Stratton, Thomas - Hispaniola - 1734, 1760.

Stump, John - Hearts Delight, Gotham Bush - 1734-1766.

Sutton, John - Essex Lodge, Swan Hast[?] - 1739.

Sutton, Josia - Swan Harbour, Essex Lodge - 1734, 1760.

Sutton, Thomas (Heirs) - Suttons Forrest - 1734, 1760.

Swift, John - New Inspection - 1734, 1760.

Symons, Thomas - St. Johns Mannor - 1734, 1760.

Syms, Anthony (St. Marys Co.) - Syms Forrest - 1734, 1760.

Syms, Marmaduke - No tract listed - 1734.

Talbott, Col. George (Heirs) - Whitton Forrest, Kildare, Osmond, Netherlands, Rembergh, Portwaling, Middleton, Mellowland, New Connaught - 1734, 1760.

Tasker, Benjamin - No tract listed - 1734.

Taylor, Edward - Coxes Park, Rumseys Rambles, New Munster and Purchase - 1734, 1739, 1760.

Taylor, Matthew - Racoon Point - 1766.

Teague, William - Teagues Delight, Teagues Endeavour, New Connaught, Mount Pisgah - 1734, 1739, 1755-1760.

Temple, Ann - Perry Point - 1734, 1760.

Terry, Benjamin - No Name alias Wormust - 1739, 1749-1766.

Terry, Hugh (Heirs) - Swan Harbour - 1734, 1739, 1749.

Terry, Thomas - Addition, Bancks, Wormust - 1734, 1760.

Terry, Widow - Banks - 1739.

Thatcher, Hannah (widow) - New Munster - 1739, 1749, 1754.

They, John - Pennyworth - 1760.

Thomas, Benjamin - Griffin - 1749-1766.

Thomas, David - Griffin - 1734, 1760, 1766.

Thomas, John - Chance, Doll Dice - 1734, 1739, 1758-1761.

Thomas, Joseph - Feddard - 1734-1766.

Thomas, Joseph (Pennsylvania) - Griffin - 1766.

Thomas, Philip - Perry Point, Yorkshire - 1739, 1749-1766.

Thompson, Augustine - None So Good, Field - 1734, 1739, 1760.

Thompson, Ephraim - Bohemia Sisters - 1766.

Thompson, Jennet - Racoon Point - 1749-1761.

Thompson, Col. John (Heirs) - Choice, Thompsons Inspection, Savins Rest, Daniels Den, Middle Plantation, Money Worth, Corborough, Long Lane, Bohemia Sisters, Dunbarr - 1734-1760.

Thompson, John, Jr. - Dunbarr, Thompsons Inspection, Long Lane, Corborough, Addition, Augustines Defiance - 1739, 1749.

Thompson, John, Sr. - Choice - 1739.

Thompson, John Dockra - Addition, Augustines Defiance, Dunbar or Dunton, Long Lane, Thompsons Inspection, Corborough - 1766.

Thompson, Joseph - Lydias Jointure, Hopewell - 1734, 1749-1766.

Thompson, Joshua [or Joseph?] - No tract listed - 1734.

Thompson, Martha - Racoon Point - 1749-1761.

Thompson, Mathew - Choice - 1766.

Thompson (Thomson), Richard - Bohemia Sisters - 1739-1766.

Thompson, Robert (Heirs) - Bohemia Sisters - 1749-1766.

Thompson, Samuel - Choice, Choice Addition, Goree - 1749-1766.

Thomson, Robert (Heirs) - Moneyworth, Daniels Den - 1739, 1755.

Thoms, John - No tract listed - 1734.

Tillson, Derrick - Oyster Point - 1734, 1760.

Tilton, Humphrey - Intermixt - 1734, 1760.

Toas, John - Cross Saile - 1734, 1760.

Toby, Cornelius - Hallowing Point, Mounts Field - 1739, 1758.

Toutchstone, Andrew - Harts Delight - 1766.

Touchstone, Richard - Perry Point - 1734.

Tree, John - Clemerson - 1734-1761.

Trumbull, Robert - Ariana - 1734, 1739.

Tully, Michael - Knavery Out Done by Justice - 1749-1761.

Turnbull, Robert - Clements Venture - 1760.

Underhill, Thomas - Kennedys Adventure, Underhills Endeavour - 1761, 1766.

Umberston (Humberstone), George - Heaths Outlet - 1749-1758.

Van Bebber, Adam (Heirs) - Clifton, Blankesteens Forrest, Newcastle Back Landing - 1749.

Vanbebber, Henry, Sr. - Francina - 1755-1766.

Vanbebber, Isaac - Bohemia Manor - 1734, 1760.

Vanbebber, James - Bohemia Manor - 1734, 1760.

Vanbebber, Mathias (Heirs) - Clifton, Blankesteens Forrest, Bohemia Manor, St. Augustine Manor, Newcastle Back Landing, Intention, Milcoms Island -1734-1760.

Vanderculon, Renier - Suackcocsee[?] - 1734, 1760.

Vanderhiden, Mathias - Coasters Harbour, Lee, Brownly, Rounds, Wheelers Warren, Pasture Point, Bohemia Sisters, Locust Neck, Wormust - 1734, 1739, 1755-1760.

Van Horn, Barnett - Indian Range - 1754-1766.

Vanhorne, Nicholas - Seedfield alias Sedgefield, Heaths Range - 1734-1761.

Van Pool, Jacob - Fox Harbour - 1754.

Vansant, Cornelius (Heirs) - New Munster - 1734, 1739, 1760.

Vansant, John - New Munster - 1734, 1760.

Veazey, Edward - Devidings, True Game, Addition to Campbells Dividend, Campbells Dividend, Salem - 1734, 1755-1766.

Veazey (Vesey), George - Locust Thicket - 1739, 1749-1761.

Veazey, James - St. Johns Manor - 1734, 1749-1766.

Veazey, John - Rumford, Manchester, True Game, Essex Lodge, Frisbys Prime Choice, Frisbys Farm, Addition to Frisbys Farm, Good Luck, Dividings - 1734-1766.

Veazey, William - Spernons Delight - 1734, 1760.

Vestry of St. Mary Ann Parish - Clayfall - 1749-1766.

Vestry of St. Stephens (North Sassafras) - North Level - 1734-1766.

Vestall, William - Levell - 1734.

Visitors of the Free School - Banks - 1734, 1739, 1755-1766.

Vorsman, Petrus alias Slayter - No tract listed - 1734.

Walgatt (Wallgatt), Otho - Ship Haven - 1734, 1760.

Walker, Hugh - Providence - 1734-1761.

Walker, Thomas - Sidney - 1734, 1760.

Wall, Edward - No tract listed - 1734, 1760.

Wallace, Adam (Heirs) - Blankesteens Park, Kirkminster - 1734, 1739, 1760.

Wallace, Andrew - Blankesteens Forrest, Castle Fine, Newport, Charlymount - 1734-1766.

Wallace, David - Snow Hill, Snow Hill Addition, Hail Hill - 1734, 1760.

Wallace, James - Blankensteens Park, Kirkminster, Thompsons Town Point, Blankensteens Park Resurveyed, James Venture, Suttons Forrest, Range - 1749-1766.

Wallace, John - New Munster - 1734-1760.

Wallace, Joseph - Monim, Sligo, Wallaces Scrawl, Broad Ax, Castle Fine, Charlemont, Zebulons Fancy - 1749-1766.

Wallace, Mathews - Wallaces Scrawl - 1734, 1739.

Wallace, Mathew, Jr. - New Munster - 1734, 1760.

Wallace, Michael - Goodwill, Lidias Choice, Lidias Jointure, Mount Pleasant, Providence - 1734-1766.

Wallace, William - Castle Fine, Garney Gift - 1734-1760.

Walmsley (Wamsly), Robert - Larramores Addition, Larramores Neck, Larramores Neck Enlarged, Augustines Defiance, Clemrson - 1739-1766.

Walmsley, William - Shrewsbury - 1749-1766.

Ward, Alice - Locust Thickett - 1734, 1760.

Ward, Henry - Chance Resurveyed, Addition to Chance - 1734, 1749-1761.

Ward, James Chetham - Greenfield - 1761, 1766.

Ward, John of William - Coneticutt, Neighbors Grudge - 1734, 1760.

Ward, John of Henry - Chance Resurveyed, Addition to Chance - 1766.

Ward, John, Sr. - Sarahs Jointure - 1766.

Ward, John, Jr. - Locust Thicket - 1734, 1749-1766.

Ward, Capt. John (Heirs) - Wards Knowledge, Coxs Forrest, Wards Addition, Strange, Colletton, Green Field - 1734, 1739, 1760.

Ward, Col. John - Colleton, Pains Lott, Wards Knowledge, Coxes Forrest, Wards Addition, Strange - 1739.

Ward, John (Surveyor) - Strange, Salem - 1766.

Ward, Nathaniel - Sperrons Delight - 1758, 1761, 1766.

Ward, Peregrine - Greenfield, Resurvey on Colleton, Resurvey on Wards Knowledge and Wards Addition, Pains Lott - 1734-1766.

Ward, Rebeccah - Pains Lott - 1734, 1760.

Ward, Thomas - Colletton - 1734, 1739, 1760.

Ward, William - Connecticut, Neighbours Grudge, Henricksons Addition, Henry and Ward - 1734-1766.

Ward, William (Carpenter) - Harmans Mount, Indian Range - 1734.

Ware, Robert - Range - 1734, 1760.

Warner, Edward - Grove, Hazlemore, Chance - 1734, 1739, 1760.

Warrilome, William - Carpenters Lott - 1734, 1760.

Watson (Wattson), Abraham - St. Clairs Purchase - 1734-1761.

Watson, Isaac Decow - St. Clairs Purchase - 1766.

Watson, Hannah alias Johnson - Kirkminster - 1754.

Watson (Wattson), John (Heirs) - No tract listed - 1734.

Watson, William - St. Clairs Purchase - 1739, 1749-1766.

Weatherspoon, David - Indian Range Resurveyed - 1754, 1755.

Wells, Zerobabell - Wells Point - 1734, 1760.

Whan, William - Society - 1758, 1761, 1766.

Wheeler, Ignatius - Yorkshire - 1755-1761.

Wheeler, John (Heirs) - Martins Nest, Round Stone, Moreland, Heaths Range - 1734, 1760.

Wheeler, Samuel - Browning Neglect, Bristow, Uppermost - 1734, 1760.

Whitaker, Thomas - Coxes Park, Rumseys Rambles - 1755-1766.

White, Alexander - Whites Folly, Raccoon Point, Pleasant Mount, Plumb Point - 1734, 1739, 1760.

White, John - Meant More - 1734, 1760.

White, Nicholas - Coxes Park, Rumseys Rambles - 1755-1766.

White, Thomas - Castle Green - 1734, 1760.

Whiteacre, Robert - Coxes Park - 1739, 1749, 1754.

Whittworth, Shadrick - Eagles Nest - 1734, 1760.

Wholachan, Orphans of - Woodbridge - 1734. [See "Wholachan Woodbridge," q.v., for possible genealogical connection].

Wier, Thomas - New Munster - 1766.

Wilbank (Wilbanch), Her. Frederick - Companys Fort - 1734, 1760.

Wilcox, Martin - No tract listed - 1766.

Wild, Josa - Black Marsh - 1739.

Wilds (Wiles), Samuel - Bottle, Dolevain - 1739, 1758.

Wilkinson, Christopher - Beaverdam - 1761.

Wilmer, Edward Pryce - Clifton - 1766.

Wilmer, Lambert - Wilmers Arcadia - 1760.

Wiley, John - New Castle Back Landing - 1734.

Wills, John - Black Marsh, Cafinruro - 1734, 1760.

Wills (Wiles), Samuel - Springs Head - 1734, 1755, 1760.

Williams, Elias - Bohemia Sisters - 1749-1766.

Williams, John - Anchor and Hope, Roycrofts Choice - 1734, 1760.

Willmer, Lambert - Wilmers Arcadia - 1734.

Willson, Adam - New Munster - 1755, 1761.

Willy, John - New Castle Back Landing - 1760.

Wilson, Adam - New Munster - 1749-1766.

Willson, Mathews - Nottingham - 1734, 1760.

Willson, Robert - Providence - 1734, 1739, 1760.

Wilton, Robert - No tract listed - 1734.

Winder, John - Isle of Oxley - 1734, 1760.

Winsly, Benjamin - New Munster - 1739.

Winsley, Thomas - Winsleys Lott - 1734, 1755, 1760.

Winsmore, William - Pipe Elme - 1734, 1760.

Winterberry, John - True Game, Henricks Choice - 1739.

Withers, William - No tract listed - 1755, 1758.

Withers, Zebulon - No tract listed - 1755, 1758.

Witherspoon, David - Indian Range Resurveyed - 1756-1761.

Witherspoon, Thomas - Indian Range Resurveyed, Fatigue, Buntington and Happy Harbour - 1766.

Wood, Joseph (Heirs) - Bohemia Sisters, Francina - 1734-1761.

Wood, Josia - No tract listed - 1734.

Wood, William - Bohemia Sisters - 1749.

Woodbridge, Wholachan - Woodbridge - 1760.

Worthington, William - Askmore - 1734.
Wroth (Wrath), James - Henricks Choice, Mesopotamia - 1739-1766.
Wroth (Wrath), Kinvan - Clemerson - 1749, 1754.
Wroth (Wrath), Thomas - Resurvey on Bachlers Hill, Hazle Branch - 1749-1766.
Yoeman, Thomas - Woodland - 1734, 1760.
York, Jane - St. Johns Mannor - 1734, 1760.
Yorkson [Yorkvon?], John - No tract listed - 1734.
Young, Jacob - Clay Fall - 1734, 1760.
Young, James - Beare Point - 1734, 1739, 1760.
Young, Joseph - Clay Fall - 1734, 1754-1760.
Young, Mary - Joans Adventure - 1734, 1755-1760.
Young, Samuel - Clay Fall - 1739.
Young, Robert - Hopewell - 1766.

TAXABLE PERSONS IN CECIL COUNTY IN 1752 (PAGE 1 OF 10):
William Richardson; James Nowland; Joseph Gibbs; Myrtough Shea; John
Rowls; Silvester Nowland; Benjamin Ridge; John Wilson; Hugh McCully;
Joseph Laughran; Thomas Saunders; William Hog; Philip Reily; William
Jones; Jacob Jacobs; James Reed; Daniel McVay; John Driscol; Charles
Shaddock; Isaac Alwinkle; Samuel Abbot; Michael Chambers; Benjamin
Richison; Richard McCarry; John Welch; James Weldon; Thomas Weathes-
by; Archibald Curry; John Rosser; Abraham Hollings; Charles Carty; David
Rees; Daniel Geers; John Loftus; Nicholas Kearney; John Boyd; To
Elizabeth Beaston - Jno. Beaston; John Beaston; Isaac Gibbs; John Malster;
Philip Stoops; Nathaniel Dobson; John Crosby; Robert Noble; Sylvester
Ryland; William Hogans; John Sewall; George Bland; Robert David; John
Ward and John A---- [page torn]; William Pearce; At Daniel Bryan's Quarter
- 2 slaves; Cornelius Vansant and Benjamin Vansant; Daniel McClean and
William McNeily; John Ashford and Thomas Caslin; George Humberstone
and Jonathan Humberstone; James O'Neile and Lawrence Connolly; Bartlet
Smith and John Loddum; Augustine Savina and Thomas Long; Bryan
Grimes and Andrew McDonnough; Edward Tully and Dennis McGee; Ben-
jamin Beaston and William McGorran; John Ozier, Jr. and Samuel Johnson;
William Jones and James Ruxton; Benedict Penington and John Dillon;
Gavin Hutchinson and Jacob Vanhorn; Sarah Penington's 2 slaves; Matthias
Hendrickson and John Brown; John Gears and John McClouds; Elizabeth
Jones' 2 slaves; William Bateman, Jr. and Robert Banks; John Bavington and
David Gray; Nicholas Vanhorn and Isaac Vanhorn; Charles Welding and
John Welding; To Susanah Vansant - George Vansant and Zachariah Van-
sant; Nathaniel Sappington and Francis Aaron; Samuel Akey and Neil Mc-
Fadden; Prince Snow, William Gale, and Ben---- ---- [page torn]; John Savin,
Jr., Owen Sullivane, and 1 slave; Robert Young, Patrick Hagan, and 1 slave;
William Savin and 2 slaves; James Hughes, Sr., James Hughes and William
White; Thomas Pearce, John Pearce and Hugh Craige; Henry Penington,
Hugh Carr and 1 slave; Michael Tully, Andrew Croker and 1 slave; John
Ozier, Sr., William Ozier and 1 slave; John Stoops, John Farrel and 1 slave;
John Coppen and 2 slaves; Thomas Penington, Thomas Roberts and 1 slave;

John McDermott, Robert Young and 1 slave; William Bateman, Sr., John Bateman and 1 slave; William Terry, Elisha Terry and 1 slave; Thomas Ryland, Sr., Stephen Ryland and John Ryland; Robert Penington, William Pearce and 1 slave; Clift Hemmings, James Hemmings and Darby Furey; William Mercer, Sr., William Mercer and Benjamin Mercer; James Coppen, William McCloud and 1 slave; William James, Jacob Mackey and Thomas Willinton; Daniel Nowland, Thomas Nowland and Ephraim Nowland.

TAXABLE PERSONS IN CECIL COUNTY IN 1752 (PAGE 2 OF 10):
James Macombs, John Macombs, Bartholomew Macombs and John Glaspy; Otho Penington, Nathaniel Buchanan, Matthew Dowlon and 1 slave; William Bordley and 3 slaves; Joseph Lilley, James Nowland and 2 slaves; Thomas Hynson, William Dulany and 2 slaves; Nathaniel Hynson, David Ring, John Manmuth and 1 slave; Nicholas Dorrell, Sr., Nicholas Dorrell, James Dorrell and Joseph Jones; James Porter, Michael McKough, John McCormack and John Ryland; Richard Penington, Richard Pearce, William Ladner and Richard Penington; To Ann Freeman - 4 slaves; Benjamin Benson and 3 slaves; Cornelius Brady, Bryan MacHugh and 2 slaves; Augustine Boyer, Benjamin Nowland and 3 slaves; Thomas Beard, Sr., James Beard, Lewis Beard, Thomas Beard and 1 slave; Hartlet Sappington, Daniel Aaron, John Barry, John Artagee and William Bolan; Richard Parsley, John McCan, James Webb, Matthew Hawes and 1 slave; Joseph Redgrave and 4 slaves; Robert Porter, Sr., Robert Porter, James Jones, John McCurry and Joseph Fullerton; To Mary Pearce - Andrew Pearce, Daniel Pearce and 3 slaves; Philip Stoops, Sr. and 4 slaves; John Jackson, William Jackson, John Watson, Herbert Rincer and 1 slave; John Ryland, Sr. and 4 slaves; George Millegan, John McGanner, Christopher Hardcastle and 2 slaves; Dennis Nowland and 5 slaves; George Cunningham, John Pugsby and 4 negroes; Edward Furroner, Barnet Grimes, Thomas Ryland, Thomas Harley, Edmond Kelly and John Standford; William Abbot, James Penington, Patrick Coyne and 3 slaves; Nathan Dobson and 6 slaves; David Rickets, Thomas Keys, Stephen Kennard, Richard Caulk and 3 slaves; John Caulk, Oliver Caulk, Oliver Caulk, Sr. and 4 slaves; John Cooper, John Chambers, John Edwards and two other names missing [page torn]; Timothy Brannan, Dominick McDermott, William Aggin, Thomas O'Lahan, Charles Hillyard, William Gudgeon and William Brannan; Thomas Savin, William Savin, Thomas Savin, Jr., Richard Savin and 4 slaves; George Douglas, James Douglas and 6 slaves; Hugh Matthews, John Williams, Patrick Matthews, Patrick Brogan and 4 slaves; Peter Noxon, Peter Hendrickson, Isaac Cartwright and 6 slaves; John Brown, Nicholas Vanhorn, Henry Hase, John Bell, Simon Newcomb and 7 slaves; Michael Earle, John McDuff, John Ward, Bartholomew Headon, William Parks and 10 slaves; James Frisby, Clement Carty and 18 slaves; Joseph Graydon, John Lewis, Thomas Aston and 15 slaves; Peregrine Ward, Valentine Rice, Hugh Calgan and 13 slaves; John Baldwin, William Penington, Nicholas Ellis and 17 slaves; William Davis; John Hodgson (weaver); and another name missing [page torn].

TAXABLE PERSONS IN CECIL COUNTY IN 1752 (PAGE 3 OF 10):
James Campbell; John Price; Jonathan Hollings; William Lovely; James Brison; Thomas Severson; James Aires; Michael Cartwright; William Price;

William Beetle; George Thornberry; John Clark; John Roberts, Jr.; Thomas Mercer; John Maclean; Thomas Wroth; John Kimbar; Matthias Pippin; Thomas Money; Robert Money; Richard Brown; Nicholas Price; John Price; Hugh Griffen; Angus McDonald; John Drummond; Alexander McIntosh; Israel Parsley; Thomas Hollings; James Poor; Thomas Pendergrass; Stephen Gibbons; Benjamin Sutton; William Lynch; Alexander Ogg; George Wightman; John Ogg and 1 slave; John Wallace and Thomas Fitzgerald; Seth Ruley and 1 slave; William Price (Boson) and William Price; Andrew Price, Jr. and William McDowell; Thomas Scurry and Dennis Dorrell; Benjamin Penington and 1 slave; Ephraim Price and Thomas Silven; Thomas Robinson and William Robinson; John Husbands and William Darren; Nicholas Money and Alexander ---- [page torn]; Benjamin Money and George Holton; Thomas Severson, Sr. and Zachariah Severson; William Morgan and Thomas Maffett; John Roberts, Sr. and James Hinds; Otho Othoson and 1 slave; Thomas Severson, Jr. and James Camp; Robert Walmsley and 1 slave; John Morgan and Richard Wallace; Jame Wroth, Sr. and John Dunk; Samuel Beetle and John Penny; John Davidge and Alexander McCloud; John Sutton and John Price; Zachariah Kirk and Joseph Kirk; Maurice Ward and George McCoy; Anthony Lynch, George Lynch and 1 slave; John Ward and 2 slaves; John Beetle, Jr., Samuel Penington and 1 slave; Jacob McDowell, John Mc-Dowell and James McDowell; Thomas Etherington, Benjamin Etherington and 1 slave; John Lusby, Robert Lusby and 1 slave; John Tree, John Urin and John Melfort; Andrew Price, Peregrine Price and Andrew Price; John Hood, James Erwin and 1 slave; John Hayes, Michael McGowan and Evan Morgan; John Fillingham, Joseph Sevary and Thomas Richards; John Hurry, a servant James and 1 slave; William Desperet, Joseph --dford and another missing name [page torn]; John Stogdon, Thomas Price and John Winterberry; Benjamin Terry, James Cosden and 1 slave; John Hall and 3 slaves; Robert Mercer and 3 slaves; William Cox, Benjamin Cox, Richard Atwood and 1 slave; William Walmsley, Charles Hay and 2 slaves; James Wroth, John Gafen, John Summers and 1 slave; John Money, David Fitzgerald, Laughlan Hlinn[?] and 1 slave; Bartholomew Etherington, James Down, Joshua Turlington and 1 slave; Henry Burnham, John McClouds and 2 slaves; John Penington, Frederick Ryland, Edward Simmonds and a servant Thomas; Michael Ruley, Anthony Ruley and 2 slaves; Henry Henrickson, John Spalding, William Lassen and Hance York Powell; Benjamin Price, Augustine Price and 3 slaves; William Ward, William Huslar, Thomas Summers, James McDeed and 1 slave; Francis Bonner, William Little and 3 slaves; William Beetle, Sr. and 4 slaves; George Veazey and 4 slaves; Isaac Caulk, Jacob Caulk and 4 slaves; Bartholomew Parsley and 5 slaves; Thomas Davis and 5 slaves; Thomas Price, Sr., Philip Lathran and 4 slaves; John Penington, John Ford, a servant Daniel and 3 slaves.

TAXABLE PERSONS IN CECIL COUNTY IN 1752 (PAGE 4 OF 10):
John Beetle, Sr., Thomas Beetle, Stephen Beetle and 3 slaves; Benjamin Pearce and 6 slaves; Revd. Mr. Hugh Jones, Henry Moreland and 6 slaves; Henry Ward, William Cole, Charles Parker and 5 slaves; John Cox, David Eiland, John Lovely, James Essage and 5 slaves; Nathaniel Childs and 10 slaves; At Mr. Peregrine Frisby's Quarter - Hugh McDowell, George Ford and 10 slaves; William Hedgest, John Walker, James Quin and 7 slaves; John

Veazey, Edward Veazey, David Price and 15 slaves; Peter Meekins, Robert Brian, Joseph Gray, Patrick White and Con O'Neile; John O'Bryan; John Bradley; Matthew Kirkling; James Patterson; William Starling; John Starling; John McDowell; John McLacklan; James Hattery; Michael Ford; Anthony Turtada; William Short; Walter Cosley; William Smith, Jr.; James McCay; John Aul; John Clark; Patrick Harris; William McKilhony; James Hattery; Joseph Chick; Samuel Stewart; William Smith, Sr.; William White; Thomas Scott; Thomas Marr; James Cockran; Edward Rumsey, Jr.; Cornelius Eliason, Jr.; Nathaniel Baxter; Matthew Kirklen; Walter Hill; Mr. Addison; Dennis Barret; William Rumsey and 1 slave; William Penington and Daniel Brougher; Henry Penington and 1 slave; William Rumsey (cordwinder) and Jeremiah Davis; John Gullahar and Thomas Cornwall; Richard Dorrell and China Choice; Richard Canter and George Barwick; John Scott and Peter Lemon; Alexander Stewart and Michael Hudson; Thomas Stewart and Robert Feris, Jr.; John Cage and Cornelius Hukill; James O'Bryan and Cornelius Kieve; Walter Devan and Dennis Kelly; John Harper (farmer) and Hugh Douglas; Clement Flintham, Richart Flintham and James Burns; Elias Eliason, John Eliason and John Keys; Michael Manycosens, James Manycosens and 1 slave; Charles Scott, William Tweddy and 1 slave; Charles Gordon and 2 slaves; Thomas Savin, Jr., William Watts and 1 slave; William Chick, John Hill and John Ryan; Richard ----, Thomas ----, and one missing name [page torn]; John Chick, Thomas Bird and Robert Gollachar; Thomas Cox, William Harp and 1 slave; Edward Rumsey, Sr., Charles Rumsey and John Reynolds; Matthias VanBebber, Henry VanBebber, Patrick Doyle and Thomas Yorkson; Evert Evertson, Jacob Evertson and 2 slaves; Bartholomew Jacobs, Jr., Henry Thompson, John Meriam and 1 slave; John Flanagan, Robert McCully, James Crayley and 1 slave; Bartholomew Jacobs and 3 slaves; Jacob Evertson and 3 slaves; John Cazier, John Warner, Cornelius Harrigan and 1 slave; To Mary Knaesborrough - Michael Knaesborrough, Farrel McCormack, William Hoskins and 1 slave; Cornelius Eliason and 3 slaves; James O'Hagan, Cornelius Coakley, John Mahada and 2 slaves; Thomas Stewart, Alexander McFarlan, Luke Hart and 2 slaves; John Carnan and 5 slaves; Walter Scott, Sr., Walter Scott, Darby Burk and 3 slaves; To Col. Rigby's Executors - 8 slaves; At Sidney George's Quarter - Richard Chandlar, Benjamin Ellsberry, William Cook, a servant Lawrence and 18 slaves; John Clark (smith); Humphry Cahoon; John Wiley; John Alexander.

TAXABLE PERSONS IN CECIL COUNTY IN 1752 (PAGE 5 OF 10):
John Nash; Charles Quigley; Alexander Scott; William Boulding; John Mc-Garvey; Jacob Pooley; Samuel Nash; William Richison; Worrack Millar; James Ford; John Cooley; John Feris; Richard Boulding; Daniel Biggs; John Gullett; Ephraim Thompson; Samuel Adair; Walter Jackson; John Reyley; William Rodey; Thomas Flanagan; Michael Carty; James McLacklan; Richard Barnaby; Mannadoe Philips; Thomas Crosby; William Kennedy; John McCafferty; Henry Neal; Henry Hukill; Anthony Cadman; Patrick Haw; Michael McGillin; Cornelius Cowley; Thomas Nash; Thomas Nash, Jr.; John Ford; Roger Hale; Richard Beetle and James Smith; John Harper (smith) and David Henry; James Smith and William McVay; David Alexander and Elias Alexander; Thomas Bravard and Benjamin Bravard; Edward Armstrong and John Connougan; Benjamin Thomas and Richard Butler; James Harper and William Black; John Crozier and John McDaniel;

Thomas Beetle and Michael Kinsloe; John Buchannan and Michael Courtney; John Lawrence and Abraham Yoe; Nathaniel Chick and John Crow; William Whittom and Benjamin Whittom; Joseph Wood and Alexander Gorley; Elinor Campbell, Bartholomew Johnson and 1 slave; Robert Thompson and Andrew Henry; Andrew Alexander and Isaac Alexander; Thomas Malone and Jonathan Malone; John Byan [Bryan?] and John Newall; Thomas Bouldin and 1 slave; John Edwards, Manus O'Harlay and 1 slave; John Dempster, David Dempster and George Finney; Abraham Millar, William Millar and Andrew Millar; John Haltham, Spencer Haltham and Patrick Hagan; Thomas Mills, William Bird and Richard H---- [page torn]; William Armstrong, John Hyland and 2 slaves; Thomas Price, Philip Ellwood, Ephraim Welch and Daniel Golder; James Wallace, Samuel Mc-Dowell, Adam Wallace and John Erwin; James Boulding and 3 slaves; Richard Thompson, Sr., Joseph Cooper and 3 slaves; George Ford, Thomas Murphy and Hugh Hanney; Richard Thompson, Jr. and 2 slaves; Patrick Craig; James Roddy; John Ham; Henry Sluyter; Nicholas Wood; Enoch Jenkins; Arthur O'Neal; Richard Tobin; John Cox; John Can; John Sampson; Anthony Noons; Abraham Hughes; William Whaylin; Samuel McCleery; Joseph Dawson; Peter Larooe; William Whitton; Francis Reynolds; Martin Con; Baltus Starn; Thomas Franket; Thomas Foster; Cornelius Wooliston; Daniel Hukill; James Dickson; Thomas Parkinson; Christopher Hollings; Jacob VanBebber; William Kleinhoff; ---- Hardman [page torn]; Bartholomew Rudulph; Jonathan Hodgson; Matthias Barcklay; Frederick Starn; John Groves; William Crow; Bryan Buckworth; Patrick Anderson; Thomas Bowen; Absalom Bowen.

TAXABLE PERSONS IN CECIL COUNTY IN 1752 (PAGE 6 OF 10):
John Gollehorn; William Cochran; Robert Veazey, Jr.; Richard Hukill; John Hukill; Thomas Hooker; John Mullin; William Lancaster; Samuel Simmonds; Peregrine Vandergrift; Samuel Taylor; Joseph Cochran; Peter Brown; Timothy Dawsey; Michael Jaggar; Frederick Boamems; John Dare; Jeremiah Rose; Timothy Campain; Anthony Fonens; Francis Donett; Jacob Marthwright; Philip Shaw; George Beaston; Andrew Lawrenson and John Husbands; Abraham Alman and one servant man; Richard Ford and one servant man; William Furey and Dennis Duffey; Joseph Neidy and John Neidy; John Veazey and 1 slave; John Carty and John Duris; Thomas Castevens and Thomas En---- [page torn]; Robert Scury and John Wills; Thomas Moore and Philip Mark; Samuel Hughes and John Ellwood; Thomas McLacklan and Abraham Buncar; Andrew Crow and Daniel Morrison; James Reddish and 1 slave; John Lawson, Daniel Ryan and 1 slave; Richard Bowen and Robert Wiley; George Lewis and John Traner; Thomas Beaston and Ephraim Beaston; Philip Burgin and Henry Lancaster; Francis Jones and Richard Smith; Peter Kleinhoff, Joseph Hone and Abel Chaler; Frederick Elsberry, John Elsberry and Thomas Braon; Peter Lawson, a servant man and 1 slave; John Hollet, Joseph Burnham and Thomas Burnham; Henry McCoy, John McCoy and 1 slave; Manasseh Loage, Daniel Carty and Darby Crawley; John Kirk, Alexander Kirk and William Cashlehorn; Robert Mansfield, Daniel Rose and Andrew Monroe; Thomas Ebthorp, John Numbers and 1 slave; Robert Veazey, Sr., Veazey Husbands and 1 slave; Richard Taylor, Joseph Taylor and William Taylor; Isaac Ham, John McCoy and

Nathaniel Pasley; Thomas Wallace and 2 slaves; ---- --zier [page torn] and 3 slaves; Samuel Milburn, Samuel Milburn, Jr. and 2 slaves; James Robison, Joseph Zelafroe and 2 slaves; Thomas Colvill and 3 slaves; Jacob Ham, Thomas Bouchell, Thomas Pendergrass and 2 slaves; Samuel Bayard, Sr., Samuel Bayard and 3 slaves; James Boyles, Daniel Boyles, John Boyles, John Bath and 1 slave; Peter Rider, Joseph Rider, Andrew Rider, Michael Roreck and 1 slave; John Latham, John Owen and 3 slaves; John Holland and 4 slaves; Richard Price, James Price, John Price, David Price, Hugh Polk and Walter Murphy; John Cochran, Joseph Cochran, Henry McPeak, James Hamlan, George Trimble and 1 slave; Adam VanBebber, William Bass, John Smith and 6 slaves; Peter Bayard and 7 slaves; Henry VanBebber, Isaac Van-Bebber, John Campbell, Daniel Goodfellow, Adam Short and 3 slaves; Peter Bouchell, Francis Hosser, Peter Hendrickson, George Swenny and 5 slaves; Sluyter Bouchell, Alexander Rice, Philip Lancaster, Richard Ellwood and 8 slaves; At the late James Bayard's - John Saltwell, Cornelius Marhees and 11 slaves.

TAXABLE PERSONS IN CECIL COUNTY IN 1752 (PAGE 7 OF 10):
Charles Ford, Robert Ford and 5 slaves; William Mitchell; Baptist Mc-Dowell; John McCulloch; John McGarragh; James Kidd; Robert Marquis; Samuel Taggart; Tobias Long; William Cunningham; Allen Campbell; John Brown; John Bonnar; Thomas Smith; James Rowland; John Henderson; Charles Erwin; Samuel Carswell; Samuel Carr; James Creswell; Hugh Brayley; Joseph Rutherford; Christopher Jones; George Death; John Woods; Andrew McAdoe; Matthew Brown; Robert Millar; John Bowen; Samuel Breaden; William Husband, Jr.; John Death; John Duffey; Robert Dixon; Samuel Caldwell; Hugh McAllister; Joseph Jacobs; Joseph Neeper; Francis Armstrong; John Wasson; Thomas McDowell; Arthur Munday; William Carmichael; James Breaden; Dennis Mc---- [page torn]; Robert Bell; Henry Dougherty; Daniel Kieve; Robert Brotherington; Cornelius Conally; John Deal; John Gilford; Robert Gordon; Samuel McMurray; Thomas Hinds; Richard Geddings; James Geddings; Hugh Dougherty; Michael Patton; Harman Baily; Edward Jackson; James Morrison; Thomas Janney; Isaac Janney; William Wilson; Morgan Swinney; Archibald Akins; Daniel Fugan; John Guffey; James Whitlock; George Lesslie; Luke Jones; Walter Finney; Jacob Johnson; John Johnson; John Blake; Oliver Johnson; Joseph Pugh; John Maclure; Samuel White; Nicholas Kelly; two missing names [page torn]; James Hewett; Joseph Moore; Joseph Reekinson; Matthew Alexander; John Wilson; Henry Guffey; James Buchannan; Th-- ---- [page torn]; Joseph Orr; Andrew Toutchston; Andrew Poulson; Francis Anderson; William Jack; William Deval; Samuel McKewn; Joseph Hunter; David Brown; John Glasgow; Jonathan Hartshorn; Theophilus Morris; William Elliott; Robert Nicholas; William Ford; Edward Shanney; William Currer; Andrew Hollet; William Murphey; Ephraim Johnson; Thomas Watts; John Lowe; John Taylor; Henry Stump; Robert McHadden; Edward McAvinchee; Alexander Ewing; Moses Ewing; James Thompson; Charles Dougherty; Olivar Millar; William Lee; Joseph Kimsey; James Reynolds; Stephen Newall; Walter Rogers; ---- --haffey [page torn]; one name missing [page torn]; Matthew Logan; Richard Downey; Joseph Young; Richard James; William Callindar; John Callindar; James Ross; Robert McMullin.

TAXABLE PERSONS IN CECIL COUNTY IN 1752 (PAGE 8 OF 10):
James Dorawe; Peter Overstock; Daniel Lesslie; John Alinson; John Clark; Samuel McClure; Daniel Long; John Given; James Craig; Roger Dumigin; Nathan Lacklen; William Glasgow; John George; Jeremiah Williston; Daniel Brumfield; George Vickars; Benjamin Bradford; Henry Jackson; Joseph Richards; William Walker; Robert Good; Conrade Raffeir; Benjamin Crockett; John Dunn; John Nedrick; Thomas Palmer; John Lackey; Flower Greenland; Matthias Bordley; Patrick Hamilton; John Stevenson; John Currer; Dominick Fanning; Thomas Pryor; Thomas Norton; Cornelius Sullivane; Hugh Gibbony; Matthew McClintock; William Ha---- [page torn]; Jacob Northerman; Andrew Coulter; Edward Philips; William Philips; Sylvester Nugent; John Hedaburgh; William Smith; John Baine; Nathan Norton; William Mitchel; John Wells, Jr.; Richard Norton; John Cesti; John Wells, Sr.; Jonas Cooper; Robert Smith; Matthew Hodgson; James Coffee; John Thompson; Joseph Baldwin; David Dicky; Nathaniel Moore; Alexander Elliot; Simon Johnson; Richard Bradley; James McLannan; James Russell; Samuel Boggs; Robert Bolton; John Little; Thomas Kilgore; William Davidson; John Gilles; James Ritchy; David Carr; Andrew Means; Robert Huggins; John Carey; Francis McClintock; Simon Annestor; Andrew Barnett; John McCulloch; David Moore; Michael Agnew; Edward Molloy; one name missing [page torn]; ----as McC---- [page torn]; Nicholas White; Matthew Thompson; George Hall; John Lynch; William Neally; William Henry; Thomas Chesnutt; William ---- [page torn]; William Wallace, Sr.; Thomas Wilson; Matthias Johnson; Moses Fearis; Baptist Scott; Robert Fleeming; John Ware; John Jeffries; James Frazier; John Elliot; Christopher Rutlidge; David Hampton; John Simpers; Adam Dobson; Jacob Johnson; John McKonkey; John Montgomery; John Bailey; David Owens; Robert Lutton; Samuel Hall; William Ferguson; Hugh Longwill; William Longwill; James Gardner; James Holms; Daniel Cane; Richard Lanney; Nathan Boyd; James Finley; John Caldwell; James McCrackin; Phineas Hodgson; Robert Breeden; Alexander Logan; Patrick Hart; Matthias Walker; Walter Carr; Francis Carruthers; Samuel Grimes; John Smith; Edward Wilson; Isaac Buttrum; Thomas Campbell; Robert Jones; John Short; Adam Short; John Maahan? [page torn]; ---- ----ts [page torn].

TAXABLE PERSONS IN CECIL COUNTY IN 1752 (PAGE 9 OF 10):
William Starkey; Richard Hall; Moses Latham; Richard Nowland; John Kirkpatrick; William McClary; Margaret Evans' slave; Archibald McCulloch; Andrew Ryan; ---- ----ooks [page torn]; ----m Hollings [page torn]; John ----orn [page torn]; John Neal; Benedict Lorrain; John Kitely; Philip Kitely; William Grace; John Thomas Hitchcock; Samuel McKinney; John Jones; Moses Jones; James Roach; Alexander McDougan; Daniel Rice; John Rutter; Thomas Nevil; Joseph Lowman; James Buchanan; William Mainley; Robert Milburn; Joseph Mauldin; Thomas Crouch; Robert McMullin; William Newill; John Slider; James Burns; Alexander MacKinney; Peter Poulson; Edward Veazey; James Veazey, Jr.; William Rannals; Thomas Rose; John Foster; James Leeper and William McTyre; Samuel Taggart and John Taggart; Adam Meek, Sr. and Adam Meek, Jr.; George Finley and John Downey; Robert Caldwall and Alexander Caldwall; William Rowland and William Currans; Robert Finlay and James MacMullin; Samuel Ewing and

Michael Sullivane; William Brown and Joseph Brown; Lewis Lee and Joseph Foreside; Hugh Ferry and Charles Ferry; Richard Fleeming and John Ronay; James Gibson and John Gibson; William Mitchell and Thomas Mitchell; Jared Neilson and Thomas Green; James Porter and William Lockhart; John Ewing and William Ewing; Archibald Buchanan and James Buchanan; George Johnstone and Cornelius Conally; Thomas Foster and Samuel Philips; William Janney and a servant Simon; Robert Lesslie and John Lesslie; John Kilpatrick and James Leard; Samuel McKewn and Martin Norman; William Sheerwood and James Roads; John Mitchell and Andrew Mitchell; James Spear and William Williams; William Gardner and John McDowell; Samuel White and William Wilson; Robert Mitchel and John Mitchel; four names missing [page torn]; James Stinson and Nicholas Mean; George Hamilton and John Edgehill; Charles Bonner and Henry Bonner; Andrew Barrat and George Spear; Benjamin Chew and ---- [page torn]; David McCrackin and John McCrackin; William Cauther and John Cauther; James Goffey and David Veure; Amos Evans and Jarvis Jolter; David Hill and Robert Hill; Martin Wilcock and Stephen Wilcock; James Grimes and Samuel Smith; Patrick Kelly and Samuel Jackson; Murtough Mahone and Cornelius Lesslie; William Baily and Neil Baily; Henry Good and John Good; Francis Maybury and Thomas Johnson; Samuel Arnett and Joseph Arnett; James Corby and Barnet McMasters; Robert Williams and Charles Dalson; Samuel Aneram and Archibald Aneram; Andrew Gibson and James Wasson; John McCue and Samuel Love; John Green, Sr. and John Green; John Welch and William Welch; John Ash and James Chambers; Richard Cazier and 1 slave; John Wyatt and John Hill; John Springs and Peter Hicks; Joseph Edwards and John Barnaby; ---- Cochran and another name missing [page torn]; ---- Proslar and another name missing [page torn]; Sidney George and Edward Linnen; Dennis Hayes and Benjamin Read; John Hayes and John Burns; William Chipley and Moses Chipley; Richard Simpers and William Simpers.

TAXABLE PERSONS IN CECIL COUNTY IN 1752 (PAGE 10 OF 10):
Nathan Worley and Dennis Worley; Philip Cazier and Abraham Cazier; Thomas Elliot and George Hedrick; James Tuft and James McMullin; Isaac Daws and Matthew Hill; Benjamin Chew and Aquila Johns; William Poulson and Anthony Kennedy; George Lawson and John Guthery; Moses Andrews and 1 slave; Samuel McCutcheon and John McCutcheon; Simon Johnson and John Dunn; John Moody and Michael Mahon; Robert Smith and William Smith; David John and William Chambers; William Harbison and William Harbison, Jr.; Augustine Passmore and John Lawler; Samuel Thompson and Hans Yorkslaber; William Culmery and 1 slave; William Maffett and Thomas Breeden; John Douglas and Jacob Bacon; James Fryar and John Beare; John McCoy and Hugh Simpson; Archibald Armstrong and Thomas Crental; Thomas Simpers and Matthias Muckley; John Bing and Obadiah Kenny; Robert Whitaker and Thomas ---- [page torn]; Jo-- ---- and Anthony - --- [page torn]; Abraham Holmes and John Holmes; William Whan and Samuel Whan; Robert Cochran and James Cochran; David Elder and Alexander Coleman; James Macky and Richard Benson; Samuel Hill and John Erwin; Adam Wilson and John Hodgson; Theophilus Alexander and 1 slave; Moses Alexander and Daniel Alexander; James Morgan and William Morgan; John Macky and John Kelly; John Smith (sadler) and John Parker;

Hukill Guilder and Henry Guilder; Caleb Carman and Samuel Whitton; Philip Nelson and Edward Moore; Thomas Hitchcock and James Bowers; Benjamin Mauldin and 1 slave; John Bayard and Walter Solomon; John Gibson and William Foster; James Veazey and 1 slave; John Lewis and Samuel Whitaker; John Hyland and Thomas Owen; Thomas Johns and Peter Beazley; Robert Thackery and John Beazley; Samuel Philips and John Philips; Job Evertson and Job Evertson [sic]; Joseph Court and John Cannon; Moses Rutter and Samuel Brown; Sampson Currer and 1 slave; James Lowry and Lott Connell; Henry Stedham and another name missing [page torn]; James Creswell and two names missing [page torn]; Robert Fleeming, John Blackburn and Victor Craig; Joseph McNealy, Joseph McNealy, Jr. and a servant; David Patterson, John Patterson and James Brislen; Thomas Sherwood and 2 slaves; Robert Patterson, Samuel Patterson and Dennis McNemarr; William Whittinton and 2 slaves; Andrew Porter, Christopher Farral and William Scott; William Ewing, James Ewing and Patrick Cavenaugh[?]; George Glas---- [page torn]; Walter Steel, Samuel Cole and Stephen Ryan; Joseph Bass and 3 slaves; Michael McFall, John Owen and Dodea[?] McFall; William McKewn, James McKewn and James Smith; Jethro Brown and 2 slaves; John Stump and 2 slaves; Robert Givans, William Dawson and John Cummin; Richard Patten, Joseph Rickinton and John Reynolds; Thomas Millar, Sr., Thomas Miller, Jr. and Edward Cavenaugh; John Rutter, Whitton Rutter and William Rice; John Murphy, Harry Baily and Thomas Crawford; Edward Dougherty, Robert Morrison and Ambrose Momford; James Manley, Robert Manley and William Withers; Neil McNeil, William Webbe and Patrick Sourey; Edward Mitchell and 2 slaves; Matthew Quile and 2 slaves. End of 1752 list of taxable persons. Total: 2,043. (Ref: Maryland State Archives and the Cecil County Genealogical Society).

LIST OF BONDS IN THE COMMISSIONERS OF THE LOAN OFFICE WITH INTEREST DUE IN FEBRUARY, 1755 (Ref: *Archives of Maryland*, Volume 52, pp. 17-27):

Principal: Robert Gordon, Esq. Security: Joshua George.
    Commencement of the Interest: April 8, 1741.
Principal: Benjamin Pearce. Security: William Rumsey.
    Commencement of the Interest: May 28, 1740.
Principal: Benjamin Pearce. Security: Joshua George.
    Commencement of the Interest: February 16, 1746.
Principal: George Steuart. Security: William Alexander.
    Commencement of the Interest: April 6, 1743.
Principal: Joshua George. Security: Thomas Johnson.
    Commencement of the Interest: August 17, 1737.
Principal: Elihu Hall. Security: Vachel Denton (A.A.).
    Commencement of the Interest: April 6, 1738.
Principal: John Currar. Security: Nicholas Hyland.
    Commencement of the Interest: July 27, 1754.
Principal: John Baldwin. Security: John Thompson.
    Commencement of the Interest: September 18, 1754.
Principal: John Thompson. Security: John Baldwin.

Commencement of the Interest: September 18, 1749.
Principal: John Mackey. Security: Col. Thomas Colvil.
Commencement of the Interest: October 1, 1746.
Principal: William Pearce. Security: Benjamin Pearce.
Commencement of the Interest: February 19, 1746.
Principal: William Rumsey. Security: Nicholas Hyland.
Commencement of the Interest: May 29, 1754.
Principal: Nicholas Hyland. Security: William Rumsey.
Commencement of the Interest: May 29, 1754.

SUNDRY WITNESSES FROM THE NORTH SIDE OF ELK RIVER IN
CECIL COUNTY PAID BY THE MARYLAND LOWER HOUSE ON
JUNE 15, 1749 (Ref: *Archives of Maryland*, Volume 46, p. 277): James Harrison, a witness for the petitioners, 2 days attendance and itinerant charges,
2.04.0....James Tilghman, 2 days attendance, and 6 days itinerant charges,
1.16.0....William Hitchman, a witness for the petitioners, 2 days attendance
and itinerant charges, 2.04.0....David Hampton, ditto....Henry Hara,
ditto....Robert Cummings, ditto....Thomas Colvil, ditto....Benjamin Bradford,
a witness for the Sheriff, 2 days attendance and itinerant charges, 2.04.0....Wil-
liam Gaunt, ditto....John Altham, ditto....James Veasy, ditto....Zebulon Hollingsworth, ditto....John Hicks, ditto....Hugul Gildart, ditto....Michael Lum,
ditto....Andrew Bany, ditto.

OFFICERS APPOINTED IN CECIL COUNTY, OCTOBER 16, 1694 (Ref:
Archives of Maryland, Volume 20, pp. 111, 138): Quorum - Col. Casparus
Herman, Col. William Pierce, Mr. William Harris, Mr. William Dare, Mr.
Mathias Vanderhayden. Justices - Mr. John Thompson, Mr. Peter Bayard,
Mr. Robert Crooke, Mr. Edward Blay, Mr. Thomas Thackstone, Mr.
Ebenezer Blackstone. Military Officers - Col. Casparus Herman, Capt. John
Thompson, Capt. Charles James. Coroners - Mr. Edward Jones, Mr. John
James. Sheriff: Mr. John Carvile. Clerk of the County Court - Mr. Charles
Bass.

CIVIL OFFICERS AND MAGISTRATES OF CECIL COUNTY IN 1696
(Ref: *Archives of Maryland*, Volume 20, p. 545): Casparus Augustine Her-
man, William Harris, William Dare, Edward Blay, John Thompson, Robert
Crooke, Abel Blackiston, William Pierce, John Carvile (Sheriff), Charles
Bass (Clerk), John Stoope, Robert Gibson, William Gallaway, York
Yorkson, William Pierce, Jr., Edward Lademore, Thomas Church, Hugh
Douch, Robert Randull, Samson George, John Glosson, William Hubbard,
William Hill, John Stanley, and William Bowlin.

MILITARY OFFICERS IN CECIL COUNTY IN 1696 (Ref: *Archives of
Maryland*, Volume 20, pp. 545-546): Casp: A: Herman, William Pearce, John
Thompson, Peter Byard, William Freeman, William Harris, M: V: Hayden,
Edward Blay, William Dare, John James, Robert Crook, Philip Cheager, Ed-
ward Larmoore, Nathll. Hilling, Robert Hues, Hen: Eldayerly, Danll. Mack-
veall, Oliver Talmer, Richard Manary, John Duing, Peter Leverson, Ffr:

Barnett, Richard Smith, William Edwards, Philip Rasen, and Richard Kinword.

PETITIONERS AGAINST A PROPOSED BILL "TO PREVENT THE MAKING OR REPAIRING OF ANY FISH DAMS AND POTS ON THE RIVER SUSQUEHANNAH" IN 1761 (Ref: *Calendar of Maryland State Papers*, The Black Books, p. 165): John Litten, John Stepelton, Richard Wells, Jr., Joseph Morgan, Stephen Fisher, Fred. Fulton, Joseph Morgan, John Smith, Joseph Husband, John Ewing, Robert Conn, John Waller, Samuel Fulton, William Husband, Sr., Richard Gay, William Ewing, Thomas Love, William Ewing, Samuel Gillespie, Robert Gillespie, Thomas Andrews, Elihu Hall, Charles Orrick, Robert Walter, John Laughlin, Charles Worthington, Jr., John Worthington, Joseph Hopkins, Sr., Joseph Hopkins, Jr., Joseph Neeper, John Neeper, James Neeper, William Neeper, Joseph Hayward, Stephen Jay, Ephraim Gover, Edward Lewis, Jr., William Collins, Thomas Husband, Gerrard Hopkins, Jr., E. Andrews, William Cox, Nathan Rigbie, Jr., Leven Mathews, Aquila Hall, Nathan Horton, William Wells, Edward Morgan, Samuel Morgan, James Lee, Francis Downing, John Short, Jonathan West, John Ross, and Richard Wells, Jr. [Note: Petitioners appear to be from both Cecil County and Harford County].

SUNDRY PERSONS WHOSE LANDS WERE ALIENATED IN CECIL COUNTY IN 1763 (Ref: *Calendar of Maryland State Papers*, The Black Books, p. 180): John Brevard, Henry Baker, Robert Evans, Christopher Parkeson and wife Sarah Parkeson, William Beedle and wife Sarah Beedle, Thomas Simpers, Moses Latham and wife Mary Latham, James Chetham Ward and wife [no name], James Arthur, Nicholas Hyland, Robert Evans, Hugh Reynolds, William Cox, Charles Orrick, James Hays and wife Sarah Hays, Elihu Hall, Nathan Oldham, Daniel Bayley and wife Johanna Bayley, James Foster, John Manley, Thomas Kilgore, Anthony Ruley, John Money, Robert Evans, Samuel Guy, Mary Ward, Abraham Holmes, Rebecca Johnson, John Ward, Benjamin Cox, Bartholomew Etherington, John Ewing, Richard Bond, and John McCoy. Francis Key, Clerk of the Court.

PETITION BY VARIOUS INHABITANTS AND GRAIN TRADERS OF THE UPPER CHESAPEAKE BAY TO GOVERNOR SAMUEL OGLE OF MARYLAND TO REPEAL A RECENT LAW "THAT HAS PROFITED PENNSYLVANIA BUT HAS CAUSED SUFFERING TO MARYLAND FARMERS AND TRADERS" IN 1737 (Ref: *Calendar of Maryland State Papers*, The Black Books, pp. 53-54): John Veazey, John Ryland, William Walmsley, Isaac Caulk, John Beedle, John Penington, Jr., Thomas Been, John Mareen, William Beaston, J. Ward, Jr., John Holland, John Jones, William Knaresbrough, John Campbell, William Pearce, Peregrine Ward, John Baldwin, George Veazey, Jeremiah Gridley, Robert Mareen, John Ryland, Sr., Henry Penington, Sr., John Chamberlin, Barnet Vanhorn, Jacob Ozier, Peter Overstock, J. Pennington, Jr., Richard Smith, William Mercer, Peter Cooper, Thomas Spencer, John Carrington, William Pennington, John Beetle, Jr., Benjamin Torry [Terry?], Thomas Pearce, John Cooper, Thomas Pearce, Jr., John Wallace, Edward Beaston, John Cox, Phillip Cazier, Robert Croker, John Lovering, Samuel Beck, Benieman Parsans,

Daniel Whalles, John Wethered, James DeHart, Richard James, John Bennett, David Witherspoon, August Bayne, Robert Penington, Thomas Kees, J. Penington, Peregrine Frisby, Mathias Daye, William Ellis, John Wallace, William Levin, Richard Wethered, Gideon Pearce, Edward Mitchell, Richard Scise[?], John Denning, James Woodland, William Catton, Porter Jorensine[?], Phillip Holleadger, Daniell Brian[?], Edward Furron, Thomas Sinnett, Philip Jobson, Thomas Haughton, and Thomas Hynson. On verso: March 3, 1737, Levin Gale, brig "Brereton," Henry Smith, master, John Williams, Robert Henry.

EARLY INHABITANTS OF CECIL COUNTY, 1649-1774 (Gleaned from George Johnston's *History of Cecil County, Maryland* (1881). [Note: Dates are those found in the records and not necessarily the dates when the people first appeared in the county.]: William Carpender, 1658; Col. Nathaniel Utie, 1652; George Utie, 1661; Richard Wells, 1661; Augustine Hermen, 1659; Resolved (Rosevelt) Waldron, 1659; John Turner, 1659; William Hollingsworth, 1661; Garratt Rutten, 1661; Francis Wright, 1659; Samuel Goldsmith, 1664; Thomas Stockett, 1664; Col. Lewis Stockett, 1664; Jacob Clawson, 1659; John Jarbo, 1660; Anna Hack and her sons George Hack and Peter Hack, 1660; Simon Oversee, 1659; Alexander D'Hinoyossa, 1662; Jacob Young, 1678; Thomas Jones, 1690; Shadrack Whitworth, 1692; Matthias Matthiason, 1692; John Labadie, 1684; Peter Sluyter alias Vorsman, 1684; Jasper Danckers alias Schilders, 1684; Petrus Bayard, 1684; John Moll, 1684; Samuel Bowens (Quaker preacher), 1702; Hermen VanBarkelo, 1698; Nicholas de la Montaigne, 1698; Peter de Koning, 1698; Derick Kolchman, 1698; Henry Sluyter, 1698; Samuel Bayard, 1698; John Moll, Jr., 1698; Ephraim Herman, 1680; John Browning, 1680; George Holland, 1680; Joseph Chew, 1680; Edward Jones, 1684; William Dare, 1684; George Oldfield, 1784; John Cann, 1684; James Williams, 1684; John White, 1684; Samuel Land, 1684; William Hamilton, 1684; Matthias Vanderhuyden, 1692; George Talbot, 1680; Nathaniel Garrett, 1683; George Wardner, 1683; William Nowell, 1683; William Pearce, 1683; Thomas Mansfield, 1683; Mathias Wallace, 1714; James Alexander (farmer), 1714; Arthur Alexander (farmer), 1714; David Alexander (weaver), 1714; Joseph Alexander (tanner), 1714; Mary Alexander, widow of James Alexander, 1718; James Carroll, 1701; Morgan Patten, 1718; John Bristow, 1718; Joseph Steel, 1718; Roger Lawson, 1718; Rev. George Gillespie, 1720; James King, 1727; William Harris, 1727; Edward Churchman, died 1732; Henry Reynolds, 1732; Benjamin Chandlee, 1710; Able Cottey, 1706; Joseph Trimble, 1741; Cottey Chandlee, born circa 1713; Jehu Kay, circa 1718; James Brown, circa 1718; Andrew Job, circa 1710; Thomas Griffith, 1701; Enoch Morgan, 1701; Mary Johns, 1701; Margaret Matthias, 1701; James David, 1701; Reese Ryddarcks, died 1707; Peter Chamberline, circa 1701; Catharine Williams, 1696; John Lawson, died 1755; Peter Lawson, 1755; Judith Bassett, 1755; Michael Bassett and Richard Bassett, sons of Mary Lawson, 1755; Peter Bayard, 1760; Catharine Hermen married Peter Bouchell and died in 1752; Mary Bouchell married Joseph Ensor in 1757; Susanna Hermen married James Creagear (no date); Augustina Hermen married Roger Larramore (no date); Catharine Hermen married Abel Van Burkelow (no date); Herman Van Burkelow, 1683; Isaac Van Bibber and wife Fronica Van Bibber, 1702; Matthias Van Bibber, 1702; Hugh McGregory, 1682; Henry Van Bibber, brother of Isaac and Matthias Van Bibber, 1720; Isaac Van Bibber died 1723; Matthias Van Bibber died 1739; John Jawert, county surveyor in 1707, married the widow of Casparus Hermen, and died 1726; Thomas Cresap, ferry owner at Port Deposit circa 1727 (later became Maryland's Indian Agent in western Maryland); John Ryland, ranger in 1722; Thomas Johnson, ranger in 1724; James Couts, 1696; John Smith, 1696; Capt. Deane Cook, 1696; Matthias Clements, 1696; Col. William Pearce, 1696; Capt. William Surting, 1696; Benjamin Allen, 1724; Capt. Henry Elves, 1744; James Heath, 1711, father of John Paul Heath, founder of Warwick, died 1746; Rev. Thomas Mansell, 1713; Rev. Peter Atwood, 1731; Rev. Thomas Pulton, 1742; Rev. John Kingdom, 1748; Rev. Joseph Greaton died 1749; Rev. John Lewis, 1753; Rev. Joseph Mosley, 1760; Rev. Mathias Manners, 1771; Charles Blake, 1770; Rev. Lawrence Vanderbush, 1692; Peter Sluyter, 1692; Rev. James Crawford, of South Sassafras Parish, died 1713; Rev. Richard Sewell, 1697; James Smithson, 1698; Matthias Hendrickson, 1698; Charles James, 1700; Richard Lugg, 1702; Rev. Stephen Boardley, 1702; Thomas Parsley, 1724; Rev. John Urmston, 1724; Rev. Hugh Jones, 1731; John Babenhime, 1731; James Bayard, 1731; Benjamin Sluyter, 1731; Nicholas Hyland, circa 1706; Joseph Young, circa 1706; Samuel Vans, circa 1706; Samson George, circa 1706; Francis Mauldin, circa 1706; John Currer, circa 1706; Richard Dobson, 1724; John Hamm, 1721; Rev. Walter Ross, circa 1722; Rev. Walter Hackett, 1733, died 1735; Rev. William Wye, 1736, died 1744; Capt. Nicholas Hyland, 1742; Capt. Zebulon Hollingsworth, 1742; Thomas Ricketts, 1742; Samuel Gilpin, carpenter, 1751; Dominie Fanning, schoolmaster, 1752; Robert Cummings, surety, 1752; John Neal, 1763; Rev. John Bradford, 1745, died 1746; Rev. John Hamilton, pastor, 1746-1773; Nicholas Painter, 1681; Philip Lynes and wife Anne Lynes, 1681; Philip Lynes died 1709; John Smith, son of William Smith, miller, 1706; William Anderson, distiller, 1707; Rev. Ericus Biork, 1697; John Hans Stillman, 1695; Allen Robinet, circa 1711; Reese Hinton, circa 1711; Lewis Jones, 1720; Stephen Onion, 1722; Richard Dobson, 1723; William Bristow, 1723; Thomas Jacobs, 1723; Valentine Hollingsworth, 1712; Robert Jones, 1711; Robert Dutton, circa 1716; John Cousine, an orphan in 1721, age 13, bound to John Pennington; Roger Kirk, circa 1719; Daniel Davis, innkeeper, 1724; Joshua Gee, 1722; Joseph Farmer, 1722; William Russell, 1722; John Ruston, 1722; George Williams, servant to Nathan Phillips, 1729; Richard Touchstone, 1727; Charles Rumsey, 1710; Thomas Hitchcock stole a horse from Owen Hughes in 1700; James Wroth, 1688; Matthew Pope, 1688; Col. Ephraim Augustine Herman, 1717; Col. John Ward, 1719; John Jawert, 1719; James Van Bibber, sheriff, 1719; Matthias Van Bibber, justice, 1719; James Wood, constable, 1720; John Sloan, disbarred attorney, 1717; William Frisby, 1682; John West, 1682; John Ryland, Jr., 1732; Benjamin and Sarah Pearce, 1732; John Knight and William Knight, 1732; Walter Scott, 1732; William Rumsey and Edward Rumsey, 1732; Robert Pennington, innkeeper, 1733; Edward Rumsey, carpenter, 1733. French Neutrals or Acadians in 1767: Issabel Brassey and family of 8 - Eneas Auber, alias Huber, and family of 6 - Eneas Granger and family of 9 - Joseph Auber, alone - Joseph Barban and wife and family of 8 (wished to migrate to Quebec, Canada) - John Baptist Granger and family (many died of smallpox). Philip Neilson, 1758; Hans Rudulph, 1758; Richard Thompson, 1723; Rev. Alexander Hutchinson, Presbyterian, 1723; Rev. George Whitefield, 1740; William Alexander and wife Araminta Alexander, 1741; Rev. Samuel Finley, 1744; Education Board of Visitors in

1723: Col. John Ward, Major John Dowdall, Col. Benjamin Pearce, Mr. Stephen Knight, Mr. Edward Jackson, Mr. Richard Thompson, and Mr. Thomas Johnson, Jr.; Rev. James Steel, 1745; Rev. John Beard, 1762; Adam Short, 1721; Davy Evans, 1721; Samuel Brice, 1722 (resident of New Connaught Manor for 9 years); Daniel Smith, 1722; George Sleyter, 1722; James Bond, 1722; John Bond, 1722; Edward Long, 1722; John Allen, 1722; Charles Allen, 1722; Elisha Gatchell, 1722; William Brown, 1722; John Churchman, 1722; Richard Brown, 1722; Roger Kirk, 1722; Isaac Taylor, 1722; John Ward, Sassafras Neck, 1665.

CECIL COUNTY COMMISSIONERS APPOINTED ON NOVEMBER 22, 1692: Capt. Charles James, Col. Casparus Hermen, Mr. Humphrey Tilton, Mr. William Ward, Mr. Henry Rigg, Mr. John James, and Mr. William Elms.

VESTRYMEN, 1692: The first vestrymen of North Sassafras Parish were Casparus Hermen, William Ward, John Thompson, Edward Jones, Henry Rigg, and Matthias Vanderhuyden. The first vestrymen of South Sassafras Parish, or Shrewsbury, were William Pearce, William Harris, Edward Blay, William Elms, Edward Skiddimor, and George Shirton.

INDEX

The same name may appear several times on the same page. Check the entire page. For Negroes or slaves without surnames see under "Negro."

AKEN, Thomas, 72
AKES, John, 72
AKEY, Samuel, 56, 122
AKIN, Alexander, 74
AKINS, Archibald, 127
ALAWAY, Thomas, 42
ALBANS, 98
ALBANY, 1
ALBENS, 1
ALDER, James, 66
ALDRIDGE, Thomas, 1
ALDRIDGE'S LOTT, 1
ALECOCK, Antoney, 80
ALET, Benjamin, 44
ALEXANDER, Aaron, 46
  Amos, 44, 46
  Andrew, 1, 3, 4, 26, 51, 52, 56, 58, 89, 126
  Araminta, 134
  Artha, 42
  Arthor, 39
  Arthur, 31, 33, 37, 39, 40, 42, 55, 80, 87, 89, 133
  Dan, 43
  Daniel, 38, 74, 129
  David, 1, 7, 33, 46, 55, 66, 89, 125, 133
  E., 2
  Eli, 47, 66, 87
  Elias, 33, 89, 125
  Elie, 64
  Ephraim, 89
  Francis, 1, 9, 89
  Isaac, 56, 89, 126
  Jacob, 53
  James, 9, 14, 29, 33, 44, 46, 50, 58, 90, 133
  Jedediah, 50
  Jessy, 46
  John, 31, 42, 44, 50, 51, 57, 59, 61, 62, 63, 85, 86, 90, 125,

  Joseph, 14, 33, 50, 90, 133
  Joshua, 90
  Mark, 1, 31, 36, 37, 39, 40
  Marten, 53
  Martin, 1, 90
  Mary, 90, 133
  Mathew, 55
  Matthew, 127
  Moses, 33, 43, 46, 51, 66, 90, 129
  Nathaniel, 51
  Robert, 55
  Samuel, 1, 4, 24, 28, 90
  Sushana, 66
  Theophelas, 66
  Theophilis, 44
  Theophilus, 129
  Theops., 50
  William, 8, 14, 30, 90, 130, 134
ALEXANDER'S CHANCE, 1
ALEXANDER'S LOT, 1
ALEXANDRA, Amos, 77
  James, 77
  Theophlous, 77
ALEXANDRIA, 1, 89
ALIASON, Corneliuos, 88
  Elias, 88
ALINSON, John, 128
ALISON, Robert, 59-61, 68
ALLAN, Henery, 78
ALLASON, Thomas, 90
ALLEN, Benjamin, 134
  Charles, 135
  Daniel, 90
  Henry, 55, 61
  James, 73
  John, 135
  Solomon, 80
  William, 77
ALLENDER, Nicolas, 41
  William, 55

ARANART, Benjamin, 41
ARANTS, Johanas, 69
ARBUCKLE, James, 90
ARCHBALD, John, 51
ARCHER, John, 29
    Thomas, 26, 87
ARCHVANHOOFE, Cornelius, 8
AREL, John, 72
ARENSON, Cornelius, 32
ARIANA, 2, 118
ARIANNA, 90
ARMSTRONG, Adam, 50
    Alexander, 52
    Archbald, 66
    Archebald, 77
    Archibald, 1, 44, 51, 54, 59, 86, 90, 129
    Benjamin, 85
    Ed., 59
    Edward, 2, 46, 52, 60, 63, 66, 80, 87, 90, 125
    Francis, 90, 127
    James, 5, 51, 90
    Jane, 37
    John, 43, 46, 55, 59, 66, 67, 77, 79, 81, 82, 90
    Robert, 36
    Thomas, 52, 76
    William, 43, 52, 77, 126
ARMSTRONG'S FORTUNE, 2
ARMSTRONGS VENTURE, 90
ARNET, Edward, 42
    Samuel, 42
    William, 55
ARNETT, Alexander, 43
    Joseph, 129
    Samuel, 29, 55, 129
ARNIT, Edward, 80
    Samuel, 80
ARNITT, Abraham, 84

ARNOLD, John, 53
ARRANCE, Johannas, 67
    Johannes, 15
ARRANT, Johann, 29
    Johannas, 2
    Johannes, 25, 33
    John, 33
ARRANTS, Harman, 75
    Johanas, 75
    Johannes, 90
    Nathan, 75
ARRANT'S CHANCE, 2
ARRENOHA, Micheal, 48
ARRENTS, Johannes, 45
ARTAGE, John, 64
ARTAGEE, John, 123
ARTERGE, John, 78
ARTHER, Matthew, 90
ARTHUR, James, 132
    Mathew, 52
ARTHUR EHASTON, 2
ARTIGE, John, 53
ARTIGEE, John, 47
ARUNDEL, 96, 111, 114, 115
ASH, George, 77
    John, 41, 44, 80, 129
    Robert, 41
ASHBAUGH, Jacob, 75
ASHFORD, John, 53, 122
ASHMORE, 96
ASHTON, Thomas, 70
ASKMORE, 2, 90, 109, 110, 112, 115, 122
ASREALL, James, 41
ASTON, James, 19, 90
    Thomas, 123
ATHABAUGH, Hanse, 79
ATKEY, Ann, 19, 34, 90
    John, 90
ATTABOUGH, Jacob, 67

Lewis, 49, 60, 64, 65, 86, 123

Thomas, 16, 34, 39, 49, 54, 64, 69, 78, 91, 123

BEARE, John, 129

BEARE POINT, 122

BEARS, Andrew, 43, 84

BEASLEY, Edward, 60, 62

BEASLY, Jeffery, 52

BEASTIN, Ephraim, 88

George, 88

John, 48

William, 34

BEASTON, Benjamin, 40, 122

Edward, 132

Elizabeth, 122

Ephraim, 126

Ephraram, 40

Georg, 40

George, 64, 86, 126

John, 64, 122

Thomas, 41, 52, 54, 126

William, 58, 132

Zebulon, 40

BEATTLE, Thomas, 45

BEATTY, John, 74

Peggy, 70

BEATY, Thos., 63

BEAVER DAM, 3, 100, 106, 115

BEAVER DAM NECK, 3

BEAVER ISLAND, 3

BEAVERDAM, 121

BEAZLEY, Edward, 87

Peter, 130

BECK, Edward, 3, 91

Jonathan, 3, 17, 91

Samuel, 132

William, 62

BECKER, Hans, 82

BECKERS ADDITION, 92

BECKETT, Thomas, 73

BECKS, William, 75

BECK'S MEADOW, 3

BECK'S MEADOWS, 3, 117

BECKWORTH, 3

BEDDINGTON PARK, 3

BEDFORD, Gunning, 3

BEDFORD'S CHANCE, 3, 106

BEDLE, Benjman, 79

Dominick, 79

Henery, 79

Hyland, 79

John, 6

Noble, 79

Richard, 79

Thomas, 69, 75, 79

William, 53, 79

BEEDEL, Stiphen, 69

BEEDLE, Augasteen, 78

Augustine, 86

Bennidick, 82

Henry, 55, 62

Hyland, 67

John, 3, 28, 64, 67, 82, 91, 132

Mary, 62

Perrigrine, 82

Rachael, 54

Raimon, 82

Raymond, 55

Richard, 54, 66, 91

Samuel, 14, 65, 82, 91

Sarah, 132

Stephen, 64, 78

Thomas, 67, 82, 91

William, 6, 9, 28, 67, 82, 91, 132

BEEDLE'S PROMISE, 3, 91

BEEK, William, 62

BEEKS, William, 75

BEEN, Thomas, 132

BEER, Andrew, 77

BEESLY, Jeffery, 91

BIDDLE, Augustine, 49
Stephen, 49
BIGGS, Daniel, 125
Judith, 40
Nathneil, 40
BIGS, Judah, 67
BIND, John, 60
BING, George, 44, 62, 76
Jane, 35
John, 2, 44, 62, 68, 76, 92, 129
BIORK, Ericus, 134
BIRD, Empson, 56
Mr., 88
Thomas, 52, 125
William, 126
BITERS BIT, 97
BITER'S BITT, THE, 3
BLACK, Alexander, 53
George, 44, 68
Hance, 66
Hugh, 57
Widdow, 76
William, 44, 76, 125
BLACK MARSH, 3, 101, 102, 110, 121
BLACKBORN, John, 37, 39
BLACKBORNE, John, 37
BLACKBURN, John, 31, 36, 130
BLACKENSTINE PARK, 3
BLACKISTON, Abel, 131
Ebenezer, 92
BLACKSTONE, Ebenezer, 131
BLADEN, John, 92
BLADES, Benjamin, 80
BLAKE, Charles, 134
John, 92, 127
Oliver, 127
Philemon, 70
BLAKISTON, Isaac, 49
BLANCHFIELD, Lawrence, 49

BLAND, George, 122
BLANESTEEN'S PARK RESURVEYED, 3
BLANKENSTEEN PARK RESURVEYED, 89
BLANKENSTEENS PARK, 119
BLANKENSTEENS PARK RESURVEYED, 119
BLANKENSTEIN, William, 3, 4, 9
BLANKENSTEIN FORREST, 3
BLANKENSTEINS PARK, 109
BLANKENSTEINS PARK RESURVEYED, 89
BLANKENSTEIN'S PARKE, 3
BLANKESTEEN, William, 92
BLANKESTEENS FORREST, 116, 119
BLANKESTEENS PARK, 119
BLANKESTEIN, William, 21
BLASHFORD, Manuel, 53
BLAY, Edward, 89, 131, 135
BLEAK, John, 41, 42, 80
BLENHAM, 92
BLENHEIM, 3
BLUNT, Robert, 92
BOAMEMS, Frederick, 126
BOARDLEY, Stephen, 134
BOCK, G., 33
BODLE, John, 92
BODY, ---n., 65
Benjamin, 49
Peter, 49
William, 84
BODYS, Benimine, 78
BOEM, Frederick, 57
BOERNE, 111
BOGE, Hugh, 67
BOGGS, Samuel, 128
William, 92
BOGS, John, 73
BOHANAN, John, 79

BOUGHANNON, James, 68
BOUING, Absolem, 40
Richard, 41
BOULDEN, James, 46
Jessy, 46
Richard, 46, 52
Thomas, 47, 65, 92
William, 3, 46
BOULDEN'S REST, 3
BOULDIN, James, 65
Jesse, 56
Richard, 66
Thomas, 62, 63, 66, 87, 126
William, 54, 66
BOULDING, Alexander, 3
Elidgah, 79
Elisah, 79
James, 79, 126
Jessey, 79
Nathan, 79
Richard, 22, 53, 92, 125
Thomas, 79, 92
William, 9, 63, 85, 92, 125
BOULDINGS REST, 91, 96
BOULLAN, Mickell, 78
BOULTON, Robert, 44, 76
BOURK, Thomas, 49
Tobias, 49
Walter, 49
BOURNE, William, 92
BOURNS FORREST, 98
BOURNS FORREST ADDITION, 98
BOURN'S FORREST AND ADDITION, 3, 100, 117
BOUYER, Peter, 60, 86
BOVING, Richard, 41
BOW--, Nathaniel, 49
BOWDY, Richard, 4

BOWDY'S FOLLY AND GREENWOOD'S ADVANCEMENT, 4
BOWEN, Absalom, 126
Absolam, 66
John, 127
Jonathan, 81
Richard, 52, 67, 126
Thomas, 69, 81, 126
William, 52, 81
BOWENS, Samuel, 133
BOWER, Peter, 66
BOWERS, Cristian, 41
Hendry, 41
James, 130
BOWHAMAN, John, 43
BOWIN, thomas, 42
BOWINGS, Thomas, 65
BOWLDING, William, 92
BOWLDINGS NEGLECT, 92
BOWLIN, Wiliam, 92
William, 131
BOWLING, William, 29
BOWYER, John, 92
BOYD, Francis, 31
John, 122
Nathan, 128
Robert, 72
Thomas, 60, 61
William, 43
BOYD, William, 52, 68, 74, 84
BOYER, Augustine, 123
John, 92
Peter, 25, 33, 45, 50, 92
Richard, 19
BOYLE, James, 66, 87, 88
BOYLES, Daniel, 127
James, 61, 62, 127
John, 127
BOYLS, James, 40

BRISTO, John, 76
BRISTOE, John, 4
BRISTOE'S CONVENIENCY, 4
BRISTOL, 91, 92
John, 93
BRISTOLE, 4
BRISTOLL, 92, 96, 98
BRISTOLLS CONVENIENCY, 108
BRISTOW, 92, 120
George, 51
John, 93, 133
William, 25, 26, 27, 45, 51, 56, 63, 65, 75, 85, 134
BRISTOW MOYETY, 110
BRISTOWE, William, 93
BRISTOWS CONVENIENCE, 108
BRISTOWS CONVENIENCY, 93
BROAD AX(E), 4, 119
BROAD NECK, 4, 95
BROADLY, John, 77
BROAK, Thomas, 43
BROCKSON, John, 58, 69, 78
Thomas, 78
BRODERICK, Thomas, 70
BRODLEY, Gorge, 77
Joseph, 57
Neale, 77
Ritchard, 77
BROGAN, Patrick, 79, 123
BROMLEY, 101
BROMPHIELD, Francis, 78
BROOGHAR, Fredrick, 40
BROOKERS, william, 8
BROOKING, Charles, 38, 39
John, 38, 68
BROOKINS, Charles, 35, 38, 59, 62, 64, 86
John, 33, 37, 38
BROOKS, James, 4, 75
John, 4

Thomas, 75
William, 70
BROOKS' MEADOW, 4
BROOKS' RANGE NO. 91, 4
BROOM, Widow, 44, 84
BROOME, Robert, 93
BROSTOLL, 4
BROTHERINGTON, Robert, 127
BROTHERTON, Robert, 45
William, 45
BROUGHT, Daniel, 125
BROWN, Dan, 70
David, 127
Ele(a)nor, 48, 55, 58, 60, 62
Elijah, 46
Gabriel, 13
Garrett, 62
Hugh, 44, 60, 76
James, 30, 76, 133
Jeremiah, 26
Jethro, 130
John, 7, 47, 49, 51, 54, 58, 60, 63, 64, 70, 74, 77-79, 85, 93, 122, 123, 127
Joseph, 129
Joshua, 43, 74
Matthew, 127
Mosses, 60
Peter, 51, 126
Richard, 48, 49, 84, 124, 135
Samuel, 52, 130
Thomas, 46, 93
Widow, 77
William, 30, 47, 50, 57, 66, 68, 74, 129, 135
BROWNE, Daniel, 93
Hugh, 69
Peregrine, 15
BROWNING, John, 2, 4, 17, 22, 26, 28, 133
Thomas, 93

CORBIT, James, 42, 63, 69, 81, 87
  William, 42, 81
CORBITT, William, 61
CORBOROUGH, 91, 109, 111, 118
CORBROUGH, 111
CORBY, James, 129
CORD, Thomas, 29, 33, 68
CORENGEM, 6
CORENGIMM, 6
CORETHERS, John, 77
COREY, Robert, 77
CORKATINE ADDITION TO
CROUCHES OVERSIGHT, 6
CORLET, Joseph, 42
CORLETT, Joseph, 62, 81
CORLOTT, Joseph, 68
CORNAX TOWN, 116
CORNELIASTON, 6
CORNELIENSON, 108
CORNELINSTON, 6
CORNELIOUSON, 95
CORNELISON, Mathias, 32
CORNELIUS, Hugh, 7
  Mathias, 6
CORNESAL, Adam, 48
CORNISH, Adam, 48
CORNWALL, 6
  Thomas, 125
CORNWALL'S ADDITION, 6
CORNWELL, 100
  Thomas, 80
CORNWELL ADDITION, 100
COROBOROUGH, 93
COROBOUGH, 7
CORRITHERS, Francis, 77
  Robert, 77
CORSINE, John, 52
CORSS, James, 5
CORTNEY, Arther, 46
COSDEN, Alphonse, 28

Alphonso, 30, 34, 51, 95
Alphonson, 89
James, 124
COSDIN, James, 64
COSER, Simon, 81
COSIER, Simon, 45
COSLEY, Walter, 125
COSTELLO, Edward, 70
COSTER'S HARBOUR, 7
COTHEW, John, 31
COTRINGER, ---, 70
COTT, John S., 44
COTTEY, Able, 133
COUCH, Thomas, 70
COUGHRAN, John, 76
  Robert, 76
COUGHRON, Alexander, 81
  William, 81
COULTER, Andrew, 55, 56, 59, 68,
87, 128
  James, 50
  Richard, 76
COURIER, John, 39
COURSEY, Thomas, 7
  William, 7, 95
COURSEY'S TRIANGLE, 7
COURT, Joseph, 130
COURTIER, William, 95
COURTNEY, Michael, 126
COUSINE, John, 134
COUTS, James, 134
COVELL, Thomas, 95
COVILL, John, 95
COWADON, James, 53
COWAN, James, 79, 81
  John, 47, 79
COWARDIN, Ambrose, 48
  Peter, 48
COWARDING, Ann, 58
  Mary, 55

Peter, 61
Robert, 76, 81
William, 29
CREVET, J., 70
CRISP, Thomas, 51
CRISSWELL, John, 41
CROCKER, Andrew, 47, 68
Capt., 96
Robert, 15, 34
Thomas, 96
William, 55, 64, 86
CROCKET, Benjamin, 29
Mary, 29
Samuel, 42
CROCKETT, Benjamin, 128
John, 69, 81
Mr., 36
Samuel(l), 31, 62, 78
CROCKRAN, Joseph, 70
CROE, Edward, 66
CROKER, Andrew, 122
Rachel, 19
Robert, 19, 53, 132
CROMEL, James, 67
CROMWELL, James, 70, 80
CRONNEY, Jeremiah, 48
CRONWALL, Thomas, 41
CROOK, Robert, 131
CROOKE, Robert, 88, 131
CROOKSHANK, William, 31, 42
CROOKSHANKS, John, 63, 87
CROSBE, John, 69
CROSBEY, James, 70
CROSBIE, John, 78
CROSBY, John, 55, 86, 122
Susan, 70
Thomas, 125
CROSBYE, John, 70
CROSEWELL, John, 37
CROSHER, William, 31

CROSIER, John, 96
CROSS SAILE, 118
CROSSAYLE, 7
CROSSWELL, David, 51
Joseph, 50
Samuell, 50
CROUCH, Ann, 34
Isaac, 7, 33, 65, 69
Jaas, 45
John, 69, 78, 84
Rachel, 19
Richard, 78
Stephen, 75
Thomas, 19, 45, 52, 65, 69, 75, 96, 128
Willam, 45, 65
CROUCHES OVERSIGHT, 102
CROUCH'S ADDITION, 7
CROUTCH, Thomas, 96
CROUTCHES OVERSIGHT, 7
CROW, Andrew, 40, 62, 126
Edward, 44, 77
John, 40, 77, 126
Mary, 59, 60
William, 52, 126
CROWLEE, Alexander, 76
CROWMELL, James, 69, 80
CROZIER, John, 96, 125
CRUICKSHANKS, William, 73
CRUIKSHANKS, William, 68
CRUMBWELL, James, 46
CRUMMELL, James, 59
CRUMMEY, Jeremiah, 82
CRUTCHLEY, James, 85
CULBERTSON, Patrick, 87
CULLAH, George, 36
CULLEN, William, 70
CULLEY, John, 66
CULLIGAN, Maurice, 84
CULLY, ---, 70

DOE HILL, 8, 111
DOE HILL AND BEAR POINT, 8
DOGAN, Alexander, 75
DOHERTY, Patrick, 70
DOIL, Patrick, 45
DOLAND, Catherine, 70
William, 70
DOLE DIFE, 114
DOLE DYFR, 8
DOLEVAIN, 105, 121
DOLL DICE, 118
DOLLVAINE, 97
DOLLVANE, 8
DOLVAIN, 110
DOMAGAN, Roger, 61, 62
DOMAGIN, Roger, 59
DOMIGAN, Roger, 43
DONAGAN, Roger, 61
DONAHO, John, 65
DONALDS, William, 97
DONALSON, Charles, 57
DONAVE, John, 60, 61
DONAWE, John, 61
DONELSON, Major, 97
DONETT, Francis, 126
DONIHUE, Gilbirt, 42
DONLY, John, 57
DONNALLY, Neal, 61
DONNEL, William, 97
DONNELLY, Neal, 47
DONNELY, James, 66
DONNOHOE, James, 49
John, 49
DONOHO, John, 60
Joshua, 56, 59, 61, 86, 88
Mary, 88
DONOHOE, John, 61
DONOHOE'S PURCHASE, 8
DONOWAY, John, 81
DOOLING, Margarett, 54

DORAWE, James, 128
DORRALL, James, 83
DORREL, Nicholas, 47
DORRELL, Dennis, 124
James, 123
Nicholas, 17, 34, 53, 55, 86, 97, 123
Nicklas, 39
Richard, 125
DORSEY, John Hammond, 3, 97
John Hamon, 65
DORSON, William, 8
DORSON'S POINT, 8, 105
DORSY, Margaret, 70
DOUCH, Hugh, 131
DOUCHET, Dr., 70
DOUGAN, James, 43
DOUGHARTY, Edward, 64
Henry, 45
DOUGHERTY, Arsbald, 82
Charles, 127
David, 76
Edward, 33, 60-62, 130
Henry, 82, 127
Hugh, 43, 73, 127
Mikel, 42
Nathaniel, 8, 97
Phillip, 73
DOUGHERTYS DESIRE, 99, 111
DOUGHERTY'S ENDEAVOUR, 8, 99, 106
DOUGHETTY, Patrick, 48
DOUGHRTEY, Edward, 41
DOUGLAS,
Abraham, 40
Archibald (Arch.), 70, 97
George, 49, 65 (-orge), 70, 97, 123
George Sewal(l), 58, 64
George Sewel, 80
Hugh, 125
Isaac, 40

ETHERINGTON'S TRYAL, 8
ETHRINGTON, Bartholomew, 55
  Thomas, 51
ETHRINGTONS CHANCE, 98
ETHRINGTONS TRYAL, 98
EVANS, Amos, 81, 129
  Daby, 135
  Elias, 98
  Evan, 70
  James, 42, 70, 81, 98
  John, 81, 98
  Margaret, 57, 128
  Robert, 8, 9, 22, 51, 58, 61, 62, 86,
  98, 132
EVANS' PURCHASE, 8
EVANS' SUCCESS, 9
EVARDSON, Evard, 64
  Jacob, 65
EVARSON, Evart, 72
  Jacob, 72
EVENS, Robert, 43, 77
EVERARD, John, 98
  Thomas, 98
EVERARDS FORTUNE, 98
EVERDSON, Jacob, 85
EVERSON, Elias, 52, 98
  Evert, 98
EVERTON, Evert, 50
  Jacob, 50
EVERTSON, Elizabeth, 64
  Elizebeth, 48
  Evert, 53, 98, 125
  Jacob, 48, 80, 125
  Job, 130
EVINGS, Peter, 37
EVINS, Amos, 41
  Peter, 36
EWENS, James, 30
EWING, Alexander, 98, 127
  Amos, 31, 181

Ellexander, 73
George, 64, 82, 86
James, 98, 130
John, 42, 54, 62, 63, 81, 85, 98, 129,
132
Joshua, 51, 98
Moses, 31, 42, 81, 127
Nathaniel, 50, 98
Natt, 82
Patrick (Pat.), 62, 98
Patt, 45, 82
Robert, 60, 62, 82
Samuel, 42, 45, 62, 64, 81, 82, 86,
87, 98, 128
William, 13, 16, 45, 46, 50, 54, 62,
68, 82, 98, 129, 130, 132
EWINGS, Alexander, 30
  John, 65
  Moses, 30
  Patrick, 65
  Samuel, 65
  William, 65
EWNING, Alexander, 43
EYLA, 9, 115, 117
EYLER, Mary, 70
  Robert, 70

-F-

FAGAN, Daniel, 73
FAGEINGS, Patrick, 41
FAGEN, John, 38
FAIR HILL, 9, 95, 98, 102, 106, 107
FAIRES, Moses, 98
FAN, William, 45, 75
FANE, John, 53
FANNING, Dominick, 128
  Dominie, 134
FARIER, Samuel, 76
FARIS, David, 46

FRYERS NEGLECT, 109
FUGAN, Daniel, 127
FULLERTON, Joseph, 123
FULTON, Alexander, 21, 46, 99
  Ann, 1
  Frances, 82
  Francis, 1, 10, 60, 86
  Frederick, 132
  James, 46
  John, 66, 99
  Samuel, 46, 82, 87, 132
FULTON'S DESIRE, 10
FULTOWN, John, 44
  William, 44
FUREY, Darby, 123
  William, 126
FURGISON, Benjamin, 42
FURMAN, Mr., 88
FURNER, Edward, 69, 78
FURRON, Edward, 133
FURRONER, --wd., 65
  Edward, 55, 56, 59, 60, 63, 85, 86, 123

-G-

G---, John, 69
GABRIEL OLD FIELD, 102
GAFEN, John, 124
GAILY, John, 88
GALAHER, John, 68, 70
  Neal G., 70
  Peggy, 70
GALASBIE, William, 65
GALASPY, --ry, 65
  Alexander, 53
GALBRETH, Samuel, 41
GALE, George, 99
  John, 25, 99
  Levin, 99, 133

Lydia, 55
William, 122
GALLAHER, Daniel, 70
  Hugh, 70
  John, 56
GALLASBIE, Samuel, 37
GALLASPEY, Samuel, 40
GALLASPIE, James, 87
GALLASPYE, George, 100
  John, 99
GALLAUGHER, William, 82
GALLAWAY, James, 99
  John, 46
  William, 131
GALLISPIE, Michael, 88
GALLOHER, Michael, 73
GALLOWAY, William, 10
GALLOWAY'S FARM, 10
GANTLEY, James, 58, 81
GARDEN, 10
GARDENER, John, 36
GARDINER'S FORREST, 10
GARDNER, Francis, 51
  James, 74, 84, 128
  John, 51
  William, 129
GARDNER'S ADVICE, 10, 104
GARDNERS FORREST, 117
GARDNER'S GIFT, 10
GARISH, Benjamin, 45
  Edward, 75
  William, 45
GARITTY, Brian, 72
GARNELL, Daniel, 29
GARNER, James, 42, 68
GARNER'S GIFT, 10, 98
GARNEY GIFT, 120
GARRETT, Amos, 61, 99
  Nathaniel, 88, 133
GARRETY, Briant, 70

GILDER'S FORREST, 10, 100
GILES, J., 88
  Jacob, 58
  John, 66
  Thomas, 88
  Tom, 87, 88
GILESPIE, Samuel, 37
GILFORD, John, 127
GILKEY, William, 60, 61
GILLASPIE, George, 100
  John, 77, 99
GILLES, John, 128
GILLESPIE, George, 100, 133
  Jno(?0, 62
  Nat., 62
  Natt, 82
  Robert, 46, 82, 132
  Samuel, 37, 38, 46, 55, 62, 82, 132
  Steaphen, 82
  W., 58
  Will, 62
  William, 18, 46, 63, 74, 82, 87, 100
GILLESPY, Simon, 77
  William, 43
GILLETSON, William, 52
GILLIGAN, William, 83
GILLILAND, John, 77
  Thomas, 76, 84
GILLIS, John, 44, 75, 76
  Thomas, 44, 100
  William, 77
GILLISPIE, Henry, 84
GILPEN, Joseph, 38
  Samuel, 44
GILPIN, Joseph, 3, 10, 20, 22, 36, 37, 38, 39, 43, 62, 63, 66, 77, 85, 89, 100
  Samuel, 30, 37, 38, 63, 76, 85, 100, 134
GILPIN'S ADDITION, 10

GIRDLE OAK, THE, 10
GIVANS, Robert, 130
GIVEN, John, 128
GIVENS, Robert, 73, 100
  William, 73
GIVIANS, William, 42
GLANCE, 10
GLANVIL, Marius, 81
GLASAGOW, John, 81
  Robert, 81
  William, 81
GLASCO, William, 62
GLASCOW, James, 68
  William, 86
GLASGOW, 10, 93, 96, 108
  ---, 60
  James, 30, 42, 54, 73
  John, 30, 43, 60, 63, 73, 85, 87, 127
  Robert, 62
  William, 31, 42, 69, 73, 87, 128
GLASHFORD, Henry, 100
GLASHOW, William, 41
GLASPEY, Samuel, 39
GLASPY, John, 123
GLASS, John, 76
GLASS HOUSE, 10, 95, 96, 100, 107, 110-113
GLASSFORD, Henry, 100
GLEAVES, Mathew Driver, 65
GLEEB, Pharloe, 24
GLEEMIN, Robert, 77
GLEN, George, 76
  Nathaniel, 84
GLENN, Ann, 88
  Robert, 53
  Samuel, 83
GLINN, Robert, 100
GLOSSON, John, 131
GLOSTER, 10
GLOSTER MOYETY, 110

GRAHAMS, James, 42
GRAHM, Archabel, 78
GRAHMS, James, 66
GRAINGER, Lazerus, 52
  Lazors, 65
GRANBURY, Gibson, 87
GRANER, Lazers, 45
GRANGE, 103, 108
GRANGER, Eneas, 134
  John Baptist, 134
  Lazaros, 69
  Lazarus, 76
GRANT, George, 60
GRASE, Aaron, 43
GRATITUDE, 11, 99, 103
GRAVES, Jesse, 73
GRAY, Alexander, 64, 87
  David, 72, 122
  Isaac, 53
  John, 17, 51, 56, 74, 77, 84, 100
  Joseph, 53, 56, 125
  Miles, 100
  Richard, 10
  William, 56, 77
GRAYDON, Joseph, 123
GRAYHAM, William, 100
GRAYS LOT, 100
GREADY, Edward, 65
GREATON, Joseph, 134
  Mr., 71
GREEDEY, Ritcherd, 45
GREEN, Henry, 67
  James, 50
  John, 30, 42, 73, 129
  Jon., 63, 68
  Richard, 59
  Thomas, 100, 129
GREEN FIELD, 120
GREEN MEADOWS, 11
GREEN OAKE, 11

GREEN SPRING, 11, 110
GREENBERRY, 11, 100
GREENBURY, 92, 106
GREENFIELD, 11, 114, 115, 120
GREENLAND, Flower, 128
  Thomas, 58
GREENWOOD, John, 4
GREY, Alaxander, 76
  Miles, 100
GRIBBEN, Hugh, 65
GRIBBIN, Hugh, 47
GRIDLEY, Jeremiah, 132
GRIFFEE, Richard, 31, 59, 63, 81, 85, 86, 100
  William, 31, 81
GRIFFEN, Hugh, 124
GRIFFEY, John, 68, 69
  William, 60
GRIFFIN, 11, 103, 104, 109, 114, 118
  Charles, 100
  Hugh, 70
  Thomas, 100
GRIFFITH, Benjamin, 15
  Edward, 2, 19, 100
  John, 44
  Nicholas, 100
  Richard, 66
  Thomas, 133
GRIFFY, John, 42
GRIG, Aaron, 84
GRIMES, Barnet, 56, 123
  Bryan, 71, 122
  James, 38, 129
  John, 100
  Samuel, 100, 128
  Thomas, 83
  William, 100
GRISE, Isaac, 40
GRISLEY, Jeremiah, 53
GRIST, Isaac, 36, 39

Augustine, 1, 3, 17, 24, 32, 88
Casp: A:, 131
Casparus, 15, 32, 131
Casparus Augustine, 88, 131
Col., 34, 102
Ephraim, 32, 133
Ephraim August, 6
Ephraim Augustine, 17, 27, 30, 102, 134
Ephraim Augustus, 89
Francina, 32
Georgius, 32
Judith, 32
Margarita, 32
HERMANS MOUNT, 109
HERMAN'S RAMBLE, 12
HERMANS RAMBLES, 103
HERMANS RANGE, 109
HERMEN, Augustina, 133
  Augustine, 133
  Casparus, 134, 135
  Catharine, 133
  Susanna, 133
HERN, Anthony, 53
HERRICKSON, Christopher, 102
HERRING, David, 72
  John, 81
HERRING POND, 12
HERSEY, Solomon, 41
HERVEY, Andrew, 77
  William, 77
HESSEY, James, 61, 78
HESSY, ---as, 65
HETHERINGTON, Henry, 61
HEWET, James, 42, 68
HEWETT, James, 127
HEWKIN, Rebecca, 35
HEYLAND, Nicholas, 102
HIBETS, Robert, 68
HIBITS, Robert, 44

HICKMAN, Joseph, 44, 68, 76
HICKS, John, 131
  Peter, 129
HIDGCOCK, John Thomas, 45
  Thomas, 45
  Thomas John, 45
HIGH OFFLEY, 12, 105, 110
HIGH PARK(E), 12, 96, 97, 101, 110
HIGHLAND, 12
  John, 5, 12, 19, 21, 102
  Nicholas, 5, 12, 19, 102
HIGHLANDS, 99, 101, 102, 103
HIGHLANDS CHANCE, 103
HIGHLANDS FOREST, 103
HIGHLANDS PART, 103
HILAND, John, 28
  Nikolas, 12
HILAND'S FORREST, 12
HILL, David, 42, 62, 73, 129
  Francis, 83
  John, 102, 125, 129
  Joseph, 84
  Matthew, 129
  Richard, 16, 102
  Robert, 37, 42, 68, 73, 88, 129
  Samuel, 11, 44, 55, 59, 63, 77, 86, 102, 129
  Thomas, 61
  Walter, 53, 125
  William, 5, 102, 131
HILL FOOT, 12, 104
HILLAS, William, 84
HILLEN, Nathaniel, 12
HILLEN'S ADVENTURE, 12
HILLES, John, 77
  Mathew, 77
  William, 76
HILLIN, Nathan, 102
HILLING, Nathll., 131
HILLINS GROVE, 102

HOLLANDS, Jonathan, 80
HOLLAND'S DELIGHT, 12
HOLLANDSWORTH, Henry, 77
Jacob, 77
Thomas, 76
Zeblon, 77
HOLLEADGER, Philip, 1
Phillip, 133
HOLLENS, John, 48
Johnathan, 48
HOLLET, Andrew, 127
Hanah, 66
John, 126
HOLLIN POINT, 13
HOLLINGS, ----m, 128
Abraham, 53, 83, 122
Christopher, 126
John, 72
Jonathan, 64, 72, 123
Thomas, 79, 85, 124
HOLLINGSWORTH, Abraham, 8, 13, 14, 21
Abram, 9, 20, 24
H., 33
Henry, 38, 56, 60, 64, 87, 102
Jacob, 56
Jesse, 36, 66, 73, 86, 87
John, 9
Lydia, 16
Stephan, 9
Stephen, 2, 13, 18, 20, 24, 26, 102
Thomas, 5, 14
Valentine, 134
William, 133
Zebulon (Zeb.), 5, 13, 29, 30, 33, 37, 38, 51, 55, 66, 131, 134
HOLLINGSWORTH(S) INSPECTION, 13, 102
HOLLINGSWORTH(S) PARCELLS, 13, 102

HOLLINGSWORTH'S FIRST PARCEL, 13
HOLLINGSWORTH'S SECOND PARCEL, 13, 100, 101
HOLLINS, Jonathan, 71
HOLLINSWORTH, 108
Abra, 102
Catherine, 102
John, 102
Lydia, 102
Mary, 102
Thomas, 102
Zebula, 102
HOLLIS, William, 55
HOLLOWAY, John, 57
HOLLOWELL, Richard, 103
HOLLOWING POINT, 13, 18, 96, 102, 110
HOLLY, Robert, 6, 13
HOLLY'S EXPEDITION, 13
HOLMES, Abraham, 129, 132
John, 129
HOLMLEY, 115
HOLMONDSTON, 13
HOLMS, Abraham, 43, 77, 103
James, 43, 87, 128
John, 43, 77
HOLT, 13, 94, 101
George, 67, 83
Isaac, 83
Joseph, 58
Obediah, 103
HOLTEN, George, 34
Jessey, 34
HOLTHAM, John, 1, 16, 22, 103
Spencer, 62, 67
Spenser, 41
HOLTON, George, 53, 124
Jessey, 83
HOLY, Robert, 13, 103

LARENIM'S CONVENIENCY, 15
LARGANT, John, 15
LARGANT'S NECK, 15
LARIMORE, Augustine, 106
LARIMORES CONVENIENCY, 111
LARKIN, John, 5, 11, 15, 18
   Thomas, 16
LARKINS, Jermiah, 52
LARKIN'S DESIRE, 15, 97, 111, 114, 116
LARMOORE, Edward, 131
LARONSON, Andrew, 40
LAROOE, Peter, 126
LARRAMORE, Augustina, 133
   Edward (Ed., Edwd.), 34, 89, 106
   Robert, 15
   Roger, 15, 22, 89, 106, 133
LARRAMORE'S ADDITION, 15, 97, 106, 107, 120
LARRAMORES NECK, 97, 106, 109, 120
LARRAMORE'S NECK ENLARGED, 15, 101, 106, 107, 109, 120
LARRANCE, John, 46
LARRIMOR, John, 77
LARRIMORE, David, 74
   John, 84
LARRIMORES NECK, 116
LARRIMORES NECK ENLARGED, 107, 109
LASHELL, William, 37
LASHELS, William, 45
LASHLEY, Francis, 68
   George, 51
   John, 74
   Robert, 50, 106
   William, 106
LASHLY, Cornailes, 41
   Robert, 68

LASLEY, Robert, 63, 87
LASON, George, 43
   John, 43
LASSELLS, William, 75
LASSEN, William, 124
LATHAM, Aron, 53
   John, 40, 41, 58, 60-62, 68, 106, 127
   Mary, 132
   Moses, 87, 106, 128, 132
LATHAN, Aaron, 106
   Moses, 51
LATHEM, John, 52
LATHRAN, Philip, 124
LATTA, Robert, 77, 84
LAUGHLAN, John, 74
LAUGHLIN, John, 42, 132
   William, 80
LAUGHRAN, Joseph, 122
LAVIN, Thomas, 71
LAW, Michael, 44
LAWERY, Benjamin, 68
   James, 68
LAWLER, John, 129
   William, 67, 80
LAWRENCE, 125
   David, 106
   John, 54, 58, 67, 126
   Samuel, 106
LAWRENCESON, Lawrence, 52
LAWRENMORE, George, 15
LAWRENMORE'S NECK, 15
LAWRENSON, Andrew, 55, 60, 67, 86-88, 126
LAWSON, David, 106
   George, 77, 106, 129
   Hugh, 25, 50, 106
   John, 15, 77, 106, 126, 133
   Jorge, 77
   Mary, 106, 133
   Peter, 41, 52, 54-56, 88, 126, 133

LYLLY, 71
LYME, John, 88
LYNARD, Clem, 49
LYNCH, 73
  Anthony, 50, 51, 59-62, 88, 124
  Elizabeth, 60, 61
  George, 61, 124
  John, 128
  William, 60, 61, 62, 67, 83, 124
LYNES, Anne, 134
  Philip (Phil.), 107, 134
LYON, Hugh, 81
  James, 52
  John, 66, 81, 87, 107
  Robert, 31, 61, 69, 81
LYTFOOT, Thomas, 15, 26
LYTHUNAM, Isaac, 68
LYTLE, Robert, 64, 86

-M-

MAAHAN, John, 128
MABOA, Benjimin, 63
  John, 63
MABURY, Francis, 30
MACADAMS, Mary, 71
MCADOE, Andrew, 127
MCALASTER, Hugh, 50
MCALLISTER, Hugh, 127
MCARTER, John, 51
MCAVINCHEE, Edward, 127
MCAWNEKEY, John, 68
MCBRIDE, Hugh, 76
  William, 68
MCCABE, John, 43, 68
MCCAFFERTY, John, 125
  Pady, 46
MCCAFFITY, Patrick, 66
MCCAGE, Francis, 71

MCCALLA, John, 87
MCCALVEY, Owen, 64
MCCAN, John, 123
MCCANNEHAN, Robert, 78
MCCAREY, James, 43
  William, 43
MCCARQ, Richard, 53
MCCARRY, Richard, 122
MCCARTNEY, James, 74
  John, 66, 79
MCCARTY, 71
  John, 47, 85
MCCAULEY, Barnabas, 76
  Bryan, 44
  John, 76
MCCAY (MACCAY), Daniel, 62, 82
  Hugh, 31
  James, 43, 59, 108, 125
  John, 31, 43, 62
  Moses, 58
  Robert, 108
MCCAYE, Beety, 77
  James, 77
  John, 77
MCCHESNEY, Samuel, 74
  Walter, 81
MCCINNEY, Andrew, 46
MCCLAIN, Daniel, 43
MCCLAN (MACCLAN), ---nl., 65
  Daniel, 60, 61, 69, 78
MCCLANE, Daniel, 62
MCCLANN, Daniel, 59, 61
MCCLAREY, Samuel, 41, 55
MCCLARY, Samuel, 66
  William, 128
MCCLE--, ---, 57
MCCLEAN, Daniel, 55, 66, 122
MCCLEARY, Robert, 51
  Thomas, 87

Benjamin, 33, 45, 52, 64, 75, 86, 109, 130
Frainces, 45
Francies, 65
Francis, 33, 60, 62, 75, 87, 89, 134
Frans., 33
Joseph, 39, 128
Mary, 69, 75
Widow, 109
William, 33, 76
MAULDING, Benjamin, 64
Francis, 17, 109
MAULDIN'S FOREST, 17
MAULSTER, John, 67
MAXFIELD, John, 46
Robert, 82
MAXWELL, Arthur, 84
William, 81
MAY, Thomas, 64, 86
MAYBERRY, Joseph, 61
MAYBURY, Francis, 42, 57-59, 73, 88, 129
Joseph, 58, 74
Mrs., 87
MAYFORD, 17
MEAKINS, Joshua, 51
MEAN, Nicholas, 129
MEANS, Andrew, 43, 59, 66, 77, 128
Benjaben, 77
William, 82
MEANT MORE, 121
MEARN, Michael, 81
MEARS, Andrew, 60
William, 55
MECAY, Ephram, 48
MECBRIDE, William, 48
MECGREGORY, 17
Hugh, 17
MECHARY, Richard, 18
MECHLIN, John, 77

MECLAN, Danniel, 48
John, 48
MECTAGE, Thomas, 48
MEDFORD, Thomas, 21
MEDOWELL, John, 65
MEDOWL, John, 77
MEEK, Adam, 30, 42, 81, 128
James, 43
John, 29
William, 30, 41, 54
MEEKENS, Richard, 67
MEEKINGS, Peter, 57
MEEKINGS ADVENTURE, 113
MEEKINS, Peter, 17, 109, 125
Richard, 58, 75
MEEKINS' ADVENTURE, 17, 109
MEEKS, Adam, 65
James, 68
MEESE, Henry, 19
MEETAGE, Thomas, 48
MEGILLIN, James, 80
MEGOWEN, Michael, 48
MEHAFFY, Thomas, 43
MEIGHAN, Thomas, 71
MEKE, John, 51
MEKEANEY, Samuel, 45
MEKENEY, Samuell, 65
MEKINN, Garrett, 33
MEKLREY, John, 48
MELFORT, John, 124
MELLOWLAND, 117
MELOAN, Jonathan, 47
Thomas, 46
MELODY, Patrick, 43
MELON, Thomas, 66
MELONE, Jonathan, 53
MENNECOSSENS, James, 48
Michael, 48
MENNEN, Mathias, 49
MENSON, Mary, 92

Thomas, 18, 46, 76, 110

NASH'S ADVENTURE, 18, 110

NAVELL, James, 51

NAVINGTON GREEN, 93

NEAL, Henry, 125
  Jacob, 57, 87
  John, 35, 36, 42, 63, 73, 128, 134
  Terrence, 74

NEALE, Edward, 71
  Henry, 70
  John, 68

NEALEY, John, 36

NEALL, Thomas, 50

NEALLY, William, 128

NEAVEL, John, 75
  William, 75

NECESSITY, 18, 114

NEDRICK, John, 128

NEEDLE, Noble, 61

NEELE, John, 36

NEEPER, James, 132
  John, 132
  Joseph, 127, 132
  William, 132

NEESBURY, Mary, 80
  Michael, 80

NEGAL, John, 57

NEGLECT, 18, 101

NEGRO [No surname given]:
  Abelow, 41; Abner, 45, 47; Adam,
  43, 48; Aky, 44; Aleck, 55; Amos, 44;
  Andrew, 41; Andrew Rany, 41; Ann,
  40; Antheny, 48; Arah, 42; Archabel,
  45; Aries, 44; Arrer, 42; Babe, 44;
  Beck, 40; Ben, 41, 43, 44, 45, 46, 47,
  48; Benjamin, 47; Bess, 40, 42-44, 45,
  46, 47; Bet, 43, 45, 46, 48; Betey, 41;
  Bett, 41, 42, 46-48; Bette, 45, 48;
  Betty, 47; Bigs, 43; Bina, 47; Bistow,
  45; Black, 47; Bob, 40, 43, 44, 45, 46,
  47, 48, 49; Bobb, 40, 46; Boson, 43,
  47; Boston, 48; Bram, 42; Bridget,
  41; Brigget, 41; Britan, 40; Burch,
  46; Burdock, 40; Cara, 42; Cate, 40,
  46, 47; Catto, 43; Cesar, 45; Cezar,
  47; Chance, 42; Charles, 40, 41, 42,
  43, 47, 48, 49; Charming, 47;
  Clayton, 47; Coffe, 48; Coock, 45;
  Cook, 41; Cudjo, 40; Cuff, 46, 47;
  Cuggoe, 47; Dafney, 45; Dan, 41;
  Dancer, 42, 43; Daniel, 45; Dave, 41,
  47; David, 45, 47, 49; Daw, 40; Dely,
  48; Dick, 42, 43, 45-48, 49; Diddo,
  40; Din, 45; Dina, 42, 45, 48; Dinah,
  42, 44; Dine, 40; Dino, 49; Dobin,
  42; Doblen, 48; Doll, 41; Dolly, 44;
  Dover, 46; Dunkin, 49; Effy, 46;
  Emanuel, 43; Ester, 42; Fill, 42, 49;
  Filles, 41; Fillis, 44; Flint, 47; Flora,
  40, 42, 44-47; Frank, 43, 46-48;
  Gabriel, 46; Gabril, 45; Geck, 43;
  Georg, 40, 45; George, 42, 43, 47;
  Gif, 44; Glasgow, 47; Gorg, 41, 42;
  Graner, 45; Groll, 45; Gudy, 45;
  Hafer, 49; Hagar, 46, 47; Hager, 43,
  46; Hague, 47; Hanah, 40, 41, 43, 44,
  47; Hannah, 42, 44, 46, 47, 48, 49, 54;
  Hanner, 45; Harey, 40; Harp, 47;
  Harre, 48; Harry, 43, 46, 47; Hary,
  43, 49; Hector, 46; Herrey, 45; Hery,
  45; Hick, 43; Isaac, 49; Ives, 42;
  Jack, 40, 41, 42, 43, 44, 45, 46, 47, 48,
  49; Jackboy, 41; Jacob, 40, 42, 47, 48;
  Jam, 45; Jame, 42, 45; James, 46-49;
  Jan, 43; Jane, 42; Janey, 47; Jans, 48;
  Jeff, 46; Jeffry, 49; Jefry, 46; Jem, 46,
  47, 48; Jen, 42, 47, 48; Jenny, 46;
  Jeny, 41, 43; Jerey, 41; Jerry, 46;
  Jervis, 47; Jeson, 44; Jill, 43; Jim, 46,
  48; Jin, 40, 42; Jo, 41, 43; Joan, 47;
  Joe, 41, 43, 45, 47; Johana, 41;
  Johannah, 42; John, 47, 48; Jonas,
  45; Jone, 40; Joseph, 41, 45; Juba,
  42; Judah, 46; Jude, 40, 41; Judey,
  48; Judge, 47; Judy, 42; Jula, 44;
  Kadner, 48; Kate, 44; Katt, 48; Keto,
  44; Kitt, 48; Leah, 48; Lidia, 47;
  Limus, 47; Lincon, 42; Little Dick,
  46; London, 43, 46; Lonn, 41;
  Lonnon, 40; Lucy, 47, 48; Luse, 48;
  Majer, 49; Major, 47; Manta, 43;
  Manuel, 40; Marea, 41; Marget, 47;
  Maria, 47; Martilla, 46; Mary, 43, 49;

PAULSON, Paul, 111
PEACE, Henry Ward, 111
PEACOCK, Luke, 46, 82
  Michael, 61
  Richard, 23, 27
PEAK, Samuel, 44
PEAKLIN, William, 41
PEALE, Mr., 87
PEARCE, Andrew, 1, 20, 39, 47, 64, 111, 123
  Benjamin, 1, 15, 17, 19, 23-25, 28, 30, 34, 67, 83, 89, 111, 124, 130, 131, 134, 135
  Daniel, 47, 58, 64, 111, 123
  Gideon, 133
  Henry, 111
  Henry Ward, 20, 54, 61, 65, 111
  Henry Wd., 83
  James, 52
  John, 47, 65, 122
  Major, 63
  Mary, 34, 123
  Nathaniel, 20
  Richard, 47, 123
  Sarah, 15, 134
  Thomas, 10, 17, 47, 65, 111, 122, 132
  William, 5, 6, 20, 22, 39, 47, 50, 64, 83, 86, 88, 89, 122, 123, 131, 132-135
PEARCE'S BEGINNING, 20, 111
PEARCE'S HOPE, 20
PEARCE'S LANE, 20, 111
PEARCE'S LOT, 20
PEARCE'S MEADOW, 20
PEARCEY, Charles, 54
  James, 85
PEARPOINT, Abraham, 81
PEARSCE, Charles, 40
PECO, Peter, 52
PEEW, Joseph, 66
PEIRCE, Daniel, 111
  Henry, 111

Thomas, 34, 111
William, 111
PEMBROKE, 100
PEN--, Jacob, 53
  James, 53
PENDERGRASS, Thomas, 124, 127
  William, 33
PENINGTON, --na., 65
  Abrm., 79
  Akey, 48
  Araham, 78
  Augustin, 53
  Benedict, 53, 122
  Benjamin, 124
  Drake, 48
  Ebenezer, 47, 60
  Henry, 34, 47, 72, 122, 125, 132
  Hyland, 79
  Isaac, 47, 48, 72
  J., 133
  James, 65, 123
  John, 34, 80, 111, 124, 132
  John Ward, 55
  John Wd., 83
  Joseph, 43, 74
  Mary, 47, 65
  Otho, 78, 123
  Rebekah, 83
  Richard, 123
  Robert, 34, 83, 123, 133
  Samuel, 83, 124
  Sarah, 56, 65, 78, 122
  Stephen, 72
  Thomas, 122
  Urias, 83
  William, 34, 54, 123, 125
  William Bayer, 83
PENNELL, John, 56
PENNEY, John, 83

Samuel(1), 65, 68, 75, 112
Thomas, 20, 21, 44, 51, 112
William, 51, 64, 86
Zeblon, 75
PHIPPES, Mathew, 51
PHIPS, Eleanor, 3
Isaiah, 112
Joseph, 3
PICKADILLY, 20
PICKARD, William, 51
PICKELENY, Hanse Martin, 57
PICKETT, John, 61
PICKLAN, Christopher, 46
PICKLES, Nathan, 52
PICOE, Peter, 112
PICTURE PARCELS, 102
PIERCE, Benjamin, 111
William, 9, 22, 27, 131
PIG POINT, 114
PIGEON, Charles, 50
PIGG POINT LANDING, 20
PIGGOTT, Samuel, 30
Thomas, 60, 61
PILGRIM, Thomas, 112
PINEL, Benjamin, 81
PINKERTON, Alexander, 112
James, 76
PIPE ELME, 121
PIPER, Samuel, 56
PIPPIN, Matthias, 67, 124
PITCH, William, 53
PLAIN DEALING, 101
PLANTATION, 116
PLAXCO, Henry, 31
PLEASANT GARDEN, 102, 103, 108
PLEASANT MOUNT, 20, 97, 121
PLEASANT RANGE, 20
PLEASANTS, Samuel, 87, 88
PLUMB POINT, 121

PLUMP POINT FORK, 113
PLUNKET, John, 71
William, 41, 75
POA, David, 61, 62
POAK, Samuel, 77
POAKE, John, 73
POALSON, Peter, 112
POATHERMAN, Jacob, 78
POER, James, 53
POILLOUN, John, 34
POLK, Hugh, 127
POLLARD, Edward, 112
POLLATT, William, 60
POLLOCK, William, 112
POLYOUNG, John, 112
POOL, Jacob, 57
POOLE, John, 26
POOLEY, Jacob, 125
POOPE, Matthew, 134
POOR, Abraham, 55, 79
James, 53, 124
Walter, 112
POPISH CLERGY, 112
POPLAR NECK, 20, 21, 111
POPLAR VALLEY, 21, 102, 112
PORTER, Andrew, 37, 46, 59, 63, 65, 73, 82, 85, 86, 112, 130
Armstrong, 81
Charles, 41, 65, 81
David, 57
George, 48, 58, 67, 82, 112
James, 2, 11, 13, 16, 37, 46, 53, 62, 66, 71, 73, 82, 86, 112, 123, 129
John, 46, 60, 62, 82
Robert, 31, 34, 37, 46, 47, 50, 55, 58, 59, 61, 62, 65, 81, 82, 84, 112, 123
Stephen, 73
Thomas, 57, 82
William, 37, 38, 46, 47, 54, 74, 81, 82
PORTERFIELD, Andrew, 73, 81

SOUTH, Hezekiah, 77
SOUTHALL, John, 87
SOUTHAMPTON, 25
SPALDING, John, 39, 124
SPARGOE, John, 83
SPARNON, James, 4
  Joseph, 25
SPARNON'S DELIGHT, 25
SPAVOLD, James, 37
SPEAR, George, 57, 129
  James, 42, 55, 81, 85, 129
  John, 74
  William, 74
SPEEDWELL, 25
SPEER, James, 30
SPENCE, Captain, 71
  Henry, 57, 58
SPENCER, Capt., 34
  George, 7, 116
  Nicholas, 27
  Thomas, 25, 132
SPENCER'S HARBOUR, 25, 93
SPERNON, Joseph, 9, 16
SPERNONS DELIGHT, 113, 119
SPERRONS DELIGHT, 120
SPORNE, Nicholas, 27
SPRING HEAD, 25
SPRINGS, John, 57, 129
SPRINGS HEAD, 116, 121
SPROTT, John, 116
SPROWL, John, 60
SPRYE, Oliver, 25
SPRY(E)'S HILL(S), 25, 101, 107
SPURNE, Nicholas, 116
SPUWL, James, 68
SQUALL, 93
STALCAP, John, 45, 65, 75
STALKUP, John, 68
STAMPSON, Sam, 71
STANAWAY, 25

STANDFORD, John, 123
STANDLEY, Michael, 56
STANDLY, Michael, 47
STANDUP, Amos, 73
STANLEY, James, 11, 71
  John, 131
STANOP, Emor, 43
  William, 43
STANUP, William, 77
STARETT, John, 116
STARKEY, William, 29, 75, 117, 128
STARLIN, George, 76
STARLING, John, 125
  William, 47, 53, 125
STARN, Baltus, 126
  Frederick, 66, 126
STARROT, John, 51
STATE HILL, 25, 89, 93, 95
STAULKUP, Henry, 55
STEDHAM, Henry, 8, 130
  Lulef, 8
STEDMAN, John Hance, 117
  Lulaff, 117
  Rocloff, 117
STEEL, Archibald, 117
  Elizabeth, 117
  James, 10, 72, 135
  John, 3, 25, 44, 58, 117
  Joseph, 133
  Robart, 75
  Walter, 130
STEELE, Elizabeth, 30
  James, 117
  Joseph, 117
  Walter, 117
STEELE HEAD, 25
STEELMAN, John Hans, 32
  John Hause, 25
STEELMAN'S DELIGHT, 25, 109
STEELMANS POINT, 117

THIESS, John, 82

THIRD OF HEATHS PARCELS, 115

THOMAS, 124

Benjamin, 46, 54, 63, 64, 66, 73, 86, 118, 125

Caleb, 73

Christifor, 77

Cristfor, 43

David, 8, 73, 118

Hendrey, 77

Isaac, 79

James, 46

John, 3, 5, 6, 8, 15, 48, 60, 67, 83, 118

Joseph, 45, 46, 63, 66, 69, 75, 85, 86, 118

Mr., 88

Philip, 87, 88, 118

Richard, 31, 35, 36, 42, 54, 55, 59, 63, 69, 74, 75, 81, 82, 85, 87

Samuel, 30, 31, 42, 54, 81

Solloman, 80

Thomas, 88

William, 62, 77

THOMAS' LOT(T), 26, 97

THOMPSON, Abraham (Abrm.), 46, 66, 79

Alexander, 51

Augustine, 118

Ephra(i)m, 47, 62, 67, 79, 118, 125

George, 26, 51

Henry, 125

James, 30, 127

Jennet, 118

John, 11, 16, 26, 34, 47, 59, 61, 88, 89, 118, 128, 130, 131, 135

John Dockery, 59, 61, 86

John Dockra, 118

Joseph, 44, 51, 54, 76, 118

Joshua, 118

Martha, 118

Mathew, 69, 118

Matthew, 44, 76, 128

Richard, 46, 47, 55, 56, 60, 62, 66, 79, 85, 89, 118, 126, 134, 135

Robert, 34, 47, 55, 59, 61, 63, 67, 85, 86, 118, 126

Samuel, 5, 44, 61, 76, 118, 129

Thomas, 60

William, 66, 77

THOMPSON'S INSPECTION, 26, 93, 118

THOMPSON'S TOWN, 26, 27, 93, 94, 108, 116

THOMPSON'S TOWN POINT, 27, 119

THOMS, John, 118

THOMSON, James, 73

John, 42

Richard, 118

Robert, 118

Sam, 34

Samuel, 36, 68

William, 36, 44, 77

THOMSONS TOWN, 104

THORNBERRY, George, 34, 124

THORNTON, Thomas, 36

William, 36, 37, 38, 39, 73

THREE PARTNERS, 27, 95, 104, 107, 116

THREE PARTNER'S ISLAND, 27

THREE PARTNERS PART, 93

THREE PASTURES, 27

THREE PRONGS, 27

THREE TRACTS, 102

TICEN, Cornelus, 78

TICKE, William, 32

TIGNER, James, 61

TILGHMAN, James, 131

TILLEY BROOME, 27

TILLSON, Derrick, 118

TILLTON, John, 46

John, 8, 11, 27, 28, 34, 36, 40, 41, 50,
52, 54, 60, 64, 66, 67, 83, 88, 89, 119,
124-126, 132
Levi, 75
Mary, 69, 75
Robert, 41, 66, 88, 126
Samuel, 55
Thomas, 45, 52, 65
William, 33, 36, 45, 55, 65, 69, 75,
83, 119
VEAZEY'S LOT(T), 28
VENTER, (THE), 28, 91
VERBRACK, Nicholas, 32
VESEY, George, 119
VESTALL, William, 119
VESTRY OF ST. MARY ANN
PARISH, 119
VESTRY OF ST. STEPHENS, 119
VEURE, David, 129
VICARS, George, 71
VICKERS, Benjamin, 83, 86
George, 57, 128
VINCENT, Charles, 28
VIRGINITY, 28, 114, 115
VISITORS OF THE FREE
SCHOOL, 119
VORSMAN, Peter, 133
Petrus, 116, 119
VORTADE, Antony, 48
VULCAN'S CHOICE, 28
VULCAN'S REST, 28, 91, 94, 97,
108, 110, 113

-W-

WACHOB, John, 57
WADDLE, Alexander, 53
WADE, Daniel, 82
WADEMORES NECK, 115
WADMORES NECK, 101
WAGONER, John, 51

WAIDLICOFF, James, 48
WAKEFIELD, John, 36, 63, 75, 86,
88
WALDEN, Edward, 62
WALDRON, Resolved, 133
Rosevelt, 133
WALES, 28, 113
WALGATT, Otho, 119
WALKER, Andrew, 31
Hugh, 13, 40, 119
James, 50
John, 42, 65, 69, 78, 81, 124
Lewis, 78
Matthias, 128
Moses, 57
Robert, 46, 65, 82
Thomas, 119
W., 59
William, 78, 128
WALL, Edward, 119
WALLACE, Adam, 14, 15, 27, 47,
66, 79, 109, 119, 126
Andrew, 3-5, 10, 46, 54, 66, 80, 119
David, 33, 119
Francis, 28
James, 14, 46, 59, 63, 64, 66, 79, 85,
86, 119, 126
Jane, 33
John, 33, 37, 51, 58, 66, 67, 119, 124,
132, 133
Joseph, 4, 9, 44, 69, 72, 77, 119
Mathew, 33, 51
Mathews, 120
Mathias, 133
Matthew, 28
Michael, 44, 50, 59, 64, 76, 86, 120
Richard, 67, 83, 88, 124
Robert, 76, 77
Thomas, 41, 44, 51, 63, 67, 76, 85,
127
William, 10, 44, 77, 120, 128

WALLACE'S SCRAWL(E), 28, 96, 103, 105, 106, 119, 120
WALLAS, John, 26
WALLER, John, 68, 132
WALLEY, Alice, 34
WALLGATT, Otho, 119
WALLICE, John, 36, 38, 39
WALLIS, Andrew, 10
  William, 10, 50
WALLNUTT THICKETT, 108
WALLTER, John, 42
WALMSLEY, Benjamin, 83
  John, 74, 83
  Nicholas, 83
  Robert, 34, 62, 67, 83, 120, 124
  William, 59, 60, 61-64, 67, 83, 85, 86, 120, 124, 132
WALNUT THICKET, 28, 103
WALTER, John, 69
  Jon., 63
  Robert, 132
WALTHAM, ---, 49
WAMSLEY, Robert, 50
  Thomas, 11, 28
WAMSLEY'S LOTT, 28
WAMSLY, Robert, 120
WAR--, Mary, 49
WARAM, 94
  James, 75
  John, 75
WARD, Alice, 120
  Benjamin, 22
  Dorrell, Nics
  Henrietta, 72
  Henry, 1, 5, 6, 9, 15, 16, 20, 21, 54, 64, 67, 83, 84, 88, 89, 120, 124
  J., 132
  James, 54, Chem
  James Chatm., 65
  James Chetham, 47, 120, 132

  John, 12, 16, 28, 34, 39, 49, 54, 58, 59, 60, 61, 64, 67, 68, 78, 82, 83, 84, 86, 89, 120, 122-124, 132, 134, 135
  John of Henry, 120
  John of William, 120
  John Veazey, 84
  Mary, 64, 69, 78, 132
  Maurice, 124
  Nathaniel, 58, 67, 83, 120
  Peregrine, 6, 22, 34, 53, 54, 64, 120, 123, 132
  Perigren, 78
  Rebeccah, 120
  Sarah, 60
  Susannah, 34
  Thomas, 29, 34, 50, 120
  William, 6, 16, 18, 19, 21, 34, 39, 67, 83, 89, 120, 124, 135
WARDNER, George, 133
WARD'S ADDITION, 28, 120
WARD'S ADDITION AND WARD'S KNOWLEDGE, 28
WARD'S KNOWLEDGE, 28, 120
WARE, John, 128
  Robert, 120
WAREHAM, James, 35
WAREN, Peter, 47
WARMUST AND HACK'S ADDITION, 28
WARNER, Benjamin, 62, 84
  Edward, 120
  George, 28, 88
  James, 84
  John, 125
  Widow, 34
  William, 59, 78, 84
WARNER'S LEVELL, 28
WARREN, 28, 99
WARRILOME, William, 120
WARRINER, Edmond, 88
WARTEN, James, 80

-Z-

-Y-

Other books by the author:

A Closer Look at St. John's Parish Registers [Baltimore County, Maryland], 1701-1801

A Collection of Maryland Church Records

A Guide to Genealogical Research in Maryland: 5th Edition, Revised and Enlarged

Abstracts of the Ledgers and Accounts of the Bush Store and Rock Run Store, 1759-1771

Abstracts of the Orphans Court Proceedings of Harford County, 1778-1800

Abstracts of Wills, Harford County, Maryland, 1800-1805

Baltimore City [Maryland] Deaths and Burials, 1834-1840

Baltimore County, Maryland, Overseers of Roads, 1693-1793

Bastardy Cases in Baltimore County, Maryland, 1673-1783

Bastardy Cases in Harford County, Maryland, 1774-1844

Bible and Family Records of Harford County, Maryland Families: Volume V

Children of Harford County: Indentures and Guardianships, 1801-1830

Colonial Delaware Soldiers and Sailors, 1638-1776

*Colonial Families of the Eastern Shore of Maryland
Volumes 5, 6, 7, 8, 9, 11, 12, 13, 14, and 16*

Colonial Maryland Soldiers and Sailors, 1634-1734

Dr. John Archer's First Medical Ledger, 1767-1769, Annotated Abstracts

Early Anglican Records of Cecil County

*Early Harford Countians, Individuals Living in Harford County, Maryland in Its Formative Years
Volume 1: A to K, Volume 2: L to Z, and Volume 3: Supplement*

Harford County Taxpayers in 1870, 1872 and 1883

Harford County, Maryland Divorce Cases, 1827-1912: An Annotated Index

Heirs and Legatees of Harford County, Maryland, 1774-1802

Heirs and Legatees of Harford County, Maryland, 1802-1846

Inhabitants of Baltimore County, Maryland, 1763-1774

Inhabitants of Cecil County, Maryland, 1649-1774

Inhabitants of Harford County, Maryland, 1791-1800

Inhabitants of Kent County, Maryland, 1637-1787

*Joseph A. Pennington & Co., Havre De Grace, Maryland Funeral Home Records:
Volume II, 1877-1882, 1893-1900*

Maryland Bible Records, Volume 1: Baltimore and Harford Counties

Maryland Bible Records, Volume 2: Baltimore and Harford Counties

Maryland Bible Records, Volume 3: Carroll County

Maryland Bible Records, Volume 4: Eastern Shore

Maryland Deponents, 1634-1799

Maryland Deponents: Volume 3, 1634-1776

*Maryland Public Service Records, 1775-1783: A Compendium of Men and Women of
Maryland Who Rendered Aid in Support of the American Cause against
Great Britain during the Revolutionary War*

*Marylanders to Carolina: Migration of Marylanders to
North Carolina and South Carolina prior to 1800*